Nontraditional U.S. Public Diplomacy:
Past, Present, and Future

Edited by Deborah L. Trent, Ph.D.

Nontraditional U.S. Public Diplomacy: Past, Present, and Future

Published by the Public Diplomacy Council, Washington, DC

Deborah L. Trent, Ph.D., Editor

ISBN-13: 978-1533450364

ISBN-10: 1533450366

The views expressed in the chapters in this volume are those of the individual authors and do not necessarily reflect those of the U.S. Department of State or the U.S. government.

Earlier Books in the Public Diplomacy Council Series

The Last Three Feet: Case Studies in Public Diplomacy *2nd Edition*
Edited by William P. Kiehl, 2014

The Last Three Feet: Case Studies in Public Diplomacy
Edited by William P. Kiehl, 2012

Local Voices/Global Perspectives: Challenges Ahead for U.S. International Media
Edited by Alan L. Heil Jr., 2008

America's Dialogue with the World
Edited by William P. Kiehl, 2006

Engaging the Arab & Islamic Worlds through Public Diplomacy: A Report and Action Recommendations
Edited by William A. Rugh, 2004

Public Diplomacy Council

The Public Diplomacy Council (PDC)[1] is a nonprofit organization committed to the study, profession, and responsible advocacy of U.S. public diplomacy as practiced across the globe. PDC members believe that understanding, informing, and influencing foreign publics, as well as dialogue and strong relationships among Americans and citizens abroad, are vital to the national interest and core elements of 21st century diplomacy.

The PDC was founded in 1988 as the Public Diplomacy Foundation. Dedicated to fostering greater recognition of the craft in the conduct of international affairs, the Foundation evolved to serve also as a resource for the teaching, training, and development of public diplomacy as an academic discipline. In 2001, the Foundation joined with the George Washington University School of Media and Public Affairs and Elliott School of International Affairs to establish the Public Diplomacy Institute.

The Foundation was reorganized as a member-based Council in 2002. The PDC regularly conducts educational, public awareness, and cultural programs. Its key partners are: the George Washington University Institute of Public Diplomacy and Global Communication; the Public Diplomacy Alumni Association; and the University of Southern California Annenberg Center on Communication Leadership & Policy.

The PDC has no government connection and receives no financial support from any government source. As a 501(c)(3) organization, it relies on dues, grants, in-kind contributions, and corporate gifts. Donations to the Council may be tax-deductible.

---

1. See http://www.publicdiplomacycouncil.org/.

CONTENTS

ACKNOWLEDGMENTS

This volume is the result of the work of many contributors who should be acknowledged, some dating back to the fall of 2013.

That was the date of a day-long forum that was an inspiration for this book, a conference which discussed many of the themes addressed on the following pages. However, all of the authors whose work is represented here have updated or created entirely anew the chapters that follow.

And we should acknowledge those who helped create and coordinate that 2013 conference, starting with our co-sponsors, the Public Diplomacy Alumni Association and the Walter Roberts Endowment, and including Walter Roberts himself, as he was a speaker at the conference.

We also offer special thanks to Deborah Trent, who edited this book, devoting years of work to bring it into being. Her steady hand over the past three years has guided all of us to produce what follows.

On the part of the Public Diplomacy Council and its members, we acknowledge all of these contributions with sincere thanks.

Adam Clayton Powell III

President
Public Diplomacy Council

1

Introduction

Deborah L. Trent*

* I am grateful to Tara Schoenborn, former Public Diplomacy Council Graduate Fellow, for her assistance with early drafting of this chapter.

Since World War One, U.S. public diplomacy communication efforts toward audiences abroad have included information programs. Mid-20th century and into the early days of the U.S. Information Agency (USIA), exchanges of jazz greats, poets, and athletes were added to the public diplomacy landscape. The Cold War, U.S. civil rights conflict, Vietnam War, and other turbulent eras have also inspired nontraditional programs. They have complemented conventional efforts, boosting the capacity of U.S. public diplomacy to support national interests and increase mutual understanding.

Today, the U.S. Department of State's cultural, educational, and information exchanges of artists, professionals, rising leaders, scholars, journalists, and students are coupled with varied online programs involving academic coursework, scientific collaboration, cross-cultural video gaming, and virtual reality experiences. Public diplomacy practitioners engage in person and online with ever-diversifying transnational identities of non-state actors.

During Thanksgiving week in 2015, the U.S. Consulate General of Naples prepared a meal for migrants of perhaps ten countries at a soup kitchen run by a local church. Amidst the unprecedented global count of people displaced by conflict, the United Nations Refugee Agency announced in June, 2016, that ten refugees would compete in the upcoming Olympics in Rio de Janeiro. On August 5th, ahead of the opening of the games, Secretary of State John Kerry greeted Team USA. He recognized the Eritrean refugee, female Muslim American fencer, and other team members for their humanitarian work and athletic achievements. In trying to understand and manage the shifting spaces for public diplomacy, implementers, policymakers, analysts, educators, and trainers must set priorities in accordance with policy, resource availability, and the connective potential of our communication tools and processes.

This volume confronts a variety of political challenges in public diplomacy from World War One to the present, analyzes innovations that either effectively bucked traditional practices or should have, and examines other scenarios where new approaches are worth trying. Three chapters (Kovach, Trent, Carlson) draw on the Public Diplomacy Council's November 2013 Fall Forum, "U.S. Public Diplomacy: A Look to the Past, A Look to the Future." All 11 chapters convey to diplomats, analysts, and students alike that building on case studies generates evidence of effective policy and programs. We need this evidence because we are responsible for the future—in this instance, the future of programming in diplomacy's rapidly expanding public dimension.

This introduction provides highlights and recommendations of the 11 chapters, together with some concluding thoughts. The chapters are sequenced by topic rather than chronologically. Each presents cases or vignettes from around the world. The authors describe, evaluate, and/or develop implications for the overall craft and practice of international diplomacy across the U.S. government.

Our opening chapter, by Anthony Quainton, wrestles with the ongoing question of defining public diplomacy and goes to the heart of the matter: how to practice it effectively. Almost 40 years of service in the U.S. Foreign Service, including four ambassadorial tours and more than a decade teaching the craft, have taught him the importance of listening to understand global publics and particular public diplomacy audiences and participants. Quainton's experience in Kuwait, Peru, Nicaragua, and the Central African Republic taught him to keep focused on the policy goals relevant to local hosts and to strive to create an advantageous "climate of opinion."

He ponders the nuanced differences between public diplomacy, propaganda, public affairs, and public relations. He illustrates tradecraft for effective public diplomacy through both tried-and-true and unconventional programs tailored to convey resonant messages and increase mutual understanding. He notes that applying social science-based analytical tools bolsters program performance. These steps must be combined, he writes, with skillful use of locally accessible communication tools to help diplomats gauge "the appropriate moment for action" in order to advance foreign policy goals.

Quainton closes with a call for "development of more sensitive antennae among diplomats within and outside the public diplomacy cone, making them more capable of listening to the voice of the mob, to understand the historical context and emotional context within which people operate, and thereby to develop new tools to influence as well as inform."[1] His emphasis on understanding audience and participant context is related to the next chapter, on the professional and personal rivalry between the World War One-era officials, Walter Lippmann and George Creel.

John Brown's rich analysis of two of President Woodrow Wilson's key and colorful appointees elucidates the roles and tensions of political rhetoric and grounded reality in the study and practice of public diplomacy. Brown served more than 20 years in the Foreign Service, and it is as much his prior credential of a doctorate in history and attention to the personalities of actors on the political stage that drives the chapter, "Janus-Faced Public Diplomacy: Creel and Lippmann During the Great War."

Brown explains how George Creel's public relations and advertising experience served him well as chair of President Wilson's Committee on Public Information. Both he and Walter Lippmann were trained journalists. The latter's more scholarly orientation suited him on the team that drafted Wilson's post-War plan, "Fourteen Points," and as executive assistant and intelligence analyst both stateside and in the European theater.

---

1. Page 41.

Each of their contrasting, yet effective, approaches to public diplomacy arose from their backgrounds and temperaments. Creel traded in public mood and passionate rhetoric (felt by some to be the most inaccurate of propaganda) and Lippmann in philosophy and high-minded democratic ideals. They shared only a dedication to the goal of winning minds and hearts. Together, their emotional and analytical approaches to shaping public opinion were a necessary and unconventional mode of operation, particularly in a war when propaganda and anti-propaganda campaigns were central to success. One of Brown's insights on the clashing communication styles of Lippmann and Creel resonates with the current era of social media-dominated newsfeeds: that reading the relevant public's "mind" and feeling its "heart" are equally essential.

Conducting public diplomacy to respond to global demands for human rights, food security, and environmental justice in the face of domestic politics that today are so ideologically polarized is challenging. However, as long as the United States continues to stand for social justice and democratic self-government for all, the role of public diplomacy will be not only to listen to, understand, and influence global publics in the name of U.S. interests, but also to promote relationships with them that are generated by the creative tension of a heartfelt and reasoned communication approach.

In "The Uses and Abuses of Public Diplomacy: Winning and Losing Hearts and Minds," Richard Virden probes successes and failures in the counterinsurgency in Thailand, war against the Viet Cong, and Poland, both under communism, and later, after achieving independence following the fall of the Berlin Wall. Virden draws on 38 years in the U.S. Foreign Service and later teaching the craft of diplomacy. He argues that listening, understanding, humility, and selectivity about missions in each host country may be unconventional for a superpower, but they are the roots of a nation founded by immigrants seeking freedom to determine their own futures.

In the Thailand of the late 1960s, U.S. policy was to join with the Thai government to prevent a takeover by communist insurgents. The large corps of U.S. military, diplomatic, and development personnel supported Thai officials and citizens by working in the background. The U.S. role "wasn't to make the village people pro-American, but rather pro-Bangkok."[2] Virden reflects that the mission was successful because Thailand was a unified country and that the King and the government addressed the socioeconomic needs in most rural areas before unrest could develop.

In the next decade, however, the United States Information Agency (from 1953 to 1999 the public diplomacy arm of the U.S. government) was unable to persuade either Vietnamese citizens or U.S. allies to back the Saigon government. The strength of Vietnamese nationalism and yearning for independence were lost on U.S. policymakers. The crucial public diplomacy tools of listening, understanding, and respecting the people of a host country were left unused.

Virden's two tours in Poland, in the late 1970s and mid-1990s, straddled the breakup of the Soviet Union and Soviet domination of Eastern Europe. He contrasts the experience of being considered a hostile actor supporting dissidents in a closed society with being in an open society, able to work with the same actors and many more on high-level mutual interests (e.g., acceptance into NATO in exchange for democratic governance reforms) and people-to-people ties. Especially on the first assignment, Western broadcasting and publications were key modes of communication, albeit one-way.

---

2. Pages 81-82.

Through Virden's analysis, we are reminded that it is risky to base a government's public diplomacy on convincing a host nation to rise up against its government. Such a goal should only be pursued with considerable cultural competency, relationship-building, and knowledge-sharing. As non-state militias and other insurgents proliferate, and as the current U.S. military engagements in Iraq and Afghanistan drag on, assessing which to back or oppose will become harder. With no shortage of hot, small conflicts and splinter-insurgency groups rising to power, considerably more clear thinking and realistic assessments of what is possible will be needed to decide how to wage effective public diplomacy campaigns. Information, cultural, and educational programs will become more difficult. Programs will have to be increasingly tailor-made for rapidly shifting environments.

Like Virden's chapter, the next one underscores the need for a program that shows cultural respect, although in a different setting. Carol Balassa's "America's Image Abroad: The UNESCO Cultural Diversity Convention and U.S. Motion Picture Exports," reflects the longstanding debate over unhindered movement of cultural goods and services and trade restrictions ostensibly imposed for cultural sovereignty reasons. Ms. Balassa's 27 years with the Office of the United States Trade Representative focused on the motion picture, telecommunications services, and energy services sectors.

Four years of post-9/11 anti-terrorism campaigns by the U.S. military had seriously eroded the U.S. government's global reputation by October 2005, when the United Nations Economic, Scientific and Cultural Organization vote on the Cultural Diversity Convention took place. Although the United States was funding 22 percent of UNESCO's budget, protecting the diversity of cultural expressions ranked low among U.S. priorities and the vote to adopt the Cultural Diversity Convention received little attention in the U.S. media. Noticeably but unsurprisingly quiet was the Motion Picture Association of America, whose members had for decades held perhaps the largest share of the global motion picture market.

Led by the Canadian and French governments, the Convention was intended to create a new body for deliberating any issues related to commerce linked with national cultural expressions, as an alternative to addressing the issue in the World Trade Organization. Years of lobbying among UN member states by France and Canada generated broad support for the Convention; it was adopted by 148 votes in favor, two opposed, and four abstentions. As Balassa details, the U.S. government largely neglected the issue and missed opportunities to address effectively the widespread perception of U.S. indifference to cultural relations. Hollywood today continues to dominate film markets worldwide, and in trade negotiations diplomats still grapple with sensitivities over the dominance of U.S. films in foreign markets.

The end of Balassa's story offers the prospect of cooperation between the U.S. and the countries sensitive to the domination of U.S. films in their domestic markets. She calls on policymakers, industry advocates, and public diplomacy practitioners to consider the deeper, underlying issues that galvanized support for the Convention – "complaints that the U.S. market was unreceptive to foreign films.... [and] deep resentment attendant to the power of U.S. film exports."[3] Since film distribution and marketing are key assets for Hollywood's global success, Balassa recommends training in those areas, designed and delivered by representatives from the U.S. film industry and nonprofit film organizations such as the American Film Institute. This approach departs from the traditional one-way outreach and messaging program to one that provides filmmakers a commercially viable way to reach audiences worldwide.

---

3. Page 115.

Anthropologist Rob Albro's chapter introduces an approach to cultural diplomacy practice that also expands the field's trend in collaboration. "Diplomacy and the Efficacy of Transnational Applied Cultural Networks" explains that "[r]ather than promotion of one's own cultural community or national cultural identity, applied cultural networks facilitate relationships of collaborative storytelling and the co-creation of cultural knowledge."[4] Similar to participatory, inclusive practices discussed in several other chapters, Albro's approach recognizes cultural diplomacy as a process for participants to determine together how they express their work. He explores several theoretical concepts underpinning transnational applied cultural networks and demonstrates how they have been recently and can in the future be enacted in both friendly and fraught diplomatic settings.

The transnational applied cultural network approach seems to have crystallized for Albro through his participation in the three-day "GLOBALLAB" convening in 2012. This gathering of artists, performers, diplomats, and human rights and social justice advocates emphasized artistic creativity across diverse cultures through joint expression. Among examples discussed was "Theatre Without Borders," a university-based peacebuilding program, which fostered original dialogue on human rights and the arts.

Albro also describes three partnerships that exemplify the benefits of transnational applied cultural networks. One involves organizations in the United States and Haiti, and two conjoin organizations in the United States and China. The Haiti Cultural Recovery Project involves many U.S. partners that, since the 2010 earthquake, have responded to Haitian cultural professionals'

---

4. Page 126.

requests for assistance in preserving their nation's heritage. The U.S.–Chinese projects have promoted public dialogue among scholars and folklorists, shared modes of operation, and policies for heritage conservation.

The emergent, unanticipated results of these projects hold the promise of sustainability because of their mutuality, but time will tell. Especially between countries with comparatively challenging bilateral relations, diverse and participant-driven networks receiving a light touch from government rather than an imposing hand have more credible standing among stakeholders. Carol Balassa's recommendation of a film distribution and marketing training program presented by a private or nonprofit organization is another example. They are less transactional and more collaborative projects, allowing space for differences and creativity, more of which will be needed, as Albro concludes, in regions of the hottest conflicts, including in the Middle East.

Mediation of the violent extremism driving the Islamic State's destruction of ancient ruins in Iraq and Syria requires inclusive participation of local professional and community stakeholders, military personnel, international heritage organization officials, and, of course, clerics. Diplomats often have coordinating roles in this political-humanitarian-peacebuilding work. The next chapter describes outreach and engagement among religious leaders and followers that lays the groundwork for perhaps, eventually, dispelling the Islamic caliphate narrative and advocating the preservation of shared cultural heritage and inter-religious cooperation.

In "Public Diplomacy Engages Religious Communities, Actors, and Organizations: A Belated and Transformative Marriage," Peter Kovach reviews the overall successful efforts of the administrations of George W. Bush and Barack Obama to institutionalize religious engagement in U.S. diplomacy. Kovach is a retired U.S. Foreign

Service Officer, among whose roles was to lead State's Office of International Religious Freedom.

Although many perceive governmental relations with clergy to be outside the bounds of the Constitution (a perception Kovach calls "First Amendmentitis"), the U.S. Agency for International Development (USAID) worked out, through intensive internal deliberations and public rulemaking, regulations stipulating how agency programs could legally solicit cooperation and partnership among faith-based civil society organizations. Since its implementation in 2004, this groundbreaking regulatory regime has gradually generated similar Department of State and other key agency regulatory reforms. At State, they are currently overseen by the Office of Religion and Global Affairs and various program entities including public diplomacy structures. Training by USAID has been part of the effort to overcome hesitancy to engage in programmatic partnerships with faith-based partners that advance secular developmental and diplomatic foreign policy goals.

The author also argues that officers should gain a working knowledge of the various religious identities, from youth to elders, in host countries to develop more

> *2004 USAID regulations stipulate how agency programs could solicit cooperation and partnership among faith-based civil society organizations.*

creative, resonant information and exchange programs. Establishing collegial relationships with Shi'a and Sunni members of the Muslim Brotherhood and the Baathist party in Yemen, and with the majority Shi'a as well as the ruling Sunni in Bahrain, Kovach developed local media, speaker, and sports programs and helped him understand "political Islam" during the 1990s, when democracy-building was a major diplomatic goal.

More recently, faith-based educational and cultural exchanges, as well as advocacy campaigns sponsored by various State Department bureaus and several U.S. embassies in the Middle East, North Africa, and Europe, have expanded efforts to foster interfaith understanding, pluralism, dialogue, and conflict mediation. Some have been conceived by Imam Bashar Arafat, a Syrian–American cleric, one of the discussants at the 2013 Public Diplomacy Council Fall Forum session on religion and diplomacy that Peter Kovach moderated. Imam Arafat has worked with the State Department to host Islamic clerics from abroad and return home better prepared to teach world religion comparatively and ease conflict.

Kovach recommends several steps to sustain the faith-diplomacy marriage. First, he recommends training around engagement with religious communities emphasize developing awareness of one's own religious or spiritual identity as it affects cross-cultural interaction and an awareness of the rationalist bias of bureaucratic culture. Second, he recommends training on the reformed regulatory regimes at State for programmatic cooperation with faith-based organizations. Third, complementing the first two steps, would be training in how to determine whether entering into such a partnership serves policy. In summary, proper regulation, training, needs assessment, and interagency cooperation reinforce this new approach's value. The next chapter also examines communication strategy among diverse publics, but because of an interagency turf battle, the story does not have as promising an ending.

Strategic communication is dead. Long live strategic communication. In "Nontraditional Public Diplomacy in the Iraq-Afghan Wars Or the Ups and Downs of Strategic Communicators," Helle Dale compares the unconventional Office of Strategic Communication (OSC) within the U.S. Department of Defense and State Department outreach to Muslim-majority countries post-9/11. Strategic communication is defined as "specifically tailored outreach informed by cultural understanding."[5] Although developed through a different lens, this chapter sends a message similar to that of Brian Carlson in the final chapter. Since 9/11, programs and policy have needed better alignment, and State and Defense, in particular, have needed better coordination.

A widely published commentator on U.S. diplomatic and defense communication, Dale contends that OSC should not have been abolished in 2012 after a six-year run, because OSC was needed to synchronize outreach programming to engage Muslim audiences and because strategic communication in wartime is the shared domain of Defense and State.

The author explains that since 9/11, both Foggy Bottom and the Pentagon ran traditional and experimental communication programs, at great expense and with mixed results. Fifteen years later, after troop drawdowns in Iraq and Afghanistan, the rise of the Islamic State in Iraq and Syria, and the rejuvenation of the Taliban in Afghanistan and Pakistan, Dale argues that the Defense Department has lost the turf battle over leading the effort to counter extremist narratives and improve America's image across the globe. All the while, Congress continues to aggressively investigate expenditures.

The power shift appeared most certain when the Center for Strategic Counterterrorism Communications,[6] within the State Department's office of the Under Secretary for Public Diplomacy and Public Affairs, was launched early in the Obama administration. Meanwhile, the Pentagon continued the embedded journalist and other media programs that amount to "lower-case" strategic

---

5. Page 176.
6. The Center for Strategic Counterterrorism Communications has been reorganized as the Global Engagement Center. (See http://www.state.gov/r/gec/.)

communications informed by local context. A decade and a half of intermittent cross-agency coordination efforts, however, has leveled off. Dale concludes with concern that it is up to the civilian side of the U.S. government house to mount "a massive synchronized Strategic Communication effort to reach Muslim populations."[7]

Helle Dale's chapter is a story of contemporary political and bureaucratic struggle to fortify military action with nonviolent tactics, amid unrelenting media coverage of domestic discontent over war losses. The next chapter is also situated in the post-9/11 era, but it tugs a bit harder on the thread of cultural understanding needed for strategic communication and public diplomacy to bolster the government's image abroad.

In "Cultural Diplomacy Partnerships: Cracking the Credibility Nut with Inclusive Participation," I examine the work of diplomats and implementers to forge and sustain partnerships with nonprofit and commercial organizations collaborating globally in the arts and humanities. Public-private partnerships (PPPs) have long been a mainstay for pursuing mutual understanding in public and cultural diplomacy; the majority of the chapters in this volume refer to PPPs. Because of their potential for wide reach, cultural co-production with a light governmental touch, innovative achievements, and funding leverage, they are increasingly the choice of diplomacy and development policymakers and implementers.

PPP's potential to enhance governmental credibility is in high demand as U.S. society seeks to understand, engage, and influence audiences wary of or opposed to U.S. government policies but favorable toward American culture and private enterprise. I offer a case study of a partnership, sponsored by the Department of State's Cultural Programs Division, with modern dance Company E and the International Writing Program of the University of Iowa. This PPP has assembled participants from around the world to further

7. Page 190.

creative expression and mutual understanding, in spite of existential political and ethnic conflicts, e.g., the Arab-Israeli crisis.

I draw on experience at the U.S. Information Agency as a manager of Fulbright programs and postsecondary institutional partnerships, subsequent research on cross-sector partnerships, and lessons from the 2013 Public Diplomacy Council Fall Forum, to show how PPPs bridge deep cultural chasms. This chapter also explains how the increasing number of diverse voices in nonprofit and commercial corporations will continue to challenge government's capacity to convene PPPs that advance credibility and national interests. I argue that cultural diplomacy practitioners should follow the trend in participatory, socially inclusive programming in development and peacebuilding and engage PPP stakeholders more widely in framing, monitoring, and evaluating program impacts. The chapter also notes that the recently established evaluation policy and evaluation unit in the office of the Under Secretary for Public Diplomacy and Public Affairs presents an opportunity to expand and systematize holistic impact assessment.   The bi-partisan Congressional International Exchange and Study Caucus, formed in 2015, is another opportunity to promote stronger cultural diplomacy partnerships and their evaluation.

I conclude that engaging more diverse stakeholders from the program formulation to evaluation stages informs and supports program goals, "reducing the need for a firewall between their collaborations and policy."[8] Such practices strengthen the U.S. image abroad, the potential of people-to-people relationships, and the capacity of public diplomacy to counter violent extremism.

---

8. Page 216.

Next, Craig Hayden, an expert on foreign policy rhetoric and public diplomacy discourse, presents "International Education and Public Diplomacy: Technology, MOOCs, and Transforming Engagement." Like the prior chapter, this one treats the related projects of credible public diplomacy programming and reliable, accurate measurement and evaluation of public diplomacy activities. Both draw on research and practice in collaborative public diplomacy including PPPs, but Hayden focuses on new and social media technology in educational exchanges, asking how they "result in differing forms of public diplomacy practice and organizational thinking."[9]

Hayden frames the concepts of public diplomacy and soft power, noting that public diplomacy comprises communication tools and processes for meeting governmental interests and informational, advocacy, and relational objectives, whereas soft power consists of the resources of a society (e.g., cultural, educational, scientific) used by government toward those ends. Because public diplomacy and soft power are often conflated, distinguishing the two both theoretically and in the context of geopolitics and educational exchanges using new technology is welcome. This chapter also complements the framings of public diplomacy developed by Tony Quainton, John Brown, and other contributors to this volume.

Hayden explains that measuring soft power and public diplomacy is difficult, because isolating the causes of behavioral change is difficult. Just as significant in the transformational engagement project are the conflicting purposes of building interpersonal relationships while seeking to influence people and evaluate their participation in programs. To explore how the growing use of new and social media affects the gradual process of intercultural understanding, Hayden looks at State's Bureau of Educational and Cultural Affairs (ECA) Collaboratory.

---

9. Page 228.

We learn that the Collaboratory's "'human-centered design' approach" is driven by embassies and program participants rather than explicitly by policy. The approach links massive online open courses (MOOCs) and social media groups with embassies and their local contacts and audiences, 'spreading rather than scaling' outcomes and impacts and working to "incorporate the 'human being to human being part.'"[10] The Collaboratory develops partnerships with educational software firms around the world to mount MOOC Camps for students abroad.

On balance, the chapter favorably assesses the inculcation of new and social media in educational exchanges. The Collaboratory's participant- and field-centric approach is decentralized and privileges the end user, a strategic response to rapidly more empowered global publics. Yet, the growing proportion of virtual learning in ECA exchanges is raising new questions about how to use and measure this kind of soft power. They are questions not only for researchers, but also for policymakers inside, and perhaps more importantly outside, the State Department, where most of the forces driving international education are at play.

Chapter 11, "Funding International Scientific Research Activities as Opportunities for Public Diplomacy," is authored by Jong-on Hahm, whose career in science diplomacy has included serving in the National Science Foundation (NSF) Office of International Science and Engineering. The contributions of Hahm, Hayden, and Albro dovetail on the value of institutional linkages, and virtual and face-to-face exchanges, to collaborate in the realms of science, education, and culture, and to develop, rather organically, areas of mutual interest. From astronomy to zoology, Hahm's narration of

---

10. Page 242.

science as "a natural ground for cultivating public diplomacy" is premised on the shared goals of sustaining the earth and nature while improving the quality of human life. To demonstrate this, she examines two U.S.-based international partnerships and another funded by the European Union.

NSF's Partnerships for International Research and Education (PIRE) was established in 2004, and the NSF-USAID Partnerships for Enhanced Engagement in Research (PEER) in 2011. PIRE was the first U.S. institutional partnership program for scientific research and education abroad. Foreign government laboratories, astronomical observatories, and multinational firms have joined some of the partnerships.

A particularly clear example of public diplomacy was the 2012 PIRE project — Science, Engineering, and Education for Sustainability (SEES) — in which U.S. and foreign students team at overseas research locales and foreign scientists host U.S. students at training workshops. One project involves three U.S. universities and five in France, Turkey, and Singapore, plus multinationals with prior ties in the United States. As signs of effective PPP in U.S. public diplomacy, "the SEES focus threw into relief the increasing universality of challenges across the world, and the need to look beyond U.S. borders for solutions to global problems";[11] many of the projects have endured beyond the original grant period with new funding, including from non-U.S. agencies.

Resources for SEES and PIRE generally have been imbalanced in favor of U.S. partners, affecting project activities. In general, U.S. partners have greater access to equipment, facilities, and travel funds. Also, NSF does not provide support to foreign researchers or institutions. Finally, unlike USAID and the National Institutes of Health's Fogarty International Center, NSF does not maintain any research operations abroad. PEER was launched to address these

11. Page 257.

issues, with USAID furnishing funds to foreign partners. This interagency collaboration was a win-win for U.S. and overseas partners, bringing to fruition 205 projects, including investigations of cassava virus, genetic defects of fish in Indonesian waters, and low-quality water usage in Uzbekistan. Hahm recognizes that financial and in-kind resources do not have to be equivalent from all partners, but that investment commensurate with resource base is needed to demonstrate commitment.

The third case in this chapter is the European Union (EU) Horizon 2020 program. Begun in 2013, it is perhaps the most integrative and ambitious of the three Hahm discusses. The grant competitions are open to all scientists, regardless of nationality, so long as their research occurs in the EU. The program is to invest around €80B in research and innovation development by the end of the decade. It includes mobility fellowships to support graduate students and recent graduates in working around and outside the European Union.

Many of us with experience in international research administration are humbled by the virtues of science diplomacy. Whether at the cross-national, regional, or global level, multi-sector, interagency scientific collaboration speaks volumes as soft power for enhanced diplomacy with some of the most positive benefits to both society and the natural world. We see in this chapter how recent innovations in cross-disciplinary engagements, administrative flexibility, and researcher mobility are improving collaboration quality. In addition, because of built-in mutuality that is at once cross-cultural yet relatively de-politicized, science diplomacy is about as close to paradise as is imaginable in a world of conflict.

Interagency collaboration in the embassy amidst violent conflict is the subject of our last chapter, "Turning Point." Author Brian Carlson begins with the Departments of State and Defense but weaves an argument for a whole-of-government approach that hinges on improved leadership capacity among ambassadors and embassy section chiefs. Informing the analysis is Carlson's Foreign Service career, which culminated with a liaison position between State and DOD on strategic communication and public diplomacy and participation in the 2008 Defense Science Board study of the two fields of practice. The chapter also benefits from field experience of discussants at the breakout session Carlson led on interagency collaboration of the 2013 PDC Fall Forum.

The first of the two turning points to which Carlson refers is World War One. The second is the terrorist attacks of 9/11. After narrating how technological innovations before World War One changed the ways in which battles were fought and U.S. communication with global publics was conducted, the author pivots to the current information and military operations against terrorism. Commercial jets were used by the non-state militia of al Qaeda as weapons of mass destruction to instill fear more than to wreak the havoc they did. Al Qaeda has expertly exploited the Internet and social media to sharpen and spread their information and recruitment campaigns.

Carlson recaps 20th century history on the stand-up and dismantlement of the Committee on Public Information, Office of War Information, and Cold War-era USIA. These episodic organizational innovations are evidence of the United States' "attention deficit disorder."[12]

He notes that by 2006, around the time that he became a liaison between State and DOD, both the front-line and information wars in Iraq and Afghanistan were escalating. Both agencies were trying to

---

12. Page 272.

connect the dots between al Qaeda's success in battle and their methods of recruitment and how to organize counter-propaganda. Carlson observes, as does Helle Dale, that State's analytical and programming efforts were faltering and DOD stepped in to do more "strategic" communication. Finding that the roles and activities of public diplomacy and DOD information operations "intentionally or unintentionally overlap," [13] Carlson suggests an interagency or whole-of-government approach to U.S. communication overseas. He concludes that the Department of State and embassies abroad are best situated to lead both public diplomacy and other information operations among civilian audiences overseas.

Carlson offers five recommendations on interagency collaboration at the embassy. One is for the ambassador and public diplomacy officer to lead by example instead of by issuing orders to other agencies' representatives. A discussant from DOD at the 2013 Public Diplomacy Council Fall Forum said that leadership like that is in short supply. Three other recommendations center on: the need for adequate training and budgeting; avoiding unfunded project mandates and requests; and grounding stakeholder-endorsed program design in clear, measurable impacts, ongoing monitoring, and impact evaluation. The fifth recommendation: although these rules are State's to enforce in Washington, the ambassador and the public diplomacy officer bear the task in the embassy.

Conclusion

U.S. public diplomacy is a big tent, crowded with demands and potential but short on resources. With so many diverse performers and acts under the cover, generalizing about them is risky. This volume aggregates nontraditional approaches to public diplomacy

---

13. Page 276.

that have managed or might have managed particular international relations scenarios well, despite political and resource constraints. From the reflections of our contributors, several common themes emerge.

First, a clear requirement for successful innovation in public diplomacy is fostering better listening to global publics. The more we hear and synthesize in context, the better we understand and generate shared interest.

Second, the craft is becoming more collaborative across sectors as well as intergovernmentally. Beyond one-way messaging and two-way exchanges, the demand for multi-directional and multi-stakeholder dialogues, convenings, alliances, partnerships, and networks will only increase. Because every collaboration differs, but is part of a whole-of-government or even whole-of-community effort, practitioners and analysts need to share experience and research about what makes for successful collaborations throughout the big tent of public diplomacy.

Third, public diplomacy and strategic communication complement each other and can be practiced together and evaluated for their impacts. Organizational innovations at the National Security Council, Department of State, Pentagon, and other agencies should be developed to better align policy and programs for delivery abroad and allowed sufficient time to yield results. The peaceful and violent power of non-state actors should be a central consideration in policy and program design with measurable outputs, outcomes, and impacts on which key stakeholders agree.

Fourth, international programs should not only empower people with personal and professional growth opportunities, but should also be inclusive across generations, cultures, genders, religions, physical ability, level of access to technology, and economic background. Empowerment and inclusiveness strengthen U.S. government credibility.

This volume covers key topics in depth, but like every book, it has limits. It does not focus on big data generated by new media or on social marketing and their implications for public diplomacy. Subnational public diplomacy, arguably predating the nation-to-nation variety, is also not part of this effort. Other potentially compelling topics include sports diplomacy, the dramatic rise in popularity of gastrodiplomacy, and live-streaming via social media. And a whole future volume could be devoted to the impact on public diplomacy of the renewed interest in storytelling traditions and adaptations for the Internet.

With these opening remarks, I invite you to explore the authors' work directly. Let us know your thoughts on nontraditional U.S. public diplomacy at pdc@publicdiplomacycouncil.org.

2

Public Diplomacy: Can It Be Defined?

Anthony C. E. Quainton

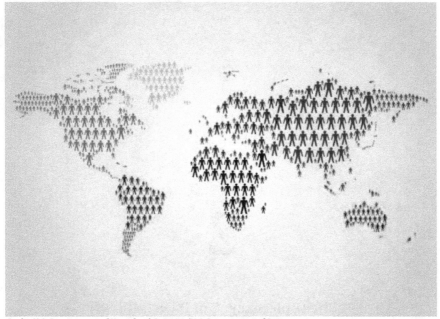

Credit: U.S. Department of Homeland Security/U.S. Department of State

No two words are more fashionable or less clearly understood in the lexicon of international relations than *public diplomacy*. Ever since Joseph Nye wrote his book *Soft Power* in 2004 there has been an academic and bureaucratic debate about how soft power should be projected, with what purposes and with what audiences in mind.[1]

An extraordinary array of programs has been lumped into the tool box of governmental (and private) activities in the international arena and labeled public diplomacy. Some of the activities might more properly be called public affairs or public relations or strategic communications or even propaganda. Or is public diplomacy all of these and more? Are we like the blind man and the elephant identifying parts of the beast without understanding the whole?

---

1. Joseph Nye, "Soft Power and Higher Education," in *The Internet and the University: Forum 2004*, (EDUCAUSE, 2005), 33-60, accessed July 6, 2016, http://www.educause.edu/ir/library/pdf/ffpiu043.pdf.

Some would say this is a futile exercise in definition. Like pornography, one knows it when one sees it.

In the late 1980s the United States Information Agency (USIA), then the guardian of public diplomacy, had the idea that the best way to sell contemporary America was to send young graffiti artists from the Bronx around the Middle East to demonstrate their "art." In due course they arrived in Kuwait, and since we had a pristine security wall around our Embassy, I invited them and a group of distinguished Kuwaitis to come and see the artists at work.

To the amazement and surprise of the audience they successfully defaced a large section of wall near the Residence garden. Kuwait was then a city of white concrete and marble walls and the thought that covering them with what seemed outlandish designs and inscrutable messages bewildered and then horrified my guests.

After it was all over I began to ask myself, what were we thinking of? Was this really public diplomacy? The Public Affairs Officer assured me it was and that we had made a powerful statement about artistic freedom in the United States. I was not so sure. In what sense had we reached a significant public and how, if at all, had we advanced United States interests in the Persian Gulf? Was this bad public relations as well as bad public diplomacy? Was this propaganda for a set of values that had little resonance in Arab society?

Public Diplomacy as Propaganda?

Perhaps one needs to stand back from a relatively insignificant exhibition and ask how we can best differentiate among the congeries of concepts that are related to and occasionally subsumed by the term public diplomacy. The best place to start is with the concept of propaganda. Most recognize that propaganda is bad; the Nazis and the Communists used it to distort truth and promote the values of their evil empires. President Putin of the Russian Federation is said to be a master of propaganda. To the general public it is all about lies. However, in its origins as the office for the Propagation of the Faith, the Catholic Church designed it to project the truth of Christianity as Rome understood it.

Several years ago I asked my graduate students to do a study of another country's public diplomacy; one pair chose the Vatican. On presenting themselves at the nunciature in Washington they were told in no uncertain terms that the Vatican did not "do" public diplomacy; it "did" truth. For the Vatican, public diplomacy was a duplicitous and manipulative technique, not something which could be used to advance religious or bureaucratic interests.

The Oxford English Dictionary confirms the negative stereotype of propaganda, noting that is "the systematic propagation of information by an interested party, especially in a tendentious way in order to encourage or instill a particular attitude or response."[2] Leaving aside the word "tendentious," this definition would not necessarily be uncongenial to public diplomacy practitioners.

Public Diplomacy—What's In a Name?

In the 15 years since the integration of USIA into the Department of State, the problem of definition has become even more confused. A new under secretary position had to be created and the incumbent was made responsible for both public diplomacy and public affairs. The USIA Integration Planning Group defined public affairs as:

the provision of information to the public, press, and other institutions concerning the goals, policies and activities of the

---

2. Simpson, J.A., and E.S.C. Weiner, "Propaganda," *Oxford English dictionary*, Vol. 12, (Oxford: Oxford University Press, 1989), 632.

U.S. government. Public affairs seeks to foster understanding of these goals through dialogue with individual citizens and other groups and institutions and domestic and international media. However, the thrust of public affairs is to inform the domestic audience.[3]

In the pre-integration days, a contrast was between the State Department's focus on informing the American people about the purposes of policy decisions and actions (public affairs) and USIA's focus on forming foreign audiences about those same policies (public diplomacy). The gap was reinforced by the 1948 Smith–Mundt Act, which prohibited the dissemination of USIA-produced materials inside the United States for fear that such dissemination would be seen as government propaganda targeting our own citizens.

The only exception, which required special congressional action, was the dissemination of the film *"Years of Lightning—Day of Drums*, which outlined the six strategic themes of the Kennedy administration and which payed tribute to JFK's life against the background of his funeral.

Public Diplomacy: A Dimension of Diplomacy

The fundamental question is whether public diplomacy is in some way fundamentally different from diplomacy itself. Sir Charles Webster defined diplomacy in words that clearly include what we now understand to be public diplomacy:

Diplomacy is a transaction between individuals or groups and successful diplomacy depends mainly on three things; first, on producing a climate of opinion in which desired ends

---

3. "Public Affairs," *United States Information Agency Planning Group* (1997), accessed July 6, 2016, http://pdaa.publicdiplomacy.org/?page_id=6.

can be most easily obtained; secondly, on devising the forms of agreement in which these ends can be translated into practical accomplishments; and thirdly on creating or perceiving the right moment at which the maximum effort can be applied. For these purposes it is, of course, necessary to possess skill in the presentation of argument and a complete knowledge of the facts.[4]

The key to successful diplomacy is clearly the creation of that "climate of opinion" within which essential policy goals can be achieved.

When USIA set about explaining its mission, it used the following definition: "Public diplomacy seeks to promote the national interest and the national security of the United States through *understanding, informing and influencing foreign publics* [emphasis added] and broadening dialogue between American citizens and institutions and their counterparts abroad."[5]

The private sector approaches the issue somewhat differently. It is not self-consciously in the diplomacy business, although there is increasing awareness of the private sector's role in citizen diplomacy. For the business community, the key issue is public relations: "the business of inducing the public to have an understanding for and goodwill toward a person, firm, or institution."[6]

Former Under Secretary Charlotte Beers was brought in to the Department of State because she was a public relations expert who had successfully marketed Uncle Ben's Rice. A recent Uncle Ben's animated video catches the marketing spirit by enticing viewers to

---

4. Sir Charles Webster, *The Art and Practice of Diplomacy* (New York: Barnes & Noble, 1962), 3.

5. "Public Diplomacy," *United States Information* Agency (1999), accessed July 6, 2016, http://pdaa.publicdiplomacy.org/?page_id=6.

6. "Public Relations," *Merriam-Webster*, October 7, 2014, http://www.merriam-webster.com/dictionary/public relations.

eat rice with the tuneful refrain: "I want you to show me the way." Getting foreigners to ask America to show them the way has never been easy. Under Secretary Beers' efforts at branding America for foreign audiences were not notably successful.

The Importance of Understanding

Repeatedly one hears one key word throughout these definitions: *understanding*. Diplomats, we assert, need to understand the world in all its complexity, including the motivations, behaviors, and objectives of our adversaries in order to devise effective solutions for issues about which decisions need to be taken. This task of understanding is the responsibility of many members of an ambassador's country team, for example, the political and economic officers, the commercial attache, the CIA station chief, the USAID mission director. There is, however, an explicit role for public diplomacy specialists, since they are expected not merely to be able to explain the politician and economic policies of the home government, but to understand the historical and cultural dynamics that underlie those policies.

I remember on arriving in Peru as ambassador in the midst of a highly contentious presidential electoral campaign, the Public Affairs Officer took the initiative to propose a series of lunches at which I could meet academics, think tank analysts, journalists, and politicians so that I, who had no previous experience in the country, could understand what was going on. Those initial contacts and connections proved to be invaluable in the course of the ensuing three years as all of us on the country team struggled to understand the rapidly changing political and economic policies of the Fujimori government.

On the other side of the coin, we want outsiders, foreign publics, and foreign governments to understand our values, culture, and policies. Without such understanding, we face opposition to many of the initiatives we take and programs we seek to implement.

I found that seeking opportunities to go on TV talk shows and to give press and radio interviews were extremely useful, particularly in Nicaragua where Reagan Administration policies were often misrepresented and caricatured. The American people need to understand the rationale for what its government is doing in the world, how it is using the taxpayers' money, and, increasingly, why and how we are using coercive force to achieve our policy objectives.

Understanding is the central task of public diplomacy. From it flow the informing and influencing of foreign publics and the broadening of dialogue between American citizens and institutions and their counterparts abroad. The global and domestic dimensions were at the heart of USIA's self- definition.

The Blessing and Curse of New Technologies

The other two points of the definitional triad, informing and influencing, also play a vital part in public diplomacy. In order to achieve the understanding by foreign target audiences, we need information and communication tools (ICTs). Historically, informing and influencing were the preserve of the press office of an American embassy, and the tools were press releases and distribution of copies of the "Wireless file," USIA's daily synopsis of critical events, speeches, and policies statements by the Administration.

In the digital age, much of that dissemination is done electronically, whether by e-mail or through social media. Given the ready availability of different technologies, the task of informing would seem to have become much easier. In reality it has become more difficult, especially considering the many world regions where radio and television are still dominant. The world suffers from information overload and fatigue. Reaching target audiences, indeed deciding on target audiences has become increasingly difficult. Tweets, blogs, Facebook likes and dislikes all clog the Internet. Yet we must go on trying, since, as the definition clearly implies, informing is an essential and integral part of the understanding which we seek and ultimately of the influencing which we try to achieve. The role of electronic social media in the context of mass demonstrations in Cairo, Kiev, and Hong Kong reminds us of ICTs' power to mobilize.

Breaking Traditions, Opening Political Spaces

Diplomacy used to be the preserve of diplomats. the members of the Foreign Service employed by the Department of State and its sister agencies the United States Agency for International Development (USAID) and USIA. However, since the end of the Cold War and the evolution of the Global War on Terrorism, colleagues in the military establishment have come to see themselves as having a critical role in the public diplomacy arena. For the Pentagon, public diplomacy is not of itself a popular term. It sounds too much like Joseph Nye's less aggressive soft power. While the State Department has tried to downplay soft power, and instead elevate the more recent framing of "smart power," the military has gone its own way emphasizing "strategic communications" as an adjunct of hard power.

The military has always seen itself as having a role in influencing target audiences in combat, usually referring to these activities as *psyops*, for psychological operations. More recently it has moved to *strategic communications*. Two definitions of that have emerged from the military establishment make their view clear. Strategic communications is:

those overt international public information activities of the United States government designed to promote United States foreign policy objectives by seeking to understand, inform, and influence foreign audiences and opinion makers, and by broadening dialogue between American citizens and institutions and their counterparts abroad.[7]

and

focused United States government efforts to understand and engage key audiences in order to create, strengthen, or preserve conditions favorable for the advancement of USG interests, policies, and objectives through the use of coordinated programs, plans, themes, messages, and products synchronized with the action of all elements of national power.[8]

The first of these definitions contains all the elements of traditional public diplomacy by focusing on the triad of understanding, informing, and influencing. The second, however, is much more hard-headed, focusing on information operations as instruments of national power and the explicit advancement of national interests, policies, and objectives. This does not sound like soft power at all, but rather a clear definition focused on strategic objectives, in effect linking public diplomacy activities and programs to narrow foreign policy objectives, rather than to the rather fuzzier objective of creating a general climate within which U.S. interests can be protected and policies advanced.

It is interesting that in a September 2014 meeting at the American Security Project Under Secretary for Public Diplomacy and Public Affairs Richard Stengel talked about hardening soft power,

---

7. "Strategic Communications," *U.S. Department of Defense Dictionary*, accessed October 9, 2014, http://www.dtic.mil/doctrine/jel/doddict/data/p/11548.html.

8. Chairman of the Joint Chiefs of Staff, "Joint Publication 5-0," *Joint Operational Planning* (Washington, DC: August 11, 2011).

suggesting a somewhat more aggressive approach to the use of the media (social and other) in projecting America's message to the world.

The challenge all of these definitions pose is that they presuppose a capacity to understand, a desire to inform, and an ability to influence. These assumptions need to be questioned because it is by no means evident that in the real world of diplomacy we can, in fact, mobilize our public diplomacy resources to do what the definitions suggest.

Understanding would appear to be straightforward. We recruit and train officers with language skills and area knowledge. Unfortunately, however, in the most critical areas of the world, notably in Iraq, Afghanistan, and Pakistan, we limit tours of duty to a year with multiple leaves of absence for rest and recuperation. Officers—unless they are willing to reapply or have a second tour of duty—rarely acquire the expertise required to understand these very complex, tribal, patriarchal societies. Even more problematic is the problem of understanding our adversaries. They are hard to penetrate, highly secretive, and yet inspired with a fervor that makes possible the mobilization of hundreds if not thousands of young people behind their cause.

Our public diplomacy strategy seems to rely heavily on a western understanding of Islam. We repeatedly assert in our public diplomacy messages that Islam is a religion of peace and that our adversaries are in effect heretics. However, most of those making such statements come to Islam from outside, from a Judeo-Christian understanding of the world, and from a Western reading of the bits of the Quran that we find compatible with our own world view. We may not, in fact, be understanding very well at all the motivation and religious fervor of our adversaries.

Indeed understanding is a two-way street. We want friends and foes alike to understand us: to understand our policies, our motivations, and our culture. However, we are very unsure about what aspects of our culture we want them to understand. Is it our freedom, our openness, our diversity? Clearly the answer is yes. But how are we to explain to them those aspects of our culture that are not immediately saleable, particularly in the Muslim world: our consumerism, our materialism, and our evolving sexual mores. How are they, the radicalized youth of the Middle East, to understand us and our values?

The task of informing may also be equally problematic. We carefully craft messages designed to provide information about our values and our policies. We want our target audiences to know the truth and subscribe to our point of view. We know what the tools are available to us: print media, radio, television, and a range of social media as well. But we are less certain about who is listening and about the degree to which those who are listening are truly informed about our action and intentions.

In the ill-fated Central African Empire, when I was ambassador, I was thrilled to be asked to speak at prime time on national television about President Carter's human rights policies and the Universal Declaration of Human Rights. This was a chance to inform the people subject to His Imperial Majesty Bokassa I of their rights. Washington was pleased. This was what ambassadors were supposed to do. However, in truth, the audience with access to television was small, and the ruler, who made all the human rights decisions and who carried out or ordered the human rights abuses, paid no attention whatsoever.

So we can try to inform; we can develop coherent, well-sourced and accurate messages, but the audience we wish to reach may not be listening. Even if they listen, they may not want to believe what we say. Even if they have their cellphones and iPads on, they may not really be listening. There is a concept of what Catholic theologians used to call "invincible ignorance," which may explain why it is that when presented with the truth so many refuse to accept it.

If it is hard to inform, it is also likely to be hard to influence. At the heart of this dilemma is that we are constantly torn between the desire to inform and influence elites—the power brokers in a society—and the publics who tend to be young, impressionable, and politically motivated. In the struggle against the Islamic State in Iraq and Syria, it is clear we have little chance of reaching the leadership of the movement. ISIS leader Abu Bakr al-Baghdadi pays little attention to our words. He may, of course, be analyzing our actions and evaluating the costs imposed on his movement by the use of kinetic force against him and his followers.

We want to influence elites in other Muslim countries. They may feel threatened by the changes going on around them and by the reality that many of their citizens may have sympathy for the radically rigorous version of Islam symbolized by the black flag of ISIS. The result is that much of our public diplomacy strategy focuses on informing and influencing the "street," where disenfranchised and unemployed youth become the recruits of the future.

It remains to be seen whether we can apply the definitional public diplomacy strategy of informing and influencing, or of getting them to understand the world through the same lens that we view it. What is clear is that we need a greatly expanded strategy of engagement, including reciprocal exchanges, creative engagement of our own Muslim fellow citizens, and an effort by all of our diplomats to use social media to listen and respond to the latent grievances in these societies.

At some level of analysis, focusing on these definitions can lead to a certain discomfort or hopelessness. The world will never understand us; we will never understand it. We can never fully inform or adequately influence. Is it all then an exercise in futility? Clearly this is a defeatist attitude that neither advances a nation's interests nor enhances its security. It may be best not to try to be overly precise in defining public diplomacy. We do need to know what we are talking about. We cannot blithely wish public diplomacy away because the definitions do not match the reality or clarify ends and means.

Deconstructing and Reconstructing the Craft

Perhaps then the best approach is simply to start with the two words themselves: public and diplomacy. It is fair to say that historically diplomacy was not about publics, or at, least not primarily. It was about government-to-government interactions designed to achieve mutually agreeable relations that advanced a nation's security and promoted its prosperity. What has changed is not that governments have become irrelevant. They clearly command political, economic, and military power that can be used to one's benefit or detriment.

However, beginning with the nineteenth century revolutions and accelerating through the twentieth century and on into the twenty-first, the power of publics has begun to rival that of governments. Hence, figuring out how to use the skills of diplomacy to understand, inform, and influence another government has not become irrelevant but must be extended and transferred to publics.

Credit: AK Rockefeller, Egypt Tahrir Square (February 2012)

These publics are certainly less well understood. We do not fully comprehend crowd and mob dynamics. Was it social media that mobilized young Egyptians to gather in Tahrir Square to overthrow Egypt's Mubarak regime? Or was it the more traditional medium of TV, especially Al Jazeera TV, which was watched by a vast Egyptian audience? Similarly, on Maidan (a central square in Kiev) and in the pro-democracy demonstrations in Hong Kong, what was the role of social media? Is it the Internet and its various manifestations, which lie at the heart of ISIS' ability to recruit in Arab societies, and other regions as well? We really don't know. We are uncertain how to reach these young audiences.

With the rise of social power, "audiences" may be less of an apt framing than "participants" or "partners." We are uncertain about which messages they will find credible. We are unsure how to influence their behavior. We are only sure that they are public diplomacy's destiny.

Classic diplomacy developed an array of formal tools for communicating between governments, including diplomatic notes and demarches backed by aide memoires. These tools, formal as they were, facilitated the process of accurate communication, negotiation, and ultimately conflict resolution.

The tools for reaching publics are known but are less precise and less susceptible to fine-tuning. We can now reach vast audiences through blogs, Facebook, virtual chat rooms, Twitter, and Instagram. They make it possible to communicate our words but also to listen to a wider array of voices. They also create new problems of volume and of measurement. What does it mean to have 10,000 likes on an Embassy's Facebook page? How do we assess the comments posted on a blog site or responses to an ambassador's tweeting? How do we identify the people with whom we are dialoguing and to whose voices we are expected to listen?

We have no clear answers to these questions. Cross-cultural communication, supported by the skills of psychology and sociology, will become ever more important to public diplomacy. So too will be the tools of big (and small) data and audience analysis. We know that crowd dynamics are surely different from cerebral calculations, reasoned policy analysis, and even the emotional dynamic of the decision making process of the political leaders and elites with whom we are accustomed to interacting. We know much less about the dynamics of mass culture and the ways in which it can be influenced.

What may now be needed is a not a redefinition of public diplomacy but a clearer understanding of both publics and target audiences. Then it will be possible to redefine the very nature of diplomacy to make it possible to have an impact on those publics in ways that advance national interests. The key to success may be the development of more sensitive antennae among diplomats within and outside the public diplomacy cone, making them more capable of listening to the voice of the mob, to understand the historical context and emotional context within which people operate, and thereby to develop new tools to influence as well as inform.

For this to happen, it is useful to recall again Sir Charles Webster's definition of diplomacy, which clearly includes what we now understand to be public diplomacy. His insistence on the primacy of the need to produce a "climate of opinion" is critical. So too is his recognition of perceiving the "right moment" for maximum effort. All diplomats must develop those skills of argument and presentation, timing, and that basis of knowledge, which he asserted was essential to success. These are the challenges of the future. Public diplomacy specialists have a particular role in both creating the climate of opinion and in helping governments understand the appropriate moment for action.

3

Janus-Faced Public Diplomacy: Creel and Lippmann During the Great War

John Brown

Credit: Barat PSN (April 2012)

World War I, the war that did not end all wars, was marked by governments' unprecedented diplomatic efforts to influence public opinion, an increasingly important element in foreign affairs. In the United States, there were two politically active newspapermen who played a significant role in this early form of public diplomacy:[1]

---

1. While arguably practiced by internationally oriented Americans since the Declaration of Independence (see footnote 70) public diplomacy as a term was introduced into the U.S. foreign policy lexicon in the mid-1960s by Dean Edmund Gullion and his colleagues at the Fletcher School of Law and Diplomacy to describe "the whole range of communications, information, and propaganda" in the modern world. See John Brown, "Public Diplomacy and Propaganda: Their Differences," *American Diplomacy* (September, 2008), accessed May 22, 2016, http://www.unc.edu/depts/diplomat/item/2008/0709/comm/brown_pudiplprop.html; see also Nicholas Cull, "Engagement is the New Public Diplomacy or the Adventures of a Euphemism of a Euphemism," *CPD Blog*, June 5, 2009, accessed May 22, 2016, http://uscpublicdiplomacy.org/blog/engagement_is_the_new_public_diplomacy; "'Public Diplomacy' Before Gullion: The Evolution of a Phrase," *CPD Blog*, April 18, 2006, accessed May 22, 2016, http://uscpublicdiplomacy.org/blog/060418_public_diplomacy_before_gullion_the_evol

The first is George Creel (1876–1953), chairman of President Woodrow Wilson's Committee on Public Information (1917–1919) and author of *How We Advertised America, The First Telling of the Amazing Story of the Committee on Public Information that Carried the Gospel of Americanism to Every Corner of the Globe* (1920). The second is Walter Lippmann (1889–1974), a media pundit par excellence, drafter of Wilson's Fourteen Points, who briefly served in propaganda operations of the U.S. Army Military Intelligence Branch in France (1918). Lippmann coined the well-known term "the manufacture of consent"[2] in his influential book *Public Opinion*, first published after the war (1922).

Like the Under Secretary of State for Public Diplomacy and Public Affairs and former *Time Magazine* editor Richard Stengel—whose stated goal is, among others, "to confront ideological

---

ution_of_a_phrase. According to Harold D. Lasswell, an American pioneer in the study of propaganda, it is "the deliberate forming of attitudes by the manipulation of words (and word substitutes)," as cited in George G. Bruntz, *Allied Propaganda and the Collapse of the German Empire in 1918* (Stanford: Stanford University Press, 1938), 5. Another definition of propaganda is by historian Kenneth A. Osgood: "At its core, propaganda refers to any technique or action that attempts to influence the emotions, attitudes, or behavior of a group, in order to benefit the sponsor. Propaganda is usually, but not exclusively, concerned with public opinion and mass attitudes. The purpose of propaganda is to persuade—either to change or reinforce existing attitudes and opinions." Kenneth A. Osgood, "Propaganda," *Encyclopedia of American Foreign Policy* (2002), accessed May 22, 2016, http://www.encyclopedia.com/doc/1G2-3402300123.html. For a list of studies consulted for this article, see John Brown, "Creel, Lippmann, and the Origins of American Public Diplomacy: An Annotated Bibliography," *Notes and Essays*, November 3, 2014, accessed May 22, 2016, http://johnbrownnotesandessays.blogspot.com/2014/11/creel-lippmann-and-origins-of-american.html.

2. See Sidney Blumenthal, "Walter Lippmann and American Journalism Today," *openDemocracy*, October 31, 2007, accessed May 22, 2016, https://www.opendemocracy.net/article/walter_lippmann_and_american_journalism_today.

support for terrorism"[3]—Creel and Lippmann were journalists who worked in communications for the American government in its efforts to promote U.S. national interests at a time of global conflict.

But Creel and Lippmann—strong-willed, ambitious, and well-connected to persons in power—had different views on what the public diplomacy of their day should—and should not—achieve. Creel, at heart a publicist, essentially saw public diplomacy as messaging to mobilize the populace, both at home and abroad. Lippmann, with his scholarly inclinations, viewed public diplomacy as enlightenment to educate the unlearned the world over.

The main point of this chapter is to examine the tension between Creel's and Lippmann's contrasting approaches to public diplomacy—essentially, rhetorical vs. philosophical—thereby shedding historical light on an issue that is still relevant among public diplomacy practitioners today.

Street Dog vs. House Cat

George Creel was born poor near Waverly in Lafayette County, Missouri, the son of a Catholic father and Episcopalian mother. His family was constantly on the move in the west-central section of that state, settling for short periods in Independence and Kansas City. The Creels eventually found a more permanent home in Odessa, Missouri, in 1888. Creel junior soon worked as a journalist in Kansas City and Denver, where he was also involved in local politics. He became a devoted admirer of Woodrow Wilson; his 1916 book, *Wilson and the Issues*, was an accolade to the president.

Wilson appointed Creel Civilian Chairman of the Committee on Public Information (CPI) by his Executive Order 2594, issued in the

---

3. For the current U.S Department of State definition of public diplomacy, see U.S. Department of State, "Under Secretary for Public Diplomacy and Public Affairs," accessed May 22, 2016, http://www.state.gov/r/.

second week of April 1917.[4] Secretary of State Robert Lansing, Secretary of War Newton D. Baker, and Secretary of the Navy Josephus Daniels were named ex officio members of the newly established agency. It was formally abolished by President Wilson (Executive Order 3153) on August 21, 1919.

At its peak the CPI was served by some 150,000 people,[5] by far most of them volunteers. Its wartime mission was "to make the fight for loyalty and unity at home, and for friendship and understanding of the neutral nations of the world."[6] It produced a massive amount of news releases, pamphlets, advertisements, exhibits, posters, and historical essays. Its 75,000 Four Minute men gave short speeches to mobilize popular support for the war and to encourage the purchase of Liberty Bonds. Hollywood films were significant in the CPI's groundbreaking use of visual media. Creel saw his mission as a struggle against the enemy's propaganda: "Always it was our policy," Creel wrote, "to find out what the German propagandists were doing, and then we did not do it."[7]

Lippmann was born rich (but not excessively so) in Manhattan, the son of a Jewish–German couple. After a private school education and graduation from Harvard, he contributed to reformist publications. While only in his 20s, he wrote an acclaimed book, *A*

---

4. See Brown, "When exactly was the Committee on Public Information (CPI) established?" *Notes and Essays*, October 22, 2014, accessed May 22, 2016, http://johnbrownnotesandessays.blogspot.com/2014/10/when-exactly-was-committee-on-public.html.

5. See Brown, "Update–The Committee on Public Information's 150,000: Details from a WWI Propaganda War," *Notes and Essays*, September 28, 2014, accessed May 22, 2016, http://johnbrownnotesandessays.blogspot.com/2014/09/the-committee-on-public-informations.html.

6. *Complete Report of Chairman of the Committee on Public Information, 1917: 1918: 1919* (Washington, DC: Government Printing Office, 1920), 1.

7. George Creel, "Propaganda and Morale," *American Journal of Sociology* 47, no. 3 (1941): 340–351.

Preface to Politics (1913) and became a member of the editorial board of *The New Republic*, founded in 1914.[8] He briefed Colonel Edward M. House, the White House confidant and foreign policy adviser, as well as Wilson himself, on how best to deal with public opinion in wartime.[9] On July 18, 1917, he was appointed assistant to Newton D. Baker, Secretary of War. In late September of that year, House asked Lippmann to serve as secretary of the "Inquiry," a secret government group that worked on plans for postwar peace settlements. Among his duties was producing a memorandum, "The War Aims and Peace Terms It Suggests," which President Wilson used in drafting his "Fourteen Points" speech he delivered to a joint session of Congress on January 8, 1918.

In the summer of 1918, Lippmann joined the U.S. Army, encouraged to do so by Colonel House. (He earlier had been exempted from the draft thanks to his Washington connections.)[10] In France for a few months in 1918 as an officer in the Military Intelligence Branch, his main assignments were interrogating German POWs and preparing leaflets to be airdropped behind enemy

---

8. On *The New Republic*'s editorial policy, see Brown, "Walter Lippmann on the New Republic: 'We have no ... propaganda to grind'," *Notes and Essays*, October 14, 2014, accessed May 22, 2016,
http://johnbrownnotesandessays.blogspot.com/2014/10/walter-lippmann-on-new-rep ublic-we-have.html.

9. There are claims, inadequately substantiated, that Lippmann was a member of the CPI. See Brown, "Why Chomsky is Probably Wrong: Was Walter Lippmann a Member of the Committee on Public Information (1917-1919)?" *Notes and Essays*, September 30, 2014, accessed May 22, 2016,
http://johnbrownnotesandessays.blogspot.com/2014/09/why-chomsky-is-probably-wr ong-was.html.

10. Lippmann tried to avoid conscription in World War I because, supposedly, of his father's ill health. See Ronald Steel, *Walter Lippmann and the American Century* (Boston and Toronto: Atlantic Monthly Press, 1980), 116–117. Lippmann wrote to Felix Frankfurter, see "Felix Frankfurter," Wikipedia, accessed May 22, 2016,
https://en.wikipedia.org/wiki/Felix_Frankfurter: "What I want to do is to devote all my time to studying and speculating on the approaches to peace and the reaction from the peace. Do you think you can get me an exemption on such high-falutin' grounds?" later noting that "my father is dying and my mother is absolutely alone." "As it turned out," his biographer Steel notes, "his father was not to die for another ten years, but the appeal struck a sympathetic ear"; Secretary of War Newton D. Baker added Lippmann "to a cluster of bright young assistants."

lines. While in Europe he participated in an inter-allied conference in London dealing with the coordination of propaganda initiatives.[11] After the war, he took part in the Versailles peace negotiations. On January 23, 1919, he sailed home and was honorably discharged from the military on February 3.[12]

Influential at the White House but not professional diplomats, Creel and Lippmann were both frequently annoyed by the State Department—a WASPish club that did not welcome interference by outsiders. Creel called Secretary of State Lansing a "dull, small man" who "bitterly resented my chairmanship of the Committee." The CPI chairman ridiculed U.S. overseas envoys for going native; he claimed that Walter Hines Page, posted in London, "like so many of our ambassadors, became more British than the British."[13]

As for Lippmann, he complained that, during the war, U.S. diplomatic missions, as "independent sources of information ... did not, with one or two exceptions, exist. ... The very last place to discover American policy was an American Embassy." This is what he had to say about ambassadors: "In Paris the Ambassador, after many years of service achieved, I believe, a smattering of restaurant and taxicab French. ... Mr. Francis in Russia was personally courageous,

---

11. See Brown, "The American word which is the big noise in the propaganda field is being spoken solely by our Allies," *Notes and Essays*, December 7, 2014, accessed May 22, 2016, http://johnbrownnotesandessays.blogspot.com/2014/12/the-american -word-which-is-big-noise-in.html.

12. Steel, *passim.*

13. George Creel papers, Box 3, undated notes attached to Wilson-Lansing, 6/29/17 and to Wilson-Creel, 10/17/17, Library of Congress Manuscript Division. Note: All Creel papers citations refer to Creel materials in the LoC Mss. Division. See also Brown, "Creel vs. Lansing," *Notes and Essays*, December 8, 2014, accessed May 22, 2016, http://johnbrownnotesandessays.blogspot.com/2014/12/creel-vs-lansing.html.

but his equipment for estimating Russian affairs just about touched zero."[14]

Creel and Lippmann disliked each other perhaps even more than they held their noses at the State Department. Their antagonistic relationship began several years before they joined the federal government. In a 1915 article, Lippmann, writing anonymously in *The New Republic*, had severely criticized Creel for his article on a strike at a Rockefeller-owned mine. He called him "a reckless and incompetent person … incapable of judging evidence, and determined to make a noise no matter what canons of truthfulness he violates."[15] Lippmann, 13 years younger than Creel, was also suggesting that his fellow journalist was over the hill—a passé muckraker at a time when muckraking was losing its appeal.[16] Creel, who, like Lippmann, flirted with socialism in his younger days, responded angrily in a letter to *TNR* editors:

> For fifteen years I have devoted myself to a task of agitation in politics and industry, trying always to stay close to what may be termed the "under dog." During this time I have seen oppression, exploitation, corruption, treachery and betrayal in all their forms, and it may well be that these experiences have made me less than judicial, over-quick to suspect and denounce.

---

14. Walter Lippmann, "For a Department of State," *The New Republic* 20, no. 24 (1919): 196.

15. "Paul Kellogg Muckraked," *The New Republic* 2, no. 16 (1915): 61.

16. See Brown, "Creel and Muckraking, or How War Employs Intellectuals," *Notes and Essays* (October 28, 2014), accessed May 22, 2016, http://johnbrownnotesandessays.blogspot.com/2014/10/creel-and-muckraking-or-how-war-employs.html; "Lippmann and Propaganda," *Notes and Essays*, October 8, 2014, accessed May 22, 2016, http://johnbrownnotesandessays.blogspot.com/2014/10/lippmann-and-propaganda.html. The person Creel attacked in his article was Paul H. Kellogg, whom Creel had accused of being insufficiently critical of John D. Rockefeller. Kellogg was an editor of the magazine *Survey*; see Survey Associates, Inc., accessed May 22, 2016 http://www.socialwelfarehistory.com/eras/civil-war-reconstruction/survey-associates-inc/. On Kellogg, see Stewart Halsey Ross, *Propaganda for War: How the United States Was Conditioned to Fight the Great War of 1914–1918* (Jefferson, NC: McFarland, 1996), 272.

You, on the other hand, are academic products who have to be commentators by virtue of self-election, based upon self-evaluation, aided, I believe, by an endowment fund [from the wealthy Straight family] that spares you the fear of existence. The antagonism between us, therefore, is as instinctive and inevitable as that of the house cat for the street dog [emphasis added].[17]

The hostility between Creel and Lippmann can be explained not only by their journalistic quarrels, but also by their different backgrounds.[18] Creel, of Irish-Scotch stock, was raised by his family after the Civil War in a region of Missouri known for its Confederate sympathies. Born with "a streak of vagabondage,"[19] George ran away from his impoverished home at age 15 to work at county fairs.[20] In his early twenties he dreamed of traveling to foreign lands; he actually made it to New York City, riding for free on a cattle train via Chicago to get there. To make ends meet in the big city, he wrote humorous pieces for the local press. He tried to enlist in the army during the Spanish–American War (1898) but failed.[21]

Creel's mother, Virginia, had ancestors from the Old Dominion. Her family's undemanding life in its Missouri white-pillared home

---

17. George Creel, "George Creel Replies," *The New Republic* 2, no. 21 (1915): 209–210. The Creel–Lippmann antagonism persisted for years, although the two evidently had little, if any, personal contact.

18. For details on Creel's and Lippmann's physical appearance, certainly a not insignificant part of their public personae; see Brown, "Creel and Lippmann Face-to-Face," *Notes and Essays*, October 26, 2014, accessed May 22, 2016, http://johnbrownnotesandessays.blogspot.com/2014/10/creel-and-lippmann-face-to-face.html.

19. George Creel, *Rebel at Large: Recollections of Fifty Crowded Years* (New York: G. P. Putnam's Sons, 1947), 23, https://babel.hathitrust.org/cgi/pt?id=mdp.39015028548579;view=1up;seq=9.

20. "George Creel," footnote 3, Wikipedia, accessed May 22, 2016, https://en.wikipedia.org/wiki/George_Creel.

21. Creel, *Rebel, passim.*

before the War Between the States was idyllic, even if "mother's people" were convinced that slavery was "even more of a curse to the white man than the black":[22]

> *The fertile soil yielded rich harvests, and with slave labor necessitating no more than supervision on the part of the masters, there was the ample leisure that permits culture. Every home had its library, and New York newspapers and even London and Edinburgh quarterlies were exchanged and discussed.*[23]

Creel's mother, whom he venerated, gave birth to three sons and kept him "from many a cheapness and compromise," teaching him "the dividing line between the true and the false." But papa Creel, whose Virginia roots dated to 1690, did not earn such admiration from George. When back in Missouri after serving as a Confederate captain, Henry—"reared as a 'gentleman'"—turned into a failed farmer and alcoholic.[24]

Creel's formal education was minimal. In his autobiography, *Rebel at Large: Recollections of Fifty Crowded Years*, written when he was 70, he claims he never went beyond the eighth grade, although he states that "Mother took me out of public school and put me in another that called itself a 'college.'"[25] Creel was, essentially, an autodidact, not that interested in academic learning:

> *The ideal arrangement, as I have come to see it, is this: after high school a year or so of work so as to give some idea of what is wanted out of further schooling. That is what I had in mind for myself, but somehow I could never find either the time or the money.*[26]

---

22. Ibid., 9.
23. Ibid., 4.
24. Ibid., 10, 23.
25. Ibid., 20.
26. Ibid., 49–50.

On his father's side, Creel's family was Roman Catholic. One story has it that an apparition of the Holy Mother of God encouraged George's grandfather, Alexander Herbert Creel, to complete his planned foundation of the town of St. Marys (as it is spelled in George's autobiography) on the West Virginia side of the Ohio River.[27] And it was to a Catholic school, "one of the best ... in the West," St. Xavier's in Cincinnati, that grandpa Alexander sent George's father Henry.[28] The school was run by Jesuits, an order most active in the Vatican's Sacred Congregation de Propaganda Fide, established in the seventeenth century to combat the Reformation, including in an area of Europe that became known as Germany. In his *Rebel at Large*, Creel highlights the work of "the great Jesuit missionary and pathfinder," the Belgium-born Father Pierre-Jean De Smet (1801–1873), who discovered gold in the West but threw it back into the stream where he found it. He feared the yellow metal would attract drunks and adventurers interfering in his conversion efforts.[29] De Smet founded a St. Mary's Mission on the Bitterroot River, not far from present-day Missoula; in 1968, De Smet Jesuit High School was dedicated in Creve Coeur, Missouri.

Writing during the Second World War, Creel enthusiastically evoked the mission undertaken by the Jesuits to save souls:

> *When Pope Gregory XV, back in 1622, created the Congregatio de propaganda fide, what he had in mind, and all that he had in mind, was the guidance of those sandaled missionaries who went forth from Rome to preach the gospel in foreign fields. The propagation of the faith!* The spread of the Christian doctrine! Just that and nothing else [emphasis

---

27. Ellen Dittman Pope, *Pleasants County* (Charleston, SC: Arcadia Publishing, 2009), 10, 18.
28. Creel, *Rebel*, 9.
29. Ibid., 9, 11–12.

added]. *Today, however, propaganda retains no trace of its original meanings and here in the United States particularly has come to stand only for evil, deceit, and corruption.*[30]

George asked his father if he wanted to consult a Catholic priest as he was approaching death, but Henry declined.[31] In the year of his father's passing (1907) and in order to prove to his religious mother, an Episcopalian, that he wasn't an atheist (George had refused to be confirmed, presumably as a member of his mother's faith), he published *Quatrains of Christ*, his first book. It consisted of 120 four-line verses that were a non-denominational Christian answer to the *Rubaiyat*, a volume of Persian poetry then popular "with sentimental women and self-indulgent men."[32]

While young George in Sunday school did not disapprove of the Psalms, the Old Testament struck him (in a sentiment not unknown to Catholics) by its "cruelty, even savagery ... If that was Christianity, I wanted no part of it." In 1932, after writing a book on the deist Thomas Paine, he became increasingly attracted to the *Common Sense* author's form of faith, which saw God "as a Supreme Being whose tenderness embraced all of humanity."[33]

Unlike Creel, Lippmann was an only child. He was raised by his well-off parents in their New York City residence on Lexington Avenue, which he considered home until age 27. Daisy and Jacob Lippmann, second-generation immigrants of German–Jewish background, wanted Walter to grow up as a gentleman. They took him on the obligatory European tours during the summer. But Jacob, a businessman who died of cancer in the 1920s, failed to inspire his son, who pitied rather than respected him (Walter, perhaps in search of an authoritative *pater familias* figure, kept a bust of Napoleon in his room; later, Lippmann was a great admirer of General de Gaulle).

---

30. Creel, "Propaganda and Morale," 341.
31. Creel, *Rebel*, 23.
32. Ibid., 22.
33. Ibid., 21–22.

Walter's mother Daisy, an heiress of considerable wealth (her father, a meat merchant, made a killing in real estate), paid little attention to him. In reaction, Walter's affection for her was very limited.[34]

Unlike Creel, Lippmann was Mr. Ivy League Education, although he did not complete his Harvard M.A., eager to shine in journalism. As an undergraduate at this prestigious college, he studied philosophy and languages, developing ties with distinguished thinkers among the faculty—the pragmatist William James, the Neo-Platonist George Santayana—and attending a seminar given by the Fabian Graham Wallas. Although he never made it as the assistant manager of the freshman track team, he became a big man on campus among the intellectually/aesthetically inclined.[35] (After his graduation, Lippmann made it clear that he accepted the quota system keeping Jews out of Harvard because "Jews were conspicuously different from the white Gentile mentality and should be treated differently."[36]) The far-left John Reed, a member of Lippmann's 1910 class, composed the following ode to his friend (the friendship did not survive political disagreements in later years):

Lippmann,—calm, inscrutable,
Thinking and writing clearly, soundly, well;
All snarls of falseness swiftly piercing through,
His keen mind leaps like lightning to the True;
His face is almost placid—but his eye—
There is a vision born to prophecy!
He sits in silence, as one who has said:
"I waste not living words among the dead!"
Our all-unchallenged Chief![37]

---

34. Steel, *passim.*
35. Ibid.
36. Steel, 195.
37. Ibid., 28.

Lippmann had far less religious fervor than Creel, if he had any at all. True, Walter was confirmed at age 14 at Emmanu-El, the most prominent congregation in the Reform Branch of Judaism. But, as Steel points out, "[Lippmann's] religious faith was minimal. In this sense he was like most German Jews of his class and background." In his later years Lippmann did consider converting to Catholicism, but its appeal to him was not "its promises of redemption," but "rather the sense it conveyed of communion in a moral order above the whims of transient majorities and the dictates of tyrants."[38]

Creel, who worshiped his mother perhaps no less than devout Catholics honor the Virgin Mary, was something of a feminist before his time. He repeatedly fought—both as a journalist and a controversial minor reform-minded city official—for women's right to vote; he was vehemently opposed to prostitution and red-light districts. A strong believer in the institution of marriage, at least in print, he remained with the same spouse, the independent-minded California-born actress Helen Bates (a divorcée), until her death in 1941; they had two children. As CPI chairman, Creel broke diplomatic ground when he selected a woman, Vira Whitehouse, to "spread the gospel of Americanism" (Creel's words) in Switzerland, much to the irritation of the male members of the U.S. mission there.[39]

At one point, Lippmann and Creel briefly corresponded about their participating in a New York's woman suffrage campaign.[40] But Lippmann, who did not get along with his mother and divorced his first wife (a dance teacher who in her youth "cared no more for politics than he [Walter] did for the tango"[41]) did not share Creel's

---

38. Ibid., 7, 491–492.
39. For more details on this significant episode of early American public diplomacy, see Greg Wolper, "Woodrow Wilson's New Diplomacy: Vira Whitehouse in Switzerland, 1918," *Prologue: Quarterly of the National Archives and Records Administration* 24, no. 3 (1992): 227–239.
40. Ross, 18.
41. Steel, 118.

enthusiastic advocacy for equality of the sexes; as a Harvard undergraduate, however, Lippmann did write that suffragettes may be "unladylike, just as the Boston Tea party was ungentlemanly," but "unfortunately in this world great issues are not won by good manners."[42] Walter's two marriages were both childless; Lippmann, marked by a "hatred of his Jewishness ... thought it inadvisable for his 'mixed marriage' to produce children."[43]

Papa, Please Love Me Most: Creel, Lippmann, and Wilson

Creel first heard Woodrow Wilson speak on the subject of democracy to Kansas City high school students.[44] The future CPI chairman became a fervent Wilson loyalist, never deviating, or so one surmises, from the instructions of his White House idol Wilson -- arguably for him a Southern father figure who psychologically replaced his "absent" alcoholic, "loser" Missouri male parent during George's difficult childhood in the defeated Dixie. While running the CPI, he told (reassured?) the president that "propaganda, of course, goes hand in hand with policy."[45] Both Creel and Wilson had Southern roots, and this may have solidified their ties, as Creel implies in his *Rebel at Large*:

> *I knew that he was born in Virginia, of course, but as I had never thought of him as a Southerner, the realization came as a surprise. One day during the war, while discussing the work*

---

42. Ibid., 26.

43. Alfred Kazin, "Walter Lippmann and the American Century," *The New Republic* 183, no. 7 (1980): 38.

44. Creel, *Rebel*, 101.

45. George Creel papers, Box 3, Creel-Wilson, 12/27/17. For Lippmann, with such low respect for his own sickly father, President Wilson (before his illness at the end of his second term) might have also been considered a reliable WASP guide, when Walter was still relatively young, to sturdy adult manhood/success in the then very Anglo-Saxon defined USA.

of the Committee on Public Information, I told him of my decision not to play up German atrocities, believing it a criminal blunder to base our propaganda on hate. The President approved, but added grimly that there was still another reason. "The Germans," he said, "might remind us of Sherman's march through Georgia."[46]

Creel, with ancestors from Scotland and Ireland, claimed publicly that Wilson was "half Irish and half Scotch," a statement that resulted in the following newspaper headline: "Creel's Speech Angers Crowd ... Declares Wilson is one Half Irish."[47]

Wilson, who acknowledged to Creel (perhaps too modestly) that "I am no expert in publicity,"[48] valued George's press and promotional know-how. The chief executive, who as Princeton president appointed the first Catholic to its faculty, insisted that Creel be on the CPI's payroll, from which George had "dismissed himself" when he assumed the agency's leadership."[49] During Creel's tenure as CPI chairman, the president stubbornly defended his faithful supporter from attacks by the turf-conscious State Department. When a third assistant secretary at Foggy Bottom, Breckinridge Long, suggested in a letter to Wilson (November 19, 1917) that "the government can best utilize the press by making it a part of the extraordinary war organization" (Secretary of State Lansing, who evidently couldn't stand Creel, doubtless had a hand in this proposal, which was made on official State Department stationery), Wilson replied bluntly that:

The Committee on Public Information, of which Mr. George Creel is Chairman, was created by me for the very purposes you outline, and if it had met with the cooperation of newspaper men instead of their petty jealousy, it would have answered its purpose at once. Moreover, it has been very

---

46. Creel, *Rebel*, 6.
47. Unidentified newspaper clipping, George Creel papers, Box OV 2: 33.
48. George Creel papers, Box 2, Wilson-Creel, 7/21/18.
49. George Creel papers, Box 3, Creel-Wilson, 3/1/17; Wilson-Creel, 5/14/17.

difficult to get one or two of the executive departments, notably the Department of State, to act through Mr. Creel's committee in the matter of publicity and the embarrassments of lack of coordination and single management have been very serious indeed.[50]

The highly educated Lippmann was not as close to Wilson as the undereducated Creel, perhaps because the chief executive had endured too many contentious academic colleagues while serving as Princeton University president (1902–1910). More important, though, was that Lippmann's *The New Republic* was at times critical of Wilson's policies, which the president did not take well. When Colonel House, the ever-faithful Wilson foreign policy adviser, passed on to the president in the summer of 1918 a negative missive from Captain Lippmann—then stationed in France with the Military Intelligence Branch[51]—on the CPI's activities in Europe, Wilson was quite irritated. "I am very much puzzled as to who sent Lippmann to inquire into matters of propaganda," Wilson told his Texas-born confidant, noting that "I have found his judgment most unsound, and therefore unserviceable in matters of that sort because he, in common with the men of *The New Republic*, has ideas about the war and its purposes which are highly unorthodox from my point of view."[52]

---

50. George Creel papers, Box 3, Breckinridge-Long, 11/19/17; Wilson-Breckinridge, 11/20/17.

51. A must-read on this episode in Lippmann's career, during which he had unique "real-life" human encounters that confirmed his Platonic suspicion of the unlearned, is Stephen Vaughn, "Prologue to Public Opinion: Walter Lippmann's Work in Military Intelligence," *Prologue: The Quarterly of the National Archives and Records Administration* 15, no. 3 (1983): 151–163.

52. Steel, 146.

When yet another Lippmann message castigating the CPI's activities in Europe reached the Oval Office in 1918, Wilson blew his top. (Evidently, House's earlier remark that "unlike other Jews, he [Lippmann] is a silent one" had limited effect on the president, reputedly anti-Semitic, although Princeton appointed its first Jewish faculty member under his leadership.) Wilson said Lippmann should be shipped back to the United States; his Military Intelligence Branch unit, the president ordered, should be placed under CPI authority for all propaganda activities. The president informed the secretary of state that "I have a high opinion of Lippmann, but I am very jealous in the matter of propaganda ... [and] want to keep the matter of publicity in my own hands."[53]

Told by House of the "friction" he was causing, Lippmann pleaded not guilty to the Colonel: "You know, of course, that I am a thousand times more interested in the Inquiry [see above] than in propaganda, and that I only went into it because I was told I was needed."[54]

Lines of authority between the CPI and the State Department "continued to be blurred for the remaining months of the war, but Creel kept the upper hand."[55]   Lippmann, however, eventually got his revenge on Creel through unforgiving prose, writing after the war in *The New Republic* that:

> the outfit [CPI] which was abroad "selling the war to Europe" (the phrase is not my own) gave shell-shocked Europe to

53. See Brown, "Wilson and Propaganda: 'entirely in my own hands,'" *Notes and Essays*, November 7, 2014, accessed May 22, 2016, http://johnbrownnotesandessays.blogspot.com/2014/12/wilson-and-propaganda-entirely-in-my.html.

54. Steel, 147.

55. Ibid., 130, 145–147, with citations from Lippmann and Wilson. See also Brown, "Cooperation between Committee on Public Information and the Military Intelligence Branch," *Notes and Essays*, December 7, 2014, accessed May 22, 2016, http://johnbrownnotesandessays.blogspot.com/2014/12/cooperation-between-committee-on-public.html; "World War I Propaganda Wars: War Department vs. Committee on Public Information," *Notes and Essays*, December 7, 2014, accessed May 22, 2016, http://johnbrownnotesandessays.blogspot.com/2014/12/world-war-i-propaganda-wars-war.html.

understand that a rich bumpkin had come to town with his pockets bulging and no desire except to please. One would never have dreamed from these "personal representatives of the President" who were all over the place that America had purposes and interests and ideas and reservations together with its whole-hearted determination to win the war.[56]

Several years later, in his review of *The Intimate Papers of Colonel House*, Lippmann had this to say about what he considered were Wilson's true views toward propaganda:

His real judgment he expressed several times, to the horror not only of the Allied spokesmen but of Colonel House; it was that the war arose out of obscure causes that were hatched in a sinister system and a tortuous diplomacy. Wilson never accepted the official propaganda even when it blew the hottest; he never respected it, and could hardly bear to listen to it. What he wanted above all things was to keep out of the hideous mess. House on the other hand was much too practical a politician to permit himself to stray into such a wilderness of unusable truth, even if he had not really wanted the Allies to win.[57]

Id, Ego, and Public Opinion

Creel, that admirer of the Propaganda Fide, repeatedly emphasized the importance of inspiring the "soul" in order to motivate—convert might be a better word—people. In his article, "Mobilizing America's

---

56. Lippmann, "For a Department of State": 196. See also Brown, "Walter Lippmann reviews George Creel's book on the Committee on Public Information," *Notes and Essays*, October 10, 2014, accessed May 22, 2016, http://johnbrownnotesandessays.blogspot.com/2014/10/walter-lippmann-reviews-george-creels.html.

57. Walter Lippmann, "The Intimate Papers of Colonel House by Charles Seymour" (book review), *Foreign Affairs* 4, no. 3 (1926): 384.

Resources for the War" (1918) he wrote, for example, that "We want public opinion that springs from the heart and soul." Earlier in his *Wilson and the Issues* (1916), he stressed that "the soul of the many is found in the far-flung idealism of the Declaration of Independence, not in the cautious phrases of the Constitution."[58]

Credit: Jeremy Segrott , To dress extravagantly in war time ... (August 2014)

Yet apparently contradicting himself, as he not infrequently did, Creel could also argue that public opinion was a rational process. "As a lifelong admirer of Thomas Paine," he wrote during World War II, he had learned "another fundamental of propaganda":

Many people believe that public opinion—the keystone in the arch of morale—is a state of mind, formed and changed by the events of the day; a combination of kaleidoscope and weathercock. At every point Paine dissented from this theory, denying that public opinion had its rise in the emotions and

58. George Creel, "Public Opinion in War Time," *Mobilizing America's Resources for the War, The Annals of the American Academy of Political and Social Science* 78 (1918): 185–194, 191. See also Creel, *Wilson and the Issues* (New York: The Century Co, 1916): 147, https://archive.org/stream/creelwilsonissue00georrich#page/n5/mode/2up.

*was tipped from one extreme to the other by every passing
rumor and every gust of passion. On the contrary, he
proceeded upon the assumption that [public opinion] had its
source in the minds of the people, its base in reason. ... In
every issue of the Crisis, every issue of Common Sense, he
provided "information" for the "formation" of public opinion.
True, he argued mightily in every pamphlet, but always from
the facts in the case.*[59]

In contrast to the emotional Creel, the analytical Lippmann
(more "ego than id," in Alfred Kazin's words)[60] stressed that a
person's opinions had little do with reason. Lippmann expressed his
thoughts in *Public Opinion*, a book—still influential today—that
reflects not only his reading of Plato (the order of the intellect) and
Freud (the anarchy of the subconscious), but also his real-life
experience in France as a U.S. Army intelligence officer who
interrogated German prisoners of war with limited knowledge of the
outside world.

Lippmann begins his book (first published in 1922 and
republished in 1943) by defining public affairs and public opinion:
*Those features of the world outside which have to do with the
behavior of other human beings, in so far as that behavior
crosses ours, is dependent upon us, or is interesting to us, we
call roughly public affairs. The pictures inside the heads of*

---

59. Creel, "Propaganda and Morale," 347–348. Creel during WWI argued that public
opinion was an emotional process (see footnote 58). Yet in 1941, the year "Propaganda
and Morale" appeared, he seemed cast doubt on the contention made by Lippmann in the
1922 edition of *Public Opinion* (which was republished in 1943; see footnote 61) that
public opinion was an irrational/emotional process ("the pictures inside the heads of ...
human beings ... are their public opinion"). If so, it is ironical that Creel, (inadvertently, or
to downgrade the "wisdom" of his WWI journalistic rival Lippmann) was dismissing his
very own 1918 claim that public opinion was based on emotion.

60. Kazin, "Walter Lippmann and the American Century," 38.

these human beings, the pictures of themselves, of others, of their needs, purposes, and relationship, are their public opinions. Those pictures which are acted upon by groups of people, or by individuals acting in the name of groups, are Public Opinion with capital letters.

In a passage reminiscent of critical observations on today's increasingly Twitter-defined, Facebooked communications, he adds that:

We shall inquire first into some of the reasons why the picture inside so often misleads men in their dealings with the world outside. Under this heading we shall consider the chief factors which limit their access to the facts. They are artificial censorships, the limitations of social contact, the comparatively meager time available in each day for paying attention to public affairs, the distortion arising because events have to be compressed into very short messages, the difficulty of making a small vocabulary express a complicated world, and finally the fear of facing those facts which would seem to threaten the established routine of men's lives.

He goes on to present a key argument: that public opinion, based on so many false suppositions and limited information, must be enlightened by experts. There follows a memorable series of closing paragraphs, in which Lippmann summarizes his views on how to shape public opinion objectively for the benefit of the unknowing populace:

That the manufacture of consent *is capable of great refinements no one, I think, denies ...*
The creation of consent is not a new art. It is a very old one which was supposed to have died out with the appearance of democracy. But it has not died out. It has, in fact, improved enormously in technic, because it is now based on analysis rather than on rule of thumb. And so, as a result of psychological research, coupled with the modern means of

communication, the practice of democracy has turned a corner. A revolution is taking place, infinitely more significant than any shifting of economic power.

Lippmann then speculates on the implications of creating public consent on a rational, rather than emotional, basis:

Within the life of the generation now in control of affairs, persuasion has become a self-conscious art and a regular organ of popular argument. None of us begins to understand the consequences, but it is no daring prophecy to say that the knowledge of how to create consent will alter every political calculation and modify every political premise.

What follows are Lippmann's views on the use of a certain *kind* of propaganda:

Under the impact of propaganda, not necessarily in the sinister meaning of the word alone, the old constants of our thinking have become variables. It is no longer possible, for example, to believe in the original dogmas of democracy: that the knowledge needed for the management of human affairs comes up spontaneously from the human heart. Where we act on that theory we expose ourselves to self-deception, and to forms of persuasion that we cannot verify.

And the final line of the book is Lippmann the philosopher's Q.E.D: "It has been demonstrated that we cannot rely upon intuition, conscience, or the accidents of casual opinion if we are to deal with the world beyond our reach."[61]

---

61. Walter Lippmann, *Public Opinion* (New York: Macmillan, 1943), 29–31, 248–249.

Creeling vs. Lippmanning

Few members of the Wilson Administration became as unpopular as George Creel, especially among policy- and opinion-makers in Washington. He was seen by many as arrogant and intolerant of criticism. In his role as Wilson's combative mouthpiece, he was repeatedly accused of fudging the facts, including on war-related news.[62] "Creeling"—making things up—became part of the press and congressional vocabulary. And, to make matters worse for him, Creel, seen by many as a Wilson propagandist, was linked to another activity—censorship—that contributed to his blemished reputation in a country that cherishes free speech.

Propaganda and censorship became two sides of the same counterfeit Creel coin in the public mind. But this may have been inevitable. After all, the ex-officio members of the CPI—Secretaries Daniels, Baker, and Lansing—had signed a letter to President Wilson on April 13, 1917, stating that "it is our opinion that the two functions—censorship and publicity—can be joined in honesty and with profit, and we recommend the creation of a Committee on Public Information."[63] Not long before the U.S. declared war on Germany, Creel—condemned by a scholar writing about him as an

---

62. See Brown, *Notes and Essays*: "Press and Congressional Criticisms of Propaganda Tsar George Creel, Chairman of the Committee on Public Information (1917-1919)," October 28, 2014, accessed May 22, 2016, http://johnbrownnotesandessays.blogspot.com/2014/10/press-and-congressional-criti cisms-of.html; "Criticisms of George Creel, the Chairman of the first USG Propaganda Agency, The Committee on Public Information (1917-1919), in the Intellectual Press, 1910s-1960s," October 29, 2014, accessed May 22, 2016, http://johnbrownnotesandessays.blogspot.com/2014/10/criticisms-of-george-creel-cha irman-of.html; "Theodore Roosevelt on Propaganda Tsar George Creel, Chairman of the Committee on Public Information (1917-19)," October 26, 2014, accessed May 22, 2016, http://johnbrownnotesandessays.blogspot.com/2014/10/theodore-roosevelt-on-propa ganda-tsar.html; and "FDR and George Creel's Propaganda: Not a Model for WWII," October 16, 2014, accessed May 22, 2014, http://johnbrownnotesandessays.blogspot.com/2014/10/fdr-and-george-creels-propag anda-not.html.

63. Walter E. Bean, *George Creel and His Critics: A Study of the Attacks on the Committee on Public Information, 1917–1919* (Berkeley: University of California, 1941), 66, corrected carbon copy of Ph.D. dissertation stored in the George Creel Papers, Box 7, LoC Mss. Division.

opportunist[64]—had written to Daniels, a fellow Southern journalist (from North Carolina) with whom he was on good terms: "By the way, I am in the field for a job. If a censor is to be appointed, I want to be it."[65]

In his self-promoting apologia pro vita sua, *How We Advertised America: The First Telling of the Amazing Story of the Committee on Public Information that Carried the Gospel of Americanism to Every Corner of the Globe*, Creel stressed that the CPI advocated "voluntary censorship." Its goal was expression, not repression. It was "the voice created to plead the justice of America's cause before the jury of Public Opinion." "In no degree," he emphasized, "was the Committee an agency of censorship, a machinery of concealment."[66] Regardless of his disclaimers, George Creel became known in America as *the* Censor of his time. When, as CPI chairman, he joined the multi-agency Censorship Board, established on October 12, 1917, his notoriety for shackling the media and attacking free speech was assured.

Lippmann, too discreet to ever be subjected to the public opprobrium that Creel endured, had advised Wilson early on in 1917 that censorship in wartime should be handled by people having "real insight and democratic sympathy"; "clearly," Steel notes, "Lippmann had Creel in mind as one to whom such a delicate task should not be entrusted."[67]

---

64. Ross, 222: "Creel was ... a narrow-thinking opportunist, always willing to compromise his diminishing bag of marketable ideals for expediency's sake." On a contemporary historian's evaluation of Creel and the CPI, see Brown, "Richard T. Arndt on George Creel and the Committee on Public Information (1917-1919),"*Notes and Essays*, October 12, 2014, accessed May 22, 2016, http://johnbrownnotesandessays. blogspot.com/2014/10/richard-t-arndt-on-george-creel-and.html.

65. Ross, 218.

66. George Creel, How We Advertised America: The First Telling of the Amazing Story of the Committee on Public Information that Carried the Gospel of Americanism to Every Corner of the Globe (New York: Harper's & Brothers, 1920), 4, 6, https://archive.org/details/howweadvertameri00creerich.

67. Steel, 125.

Lippmann was not against all forms of censorship, so long as it was intelligently implemented (same with propaganda). He seemed less concerned about the pernicious effects of censorship at home than about the failure of the CPI's overseas propaganda. In his 1920 review of Creel's *How We Advertised America* (a title he found "excruciating") Lippmann concluded "there is probably no healthy way in which a government based on consent can enter the business of manufacturing consent."[68]

During and after the war, Lippmann repeatedly blamed the CPI for mishandling how America should present its ideas to the world. But he did realize, sooner rather than later, that the Wilsonian policy he was so influential in shaping—the Fourteen Points proclaimed to a nondemocratic world—had not been a success in and of itself. So Lippmann pointed his finger at the propagandist (Creel). This kind of "blame game" has, of course, a long history in foreign affairs: the strategists blaming the "propagandists" for failures in implementing the strategists' very own policies.

Still, Lippmann did acknowledge, but ambivalently, the results of the work of Creel's CPI in his *Public Opinion*:

Probably this is the largest and the most intensive effort to carry quickly a fairly uniform set of ideas to all the people of a nation. The older proselyting [sic] *worked more slowly, perhaps more surely, but never so inclusively. Now if it required such extreme measures to reach everybody in time of crisis, how open are the more normal channels to men's minds? The Administration was trying, and while the war continued it very largely succeeded, I believe,* in creating something that might almost be called one public opinion all over America [emphasis added]. *But think of the dogged work, the complicated ingenuity, the money and the*

_____

68. Brown, "Walter Lippmann reviews George Creel's book on the Committee on Public Information," *Notes and Essays*, October 10, 2014, accessed May 22, 2016, http://johnbrownnotesandessays.blogspot.com/2014/10/walter-lippmann-reviews-geo rge-creels.html.

personnel that were required. Nothing like that exists in time
of peace, and as a corollary there are whole sections, there
are vast groups, ghettoes, enclaves and classes that hear only
vaguely about much that is going on.[69]

The Tense Legacy of Creel and Lippmann

Arguably, the roots of American public diplomacy go back to the
Declaration of Independence.[70] Many historians have also accurately
traced its origins to U.S. government World War I propaganda efforts,
citing the CPI's structure, programs, and use of the latest
communications technologies, including visual ones. What can also
be found in this period is the genesis of an anti-propaganda tradition
in the United States,[71] a negative reaction to the CPI which led in
part to the Smith–Mundt Act of 1948[72] that prohibited the domestic
dissemination of State Department information products intended
for foreign audiences.

What could use more emphasis in understanding the past of U.S.
public diplomacy, however, is this activity's inherent tension, as it
evolved in the twentieth century, between the rhetorically inclined
(Creel) and the philosophically minded (Lippmann) among those who
practice and advocate this form of foreign relations. Essentially, Creel

---

69. Lippmann, 48-49.
70. John Brown, "Empire of Ideas" (book review), *American Diplomacy* (April
2013), accessed May 22, 2016,
http://www.unc.edu/depts/diplomat/item/2013/0105/bk/book04_brown_empire.html.
71. See Brown, "The Anti-Propaganda Tradition in the United States," *Public
Diplomacy Alumni Association*, July 4, 2003, accessed May 22, 2016,
http://www.publicdiplomacy.org/19.htm.
72. The Smith–Mundt Act was recently amended. See Emily T. Metzgar, "Smith–
Mundt Reform: In With a Whimper? It's Now Legal to Broadcast Voice of America
Stateside, But Few Seem to Notice," *Columbia Journalism Review*, January 21, 2013,
accessed May 22, 2016,
http://www.cjr.org/behind_the_news/smith-mundt_modernization_pass.php.

told his tales with "news";[73] Lippmann argued his points with ideas. To be sure, philosophy and rhetoric cannot be surgically divided; their dichotomy, in real life, is not that clear, as I personally experienced as a Foreign Service officer (1981–2003).[74] Still, there was an emotional and intellectual tension between Creel and Lippmann (if not within themselves), a tension that shapes today's public diplomacy and that is well illustrated in Plato's *Gorgias*, a dialogue in which the philosopher Socrates asks the rhetorician Gorgias, "Shall we then assume two sorts of persuasion, one which is the source of belief without knowledge, as the other is of knowledge?"[75]

In the recent past, public diplomacy was mostly handled by the United States Information Agency (USIA), established in 1953. It was praised as "the most effective anti-propaganda institution on the face of the earth" by Secretary of State Albright upon its consolidation in 1999 into the State Department.[76] USIA's abolition repeated a recurrent historical pattern: When a global conflict ends (WWI,

---

73. See "Propaganda-World War Ii [sic]," *Science Encyclopedia*, accessed May 22, 2016, http://science.jrank.org/pages/10871/Propaganda-World-War-II.html: "When Sir John Reith (1889–1971), the former director general of the BBC, was appointed minister of information in 1940, he laid down two fundamental axioms, that 'news is the shock troops of propaganda' and that propaganda should tell 'the truth, nothing but the truth and, as near as possible, the whole truth.'"

74. See Brown, "The Purposes and Cross-Purposes of American Public Diplomacy," *American Diplomacy* (August 2002), accessed May 22, 2016, http://www.unc.edu/depts/diplomat/archives_roll/2002_07-09/brown_pubdipl/brown _pubdipl.html. I voluntarily left the U.S. Foreign Service in March 2003 in opposition to the planned war in Iraq, a senseless adventure that was marked by arguably one of the most reprehensible and mendacious USG propaganda campaigns in American history. See "Following is the text of career diplomat John Brown's letter by which he resigned from the Foreign Service," *American Diplomacy* (April 2003), accessed May 22, 2016, http://www.unc.edu/depts/diplomat/archives_roll/2003_01-03/brown_resign/brown_ resign.html.

75. See "Plato on Rhetoric and Poetry," section 4 on Gorgias, *Stanford Encyclopedia of Philosophy*, accessed May 22, 2016, http://plato.stanford.edu/entries/plato-rhetoric/; Plato citation from *American Rhetoric: Plato on Rhetoric*, accessed August 7, 2016, http://www.americanrhetoric.com/platoonrhetoric.htm/.

76. Madeleine Albright, "The Importance of Public Diplomacy to American Foreign Policy: Remarks at a ceremony commemorating the consolidation of the Department of State and the U.S. Information Agency," *U.S. Department of State Dispatch* 10, no. 8 (1999): 9; on USIA, see *United States Information Agency*, accessed May 22, 2016, http://dosfan.lib.uic.edu/usia/.

WWII, the Cold War), the U.S. government eliminates its "information" agencies.

During the USIA era, public diplomacy's inherent tensions were illustrated, among many examples, by the differing priorities of Charles Z. Wick[77] and Senator J. William Fulbright.[78] Wick (1917 [the date the CPI was founded]–2008), the longest serving USIA director (1981–1989), appointed by President Reagan, a Republican, emphasized the use of the fast media (e.g., television) in the ideological struggle against communism. (Like Creel, Wick was a confidant to the president). Arkansas Democratic Senator J. William Fulbright (1905–1995), on the other hand, fought for his "propaganda-free" State Department educational exchange program, named after him, that was created in 1946 almost singlehandedly by him to bring people throughout the globe closer together, despite his being a segregationist back home. (Like Lippmann, Fulbright was

77. See Timothy Noah, "The Rise of a Not-so-great Communicator: Charles Z. Wick, Entrepreneur," *The New Republic* 186, no. 15 (1982): 11–14. Wick did increase funding for the Fulbright program, but this program was not his first priority; "information" via television was. See Joseph O'Connell, "U.S.I.A. Is Guardian Of Fulbright Program," letter to the editor, *The New York Times*, June 27, 1986, accessed May 22, 2016, http://www.nytimes.com/1986/07/26/opinion/l-usia-is-guardian-of-fulbright-program -675886.html. Regarding Wick's use of propaganda, see Alvin A. Snyder, *Warriors of Disinformation: How Charles Wick, the USIA, and Videotape Won the Cold War* (New York: Arcade Publishing, 2012). Wick's obituary: Godfrey Hodgson, "Charles Wick," *The Guardian*, August 3, 2008: "He was born Charles Zwick in Cleveland on October 12 1917. ... He shifted the Z from the front of his name to the middle when he was working as a business adviser to the Tommy Dorsey swing band in the 1930s ... Charles Z Wick, political adviser, born October 12 1917; died July 20 2008" (note: no period after "Z"), accessed May 22, 2016, http://www.theguardian.com/world/2008/aug/04/usa; Douglas Martin, "Charles Wick, 90, Information Agency Head, Is Dead," *The New York Times*, July 24, 2008, accessed May 22, 2016, http://www.nytimes.com/2008/07/24/us/24wick.html?_r=1.

78. See Stacey Cone, "Pulling the Plug on America's Propaganda: Sen. J. W. Fulbright's Leadership of the Anti-propaganda Movement, 1943–74," *Journalism History* 30, no. 4 (2005): 166–176; and Yelena Osipova, "Fulbright on USIA," *Global Chaos*, January 11, 2012, accessed May 22, 2016, http://lena-globalchaos.blogspot.com/2012/01/fulbright-on-usia.html.

critical of the White House.[79]) In 1978, Fulbright's pet program was transferred from the State Department to USIA, which the Senator had criticized (along with the Voice of America)[80] as being a propaganda operation.

Questions raised by the Creel–Lippmann tension continue to this day: Should the U.S. government, in its overseas outreach efforts, tell America's "amazing" story (to use Creel's adjective) or should it search for, and share, universal truths? What should be the focus of public diplomacy in the future—delivering information or imparting knowledge?

Yes, the usual answer to these eternal questions has, for years, been constantly repeated: American public diplomacy should harmonize both approaches for the sake of the Republic's national interests. But the tension between these two ways of communicating (narrative vs. truth?) is not one that can be easily resolved—even with the best emotional, intellectual, and bureaucratic intentions. This, perhaps, is the most important public diplomacy lesson to be learned from George Creel and Walter Lippmann during the Great War.

79. See David Lauter and Burt A. Folkart, "Fulbright, Critic of Cold War Policy, Dead at 89: Politics: Ex-Senator, a Noted Segregationist, Created Student Exchange program," *Los Angeles Times*, February 10, 1995, accessed May 22, 2016, http://articles. latimes.com/1995-02-10/news/mn-30368_1_james-william-fulbright. "Truman dubbed him [Fulbright] 'Half-Bright'": David Greenberg, "Give 'Em Hell, Barry: Obama needs a little of the Truman touch," *Slate*, November 19, 2010, accessed May 22, 2016, http://www.slate .com/articles/news_and_politics/history_lesson/2010/11/give_em_hell_barry.html.

80. Lippmann also was critical of Voice of America; so was Creel, but no doubt for different reasons (by the 1950s Creel had become a strong anti-Communist Joseph McCarthy supporter; see Ross, 271–272). See Brown, "Walter Lippmann, 'The Voice of America Should be Abolished,' Los Angeles Times, April 29, 1953," *Notes and Essays*, September 30, 2014, accessed May 22, 2016, http://johnbrownnotesandessays.blogspot.com/2014/09/walter-lippmann-voice-of-am erica-should.html.

4

The Uses and Abuses of Public Diplomacy: Winning and Losing Hearts and Minds[1]

Dick Virden

---

1. Portions of this work draw on three of the author's prior publications: Dick Virden, "Thai Memoir~Firsthand Observations on Countering Insurgencies: Lessons for Today?" *American Diplomacy* (September 2012), accessed June 10, 2016, http://www.unc.edu/depts/diplomat/item/2012/0712/fsl/virden_thai.html; Dick Virden, "Poland During the Cold War," *American Diplomacy* (December 2011), accessed June 10, 2016, http://www.unc.edu/depts/diplomat/item/2011/0912/ca/virden_poland.html; Dick Virden, "Coming Home: Different Popes for Different Times," *American Diplomacy* (April 2014), accessed June 10, 2016, http://www.unc.edu/depts/diplomat/item/2014/0105/fsl/virden_popes.html.

Credit: Onyca, The largest display of unaltered portions of the Berlin wall outside of Germany (October 2014)

The term "public diplomacy" had not yet been invented when I started engaging in this activity by other names a half century ago. Though we seem now to have settled on what to call it, we still debate what it means, how best to practice it, and what we can expect it to accomplish. The last question is the most critical.

Some American public diplomacy efforts were dramatically different in kind, truly exceptional assignments that went far beyond public diplomacy's core function of securing popular approval abroad for the United States and its policies. In the most extreme cases—during wars both hot and cold—the task was to persuade foreign audiences to back—or resist—their own governments. This is clearly a much trickier, more controversial undertaking, whether we call it public diplomacy or include it under the category of nation-building, democracy promotion, political warfare, counterinsurgency, or, as some would have it, subversion.

The pursuit of these extraordinary, unconventional, and sometimes misconceived objectives is the subject of this chapter. These tasks were usually part of major national commitments, not the work of public diplomacy specialists alone. Some of the campaigns succeeded, while others failed. On the plus side, we can count our four decades of nurturing nonviolent democratic opposition to communist regimes in Eastern Europe. That effort ended triumphantly with the fall of the Berlin Wall. The actors in white hats—the ones we supported and who embraced our ideas and values—took power, mostly without bloodshed. An unloved communist system was tossed on the ash heap of history. Few wept (President Putin aside).

Thailand is another positive example. A counterinsurgency program that the United States inspired, funded, and helped conduct there in the late 1960s prevailed. That Southeast Asian country did not "go communist," as we feared at the time. Instead, rural residents stuck with the Bangkok government rather than join communist rebels bent on revolution.

On the other side of the ledger, however, our all-in American battle for allegiance in nearby South Vietnam failed disastrously. We did not capture the hearts and minds of the rice farmers of South Vietnam, despite a horrendous expenditure of blood and treasure. We lost a war and the admiration and trust of much of the world in the process. We also created or exposed huge ruptures in our own society and undermined trust in our institutions.

Something all too similar could be happening today with our effort to persuade Muslim believers to choose us and our local allies rather than anti-western Islamic militants. The struggle is not going well, and many Americans grow understandably tired of it. Yet this is no war of choice; it is another vital contest of ideas, one central to the war on terror and our own security. Barack Obama acknowledged the importance of this battle in the early months of his presidency when he chose to go to Cairo, the heart of the Arab world, to address Muslims everywhere. Such efforts have borne little fruit to date. But given that there are more than 1.5 billion Muslims, and that Muslims are a majority in 49 countries, folding up our tent and walking away is not an option. We will, however, need to compete more effectively than we have until now.

With that end in mind, this chapter will examine a few selective cases in which extraordinary public diplomacy efforts helped achieve a vital national objective (Thailand in the late 1960s, Eastern Europe during the Cold War), and others in which we failed (South Vietnam) or risk failing (Iraq, Afghanistan).

What can we take away from our experiences to date in this and other such contests? The Pentagon used to conduct after-action reviews or "lessons learned" sessions after every major engagement. The exercises are still done but are now more often called "lessons identified," in sad recognition, it seems, that we do not always learn what we might from our past. And yet we must—or risk more national tragedies.

Public Diplomacy and Its Purposes

Public diplomacy is the effort by governments to understand, inform, and influence foreign publics. Though more elaborate definitions are available and have merit, this one seems to me the most useful because by sticking to the basics it encompasses the wide range of jobs Americans leaders have set for our public diplomats at different times and in quite diverse situations.

For nearly four decades, I worked on many public diplomacy campaigns, conventional and otherwise, as a Foreign Service Officer with the United States Information Agency (USIA) and then the State

Department. Before entering the Foreign Service, I spent three years as a writer and editor for USIA's Wireless File in Washington, where a plaque on the wall of the headquarters at 1776 Pennsylvania Avenue said we were "telling America's story to the world."

Most observers will concede both the validity and the need for such efforts. In fact, some think this should be public diplomacy's *only* purpose, that we should mind our own business and devote our efforts to explaining ourselves. Certainly authoritarian regimes impatient with our "meddling" (on human rights, for example), have so argued, and many Americans feel we should indeed confine ourselves to nation-building at home. President Obama has said he'd like to do just that.[2]

Yet we continue to be drawn into foreign quarrels, no matter which party is in power in Washington and how much our leaders would prefer otherwise. And when we do engage in internal conflicts abroad, our strategy necessarily includes trying to affect the attitudes of ordinary people toward their own governments and pretenders to power. What ordinary citizens in big cities and distant villages think and feel about us and the side we're backing will be critical, often decisive, even if that part of our strategy gets short shrift in our calculations and allotment of resources.

Those responsible for designing and carrying out our public diplomacy campaigns must find ways to ensure that the impact of our actions on audiences abroad is taken into account by those weighing whether to invade, negotiate, or sit on the sidelines.

---

2. See https://www.whitehouse.gov/blog/2011/06/22/president-obama-way-forward-afghan istan; and http://abcnews.go.com/blogs/politics/2012/05/obamas-weekly-address-time-to-focus-on-nation-building-here-at-home/.

Edward R. Murrow's demand to be in on the takeoffs, not only the crash landings, is a worthy but still unrealized goal. In pursuit of it, public diplomacy experts cannot stand on ceremony; they should volunteer their perspectives while decisions are still in the balance, without waiting to be asked. If more observers with real understanding of Iraqis had warned how they would respond to an American invasion of their country, or if senior leaders had paid heed to those who did speak up, we might have avoided one of the most disastrous foreign policy decisions in our nation's history.

The prediction that we'd be welcomed in Baghdad with open arms when we attacked Iraq in 2003 is a particularly unhappy contemporary example. What was the basis for that false prophecy? Who challenged it? Where were the experts who actually knew something about how Iraqis might react to a U.S.–led intervention? Were the deciders for war aware of the Sunni–Shi'a divide?

If public diplomacy includes understanding your target audiences, we as a nation missed the mark in Iraq by a heroic margin. Not anticipating the insurgency that would follow the overthrow of Saddam Hussein was another disaster, even if the blame goes more to others (politicians, the media, intelligence analysts, military commanders) than to public diplomacy practitioners, who were probably not even consulted about the likely consequences of an invasion.

Nor have we fared notably better in the years since that 2003 invasion. There has been little apparent improvement in our understanding of Iraqis or our ability to persuade them to accept our point of view about how they should be organized and governed. Maybe things will yet work out brilliantly there, but you could get long odds on such a bet.

In mining my own public diplomacy experience for potential lessons, I'll start with a success story: counterinsurgency in Thailand.

Counterinsurgency in Thailand

Thailand was my first post in the Foreign Service. I landed in Bangkok in early 1967 to begin work for the United States Information Service (USIS), the field organization of USIA, then our chief public diplomacy agency, later absorbed by the State Department. Our USIS program in Thailand at that time was both unconventional and large, with a sprawling headquarters in a leafy compound in the capital and as many as thirteen branch posts. We even briefly had a post in the tiny northeastern town of Surin, known chiefly for its annual elephant roundup.

Today we've gone to the opposite extreme, leaving megacities in Brazil, India, and elsewhere around the globe with no U.S. government representative, no eyes and ears on the scene whatsoever. This feast or famine approach is neither sound nor in our own long-term interest.

The United States was engaged so intensively in Thailand in the 1960s because we feared the communist insurgency in Vietnam would spread there. We worried that a disaffected population could turn against the government here, too, as in Vietnam. Thailand was a key ally, one of only a half dozen countries with troops on the ground in South Vietnam, about a thousand soldiers at the peak. Thailand also allowed the Pentagon to set up a string of air bases in the northeast region to wage bombing campaigns in nearby Vietnam and Laos. We believed our national interest required keeping Thailand stable and on our side.

Thailand was then governed by the same political dynamic that had prevailed since the absolute monarchy was overthrown in 1932. Power was shared between the King and Army generals. The trappings of democracy were in place, but this was no Jeffersonian state. Those who pushed from within for greater democracy and deeper reforms made little headway. Rulers were aloof, and their writ rarely extended into the countryside, even in the lowland plains, much less the distant mountain regions. That many villages still lacked electricity, passable roads, and even schools was a telling indicator of long neglect. To their credit, Thai leaders recognized that the pattern had to change, and that economic development and counterinsurgency were required for their own survival.

After a half year of training in various USIS offices in Bangkok and at our consulate in the far northern city of Chiang Mai, I was assigned as Branch Public Affairs Officer in the north central river town of Phitsanuloke, midway between Chiang Mai and Bangkok. Our job was counterinsurgency, then the focus for most of the U.S. Mission in Thailand. The U.S. aim was to help bring the government and people closer together. In short, this was a battle for "hearts and minds," in the language of the day.

For our part, USIS pursued this cause in the field mainly through what we called "mobile information teams," or MITs. We traveled by Jeeps, often via ox-cart trails. The point was to get Thai government representatives out of their offices and out among the rice paddies to show villagers that their government was there for them and deserved their support. The concept seemed simple enough, but getting city-dwelling officials into the boondocks went against the grain. Traditionally, state officials stayed put; if the peasants wanted something, they should come to them. The notion of reversing the flow, of reaching out to earn the respect of the governed, was radical change, a value Americans added to the equation.

The suggestion that loyalty had to be earned—not granted automatically as their due—was a novel notion for mandarins steeped in a centuries-old authoritarian system. Some Thai officials —particularly those trained at the district academy created by the

United States Agency for International Development (USAID)—were willing enough to venture out but lacked the means. We paid for our gas and often theirs. Our supplying the wherewithal and impetus helped overcome inertia.

We wanted officials on the trips who brought meaningful help: veterinarians, doctors, or other health practitioners, agricultural specialists, and educators, along with line district and provincial officials. We encouraged them to bring items to give away: medicine, for example, or new strains of seeds.

The country had an estimated 50,000 villages in the late 1960s; most of them lacked electricity, running water, schools, competent health care, and decent roads. Vital development work was just getting started, and there was not yet much to show for it. Many areas had yet to be reached at all. Rice farmers lived out among the paddies as they had since time immemorial, and they were not used to having government officials around, much less foreigners.

The American officer in the group was often the first *farang*—white foreigner—to show up in a village, a real curiosity. We brought along sleeping bags and tossed them on the floor of the school or *wat* (a Buddhist temple). We usually brought our own food and drink. In effect, we were following Mao Tze Tung's manual on guerrilla behavior; for example, don't take anything from villagers without paying for it, treat women respectfully, and so on.

Our officers had all been given enough Thai training to get by in the language, but we tried to minimize our own presence, to stay in the background and allow Thai officials and our own Thai staff to take the lead in distributing pamphlets, showing movies, and providing practical help. Our goal wasn't to make the village people pro-American, but rather pro-Bangkok. We knew that if it looked as if we were running the show, we'd be undermining our own purposes. Our national interest in this case was the survival of an important ally.

I left Thailand for reassignment in late 1969. When I returned to Bangkok in 1980, the city and country still looked and felt familiar, but the U.S. government's priorities had changed. Rather than being concerned with rural insurgency, which was fading into the background, we were concerned about the aftermath of wars in Vietnam, Cambodia, and Laos. In particular, large numbers of refugees from all three of those countries had fled to Thailand by land or by boat, inundating camps set up to give them temporary asylum and creating a wrenching humanitarian crisis.

What of that insurgent threat that had so preoccupied us in the 1960s? Why did Thailand not go the way of Vietnam?

Thailand's own strong, cohesive culture was the decisive factor. For centuries, the country had managed to stave off would-be colonial powers, in part through skilled diplomacy, in part because of the unifying force of the royal family and Buddhism. King Phumiphon remained a revered, god-like figure for most Thais throughout this period. Only in later years would his star dim as Thais fighting for greater liberalization begin to see Phumiphon as anti-democratic and hostile to their reform agenda. But in the 1960s and 1970s, loyalty to King Phumiphon helped hold the country together.

Another key element was that rural life had measurably improved. Over the years, once poor, inaccessible villages benefitted from roads, electrical power, schools, and potable water. The development work by the Thai government and outside entities, USAID included, paid off. Villagers had started to share in the nation's progress, and, with that, to perceive a government serving them, too, not only princes and generals.

In addition, Thailand acted in time, partly because of U.S. prodding, partly because it saw the danger of what was happening nearby in Vietnam. Thailand began to pay attention to its rural citizens *before* an incipient insurgency could take hold. As in medicine, prevention is easier and better than cure.

Developments outside the country, including an end to the wars next door and a lessening of support for revolutionary parties from Moscow and Beijing, also played a role in Thailand's case, as did crackdowns against leading militants and olive branches offered to those ready to come out of the shadows. Closing the American air bases also took away an issue that had been a rallying cry for rebels.

But what of the U.S. involvement? Did it make a difference? Is there a winning formula that the United States might adopt for dicey situations elsewhere? Yes and no. Our insistence that more attention must be paid to rural citizens clearly did change official Thai attitudes. We can take some satisfaction in introducing the democratic ideal that governments must earn the consent of the governed and not take it for granted. Still, much as we might preach that gospel and regard it as universal, it might not take everywhere, particularly in societies without the heft and texture that has held Thailand together for so many centuries. It was already a nation; we didn't have to try to build it. Thailand remains a key ally today, even as it now contends with rising demand for greater democracy and King Phumiphon became too old and frail to be the stabilizing factor he once was.

Failure in South Vietnam

What worked in Thailand did not work in South Vietnam. The horse we backed there never even made it to the finish line; it faltered and fell in the face of a final push by Hanoi and the Viet Cong. Our massive decades-long national commitment to the Saigon government could not rally the citizens of the south to our proxy. We lost, even though we sent an expeditionary military force of more than half a million American soldiers, controlled the air, and had overwhelming firepower.

Actually, our fearsome military force may have been part of the problem, often acting at cross-purposes with our appeal for popular support. "Grab them by their balls and their hearts and minds will follow," one American officer sneered. Tough talk, but it didn't work out that way. When our mammoth B-52 bombers dropped their explosives from miles above, they devastated village life and land. The raids may have achieved their military objective—clearing the area, draining the swamp—but the wholesale physical destruction and loss of lives only made villagers more hostile toward the foreign giant behind them. Ditto for the burning of villages and tactics such as "armed propaganda teams."

When progress is measured by counting bodies, "soft power" has little chance to win the day. Were we trying to compel or attract Vietnamese to our camp? The two approaches are at war with each other, and we never resolved the fundamental incoherence in our strategy.

Our engagement in Vietnam, of course, was a whole-of-government approach, to use a term now fashionable in discussions of public diplomacy. Civilian agencies—USIA, State, USAID, CIA, and others—were fully committed, so disproportionally in fact that often-vital matters elsewhere were left unattended. When I was assigned to Vietnam in early 1970, I was told that about half of USIA's officers had already served there. For the Foreign Service Officers of today, Iraq and Afghanistan became similar drains on staffing, budgets, and other resources. The opportunity costs are incalculable.

USIA had two fundamental tasks concerning Vietnam: one was to convince South Vietnamese to accept and actively support the Saigon government. The second was to convince friends and allies elsewhere that our Vietnam policy was necessary, moral, legal, sound, and working. These were misguided goals—a fool's mission—and neither one was achieved, despite intense efforts. When President Johnson sent senior diplomats and military officers around the world on an intensive, "many flags" campaign, only seven nations signed up to join us on the ground in South Vietnam. It was America's war.

When the Americans withdrew, the side we'd spent so much blood and treasure building up collapsed ingloriously, the North Vietnamese and Viet Cong took over, and Saigon became Ho Chi Minh City. The mistakes that contributed to this outcome are too many to count. In a now forgotten 1966 book called "The Lost Revolution," Robert Shaplen of *The New Yorker* argued that our Vietnam fate may have been effectively sealed as far back as 1945, when we allowed the French to move back in, to regain their colonial status, as the Japanese were defeated. We put ourselves on the wrong side of history, a handicap no amount of military might, valor, and skill could overcome.

What mattered most in the end was Vietnamese nationalism. The Vietnamese people were tired of domination by outsiders: the French, the Japanese, and then the French again in recent times, and the Chinese for centuries before that. If America had experts who knew the depth of Vietnam's anti-foreign sentiment, they were never close enough to power to whisper in the ears of Kennedy, Johnson, McNamara, or the others who led us into an unwinnable war. Our diplomats as well as our military officers saluted and marched forward. The can-do attitude so characteristic of the American military is an admirable trait, but at times pointing out forthrightly what cannot be done may be the greater virtue. Would that we had practiced it.

Public diplomacy begins with understanding the people you're trying to reach. Tragically, we intervened in Vietnam knowing little of its language, culture, history, or day-to-day concerns. We saw the country's importance only in broad, Cold War terms; we did not consider the interests of the Vietnamese people. Whether out of ignorance or arrogance, we went to war in Vietnam without appreciating the sentiments of the people we were undertaking to save. Public diplomacy cannot succeed under such circumstances. We paid dearly for our folly, and unfortunately, it was not the last time we'd make such a mistake.

Liberating Eastern Europe

On the other hand, we did much better on another front of the Cold War. Using the limited public diplomacy tools available in the closed societies of Eastern Europe, we helped encourage, nurture, and sustain democratic activists while pressuring communist party leaders to grant them greater rights. When, for example, we provided Poland with hundreds of millions in agriculture credits to make up for the annual shortfall in wheat production, we conditioned our aid on liberalizing moves by the Warsaw government. (An example of the gallows humor of the day: why the chronic failure of agricultural plans under socialism? Answer: 40 years of bad weather.)

My first tour in Warsaw was as Information Officer/Press Attaché in the late 1970s, when the country was still behind the Iron Curtain, as Eastern Europe was described in those days. To Poland's government and party leaders—though not most citizens—ours was considered a hostile embassy. It was true our sympathies were with regime opponents; we did indeed want and expect communism to wither away and for democracy to emerge from the shadows.

We did our part to hasten the arrival of better days. To whittle away at the party's monopoly on information, for example, we did things like give away bootleg copies of *Newsweek*. We couldn't send them through the mail—they'd be stolen or confiscated—but slipped them directly to our friends. Since access to information was tightly controlled, uncensored news was a highly sought commodity. We also distributed USIA magazines, including Polish editions of *Dialogue* and *America Illustrated (Ameryka*, in Polish).

Broadcasting was a prime lever of state power. As elsewhere in the region, government controlled domestic radio and television, then the main source of news as well as entertainment. To counter it, Radio Free Europe, Voice of America, and BBC shortwave radio from outside the country provided a broadcast alternative, an antidote to regime propaganda. For those who dared listen—and they were legion—these surrogate stations provided factual reporting not available from their state-controlled media.

What Poles heard about their own country from their official mouthpieces was flatly contradicted by the misery they encountered in their daily lives. The bitter economic reality clashed with the party narrative about a workers' paradise. No wonder gallows humor proliferated. Some 30 years into socialism, people no longer took their government seriously. Poland's domestic credibility gap was every bit as severe as ours during the Vietnam War era.

We sought to identify open-minded people from every profession and involve them with our Fulbright, International Visitors, and other exchange programs. It often took intense bargaining with party officials to get grantees authorization to travel, but the effort paid off when many of these journalists, economists, academics, politicians, and religious leaders later helped lead the peaceful revolution and the new Poland that emerged after 1989.

When Polish friends wanted to talk about something sensitive, we met them for walks in parks, where the state's recording devices did not reach. Other times we simply showed up on public occasions to show the flag and demonstrate where we stood. During my first fall in Warsaw, in 1977, I joined other Western diplomats at the opening of the academic year at the Catholic University in Lublin (KUL), then the only private university east of the Oder. It had a long, proud tradition, including a library whose core collection had been spirited out of a Catholic seminary in St. Petersburg at the time of the Russian revolution.

In their ceremonies, KUL administrators traditionally acknowledged, one by one, each diplomatic representative. The minister of religious affairs, a Communist Party official, was usually present and could hardly miss the point about our support for principles like freedom of speech, inquiry, and religion.

Among those present for that KUL ceremony in 1977 was Cardinal Karol Wojtyla, then an adjunct professor in addition to his duties as the bishop of Krakow. A year later he would become Pope John Paul II. When he returned home for the first time as Pope in June of 1979, there was general euphoria as the first Slavic Pontiff awed and lifted up his countrymen with his charismatic persona and message of faith and hope.

Within a year of the Papal visit, a powerful trade union/protest movement—appropriately called "Solidarnosc"—would burst on the scene. It began on the Baltic coast, in Gdansk, where an unemployed electrician named Lech Walesa jumped over a shipyard wall and into history. The gathering threat to their legitimacy eventually prompted communist party leaders to impose martial law in an effort to hold back the tide. They failed. Within a decade, the seemingly invincible communist system was swept away, in Poland and elsewhere in the region.

That the 1979 Papal visit would prove to be such a transformative event was would have been beyond the hopes of the throngs that accompanied John Paul II everywhere his pilgrimage took him that week, but it was clear we were seeing something great, powerful, historic, and good. No one could have imagined what would come next, but everyone knew life would not continue on as before. The facts on the ground had changed, and the hitherto all-powerful regime would be on the defensive until its demise.

This was a long twilight struggle, as President Kennedy said, but it ended in triumph with the 1989 fall of the Berlin Wall. Quoting a Chinese proverb, JFK observed that success has a thousand fathers while failure is an orphan. Public diplomacy was one of the many fathers of that Cold War victory, a war won not by guns but by information, ideas, and values.

Credit: Roger W, Berlin - Brandenburg Gate (August 1963)

Our stress to our East European friends throughout this period had been on peaceful struggle. We were careful not to encourage violent action or suggest that we would back it. Some contend that 1956 Budapest was an exception, that Radio Free Europe incited Hungarian rebels to take to the streets with implied offers of support. Whatever the historical facts—about which fierce debate still continues—the danger of promising more than will be delivered should be clear.

My family and I left Warsaw early in the summer of 1980 for a new assignment in Thailand. By the time we returned in 1994, Poles had overcome the odds to win their struggle for independence. The Cold War was finished, as was communism, the Soviet Union, and the Warsaw Pact. Poland itself, a country that had been once been carved up by Prussia, Austria, and Russia, was back on the map and governed by leaders of its own choosing.

Our second tour in Poland, from 1994 to 1997, was dominated by the issue of NATO expansion. Poland wanted membership to guarantee its long-sought independence and security. We and our NATO allies agreed to grant it if Poland made the necessary military, political, and economic reforms. They did their part and we did ours. Poland did not miss its historic opportunity but went on to build a successful democracy and one of the strongest economies in Europe.

Fewer Resources and Shifting Priorities

With the end of the Cold war, the United States started cutting budgets and reducing our presence around the world, including in Poland. We were forced to close our consulate and USIS branch post in Poznan, in the western part of the country, leaving our consulate in Krakow as our only diplomatic representation outside the capital. Closing that USIS post saved at most a couple hundred thousand dollars a year, at great cost in hurt feelings and lost contacts. To the Poles, it looked like we had lost interest and lacked staying power. Now we are trying to put Humpty Dumpty back together again, beefing up our representation to try to reassure Poles about the strength of NATO's resolve to defend the country in the wake of Putin's threatening behavior nearby in Ukraine.

Domestic politics converged with the popular theory that we no longer required "Cold War tools" including public diplomacy, and USIA was folded into the State Department in 1999. It was as if the end of the Cold War—and history—meant America could safely ignore the rest of the world and return to 1930s-style isolation. Hollywood captured this myopia in *Charlie Wilson's War*, a film showing America coughing up billions to drive the Soviets out of Afghanistan but then begrudging even chump change for schools and roads for our Afghan friends.

Our indifference to post-Soviet Afghanistan came back to haunt us when Al Qaeda operatives, directed from their sanctuary in Afghanistan, attacked our homeland on September 11, 2001. We've been embroiled in Afghanistan ever since, once again at great cost in blood and treasure. The wars in Iraq and Afghanistan will ultimately cost U.S. taxpayers more than $3 trillion, according to estimates.[3]

U.S. civilian and military leaders have repeatedly made clear that we are in Afghanistan mainly to protect our own security, not help Afghans. The Afghans will have noted such statements as well as the overwhelming evidence that we want to leave and will, sooner rather

---

3. See E. Londoño, "Study: Iraq, Afghan War Costs to Top $4 Trillion," *The Washington Post*, March 28, 2013, accessed April 27, 2015, https://www.washingtonpost.com/world/national-security/study-iraq-afghan-war-cost s-to-top-4-trillion/2013/03/28/b82a5dce-97ed-11e2-814b-063623d80a60_story.html. See also L. J. Bilmes, "The Financial Legacy of Iraq and Afghanistan: How Wartime Spending Decisions Will Constrain Future National Security Budgets," *HKS Faculty Research Working Paper Series RWP13-006* (March 2013); National Priorities Project, "Cost of National Security," accessed April 27, 2015, https://www.nationalpriorities.org/cost-of/.

than later. They know that when we're gone, they'll have to find a way to live with the forces in and around their country, including the Taliban. Those facts of life on the ground also help explain why Afghanistan's nuclear-armed neighbor, Pakistan, resists our insistence that it join us in making all-out war against the Taliban. Some of what our friends in the region do seems confounding—and ungrateful—to Americans, but is entirely rational from the point of view of Afghans or Pakistanis acting out of what they see as their interest. Once again, there is a gulf in understanding.

In our contemporary wars in Afghanistan and Iraq, we're attempting to persuade citizens of those countries to support governments we've installed in Kabul and Baghdad. Some say we are exporting democracy and freedom, just as we did in Eastern Europe during the Cold War. Somehow, though, it feels more like we're repeating our Vietnam error by trying to prop up weak, corrupt, unrepresentative, and unstable regimes. Our very military presence, and the collateral damage caused by our use of unstaffed drones, appears to arouse more bitter anti-West resentment than gratitude, relief, or agreement. Our words of assurance are belied by the widespread death and destruction. Once again, our strategy seems to be at odds with our hope of capturing the imagination of Muslim publics.

In another trouble spot, 2014 Ukraine, pro-Western activists overthrew a president who was democratically elected but corrupt. President Putin claimed we instigated this revolution, citing evidence such as Assistant Secretary of State Victoria Nuland's intercepted phone conversations with our ambassador in Kiev cherry picking who should be allowed in and who kept out of a new government. Putin used such "interference," a phenomenon he knows well, to justify his takeover of Crimea and fomenting of separatism in eastern Ukraine.

What were we actually doing in Ukraine? Were our democracy-promotion activities there a logical and legitimate continuation of what we did throughout Eastern Europe during the Cold War? Or did we go farther this time and encourage an armed revolt, as we were accused of doing in Hungary in 1956?

Some contend we have been too interventionist in Ukraine and also in Syria, where a multitude of rebel groups are waging a civil war that may be at least partly in response to President Obama's 2011 declaration that President Assad had to go. Did our president, perhaps emboldened by the success of his earlier call for the replacement of Libya's Qaddafi, imply too much? Or was the Syrian opposition guilty of wishful thinking, hearing only what they wanted to hear?

Listen Better, Understand More, Preach Less

Answers to the difficult questions about Iraq, Afghanistan, Syria, and Ukraine are uncertain, just as our approach toward these and other troubled areas has long been ambivalent. Americans remain torn between isolationism and a belief that as the indispensable nation we have a special role to play in the world. We are a reluctant sheriff, yet we have accustomed the world to expect America to take on every new security crisis. President John Quincy Adams once said that America did not go abroad in search of monsters to destroy. But we have, often, and we continue to find new dragons we believe need slaying.

If we hope to improve what has been a mixed record of convincing foreign publics to see these adventures our way, we might start with clearer thinking and more honesty about our intentions. We often hear that we have a great foreign policy but that we don't tell our story very well. Actually, the reverse is often the case. Good public diplomacy cannot make bad policy sound.

When we do take sides in internal conflicts, our ability to influence events will likely be on the margins, a distant second in importance to the strength of local governments and societies. As outsiders, our role should be modest, subtle, and close to invisible. Otherwise, our very presence becomes part of the problem and a lightning rod for anti-foreign sentiment, as in Vietnam and much of the Middle East today.

Finally, we need to look before we leap, to take the trouble to understand where others are coming from before trying to prescribe their futures. At the founding of our own country, we declared "a decent respect to the opinions of mankind." Our prospects will improve if we honor that tradition and consider the perspectives of the people whose support we're trying to attract. That's where we came in as a nation.

5

America's Image Abroad: The UNESCO Cultural Diversity Convention and U.S. Motion Picture Exports[1]

Carol Balassa

1. This chapter is adapted from Carol Balassa, *America's Image Abroad: The UNESCO Cultural Diversity Convention and U.S. Motion Picture Exports* (Nashville: The Curb Center for Art, Enterprise & Public Policy at Vanderbilt University 2008), accessed May 23, 2016, http://www.vanderbilt.edu/curbcenter/files/Americas-Image-Abroad-final.pdf. The author wishes to express gratitude to Carol Bidault and Jonathan Levy for their detailed comments and useful advice on many points in this report. The views expressed are solely those of the author.

Credit: Marc Falardeau, DIVERSITY (April 2013)

Beginning in 1998, a consortium of cultural ministers led by representatives of Canada and France advanced a set of principles ostensibly formulated to protect creative work grounded in the cultural heritage of communities and nations. From 2003 to 2005, the informal activities of this group were debated and ultimately memorialized within the United Nations Educational, Scientific and Cultural Organization (UNESCO) as the "Convention on the Protection of the Diversity of Cultural Expressions."

Most informed observers of the UNESCO negotiation leading up to adoption of the Convention agree that the initiative was not about the integrity of "cultural expressions" but instead represented longstanding attempts by Canada and France to remove from World Trade Organization (WTO) trade rules any trade issue touching on a service, good, or agricultural product that might be viewed as being related to cultural expression.[2] Adoption of a new international agreement, whose ambiguous objectives cover a broad range of measures that governments can justifiably enact "to protect and promote the diversity of cultural expressions,"[3] was viewed by Canada and France as the appropriate instrument to attain this goal.

This chapter examines the U.S. response to the Canadian–French initiative in the period leading up to adoption of the UNESCO Convention, offering an unexplored opportunity to understand how U.S. motion picture exports affect foreigners' views of the United States. The chapter concludes with a recommendation designed to address some of the issues that formed the backdrop to negotiation of the Convention, giving special emphasis to the U.S. film industry as a symbolic and practical arena within which to address attitudes toward U.S. cultural products in the world.

Campaign to Gain Support for the Cultural Diversity Convention

The Rationale: Global Dominance of U.S. Motion Pictures

To ensure that their proposal would receive a warm reception within UNESCO, Canada and France skillfully played on resentment over U.S. motion picture dominance in most foreign markets to appeal to growing concerns over national culture and identity. In the lead up to the Convention's adoption in October, 2005, an article in Canada's *Globe and Mail* claimed that internationally, cultural diversity is "code for let's all get together and protect our national

---

2. U.S. Department of State, "The Convention on the Protection and Promotion of the Diversity of Cultural Expressions," *Fact Sheet*, October 11, 2005, accessed May 23, 2016, http://2001-2009.state.gov/r/pa/prs/ps/2005/54690.htm.
3. UNESCO, "Convention on the Protection and Promotion of the Diversity of Cultural Expressions," October 20, 2005, accessed May 11, 2016, http://portal.unesco.org/en/ev.php-unesco.org/en/ev.php-URL_ID=31038&URL_DO=DO_TOPIC&URL_SECTION=201.html.

cultures against Hollywood."[4]   According to French Culture Minister Renaud Donnedieu de Vabres, "nations had a right to set artistic quotas because 85 percent of the world's spending on cinema tickets went to Hollywood."[5]

The weak showing of foreign films in the United States exacerbated resentment over U.S. dominance in the international motion picture marketplace. The EU market for U.S. audiovisual goods, including box-office receipts, videocassette rentals, and television rights, for example, was $7.4 billion in 1998, compared with a U.S. market for European films of just $706 million (a ten to one ratio). At the time, barely two percent of films shown on U.S. screens were translated, and hardly any European productions appeared on American television.[6]

The Rhetoric: Linking Cultural Diversity to National Identity

The argument made by Canada and France to support the Convention was grounded in the concept that cultural activities are "special" in that they convey a nation's unique identity and are thus essential to the nation's survival as an independent, distinctly recognizable entity.[7] The message linking cultural diversity to national identity resonated with potential signatories to the Convention at several levels.

On an emotional level, the diversity concept was attractive to countries uncertain about the development and sustainability of their own culture in a globalized environment. Simultaneously, those

---

4. Kate Taylor, "Our Sad Little Stand to Protect Canadian Culture," *Globe and Mail* (June 4, 2005), accessed May 23, 2016,
http://www.theglobeandmail.com/arts/our-sad-little-stand-to-protect-canadian-culture/article18229094/.
5. BBC News, "Countries turn backs on Hollywood," October 20, 2005.
6. Philip H. Gordon and Sophie Meunier, "Globalization and French Cultural Identity," *French Politics, Culture and Society* 19, no. 1 (2001): 22.
7. Armand Mattelart, "Cultural Diversity Belongs to Us All," *Le Monde Diplomatique*, November 15, 2005, accessed May 23, 2016,
https://mondediplo.com/2005/11/15unesco.

concerned that their domestic cultural activities—especially their motion picture sector—were being overwhelmed by the dominant presence of U.S. motion picture imports, were drawn to the Convention's promise of protection from Hollywood's blockbusters and the other movies that, since the 1970s "have become the world's common denominators, submerging many countries' indigenous film industries."[8]

Still others likened cultural activities to the endangered species of the Biodiversity Convention, and looked to the Cultural Diversity Convention to prevent their weak culture from becoming extinct in the same way that the biodiversity initiative was intended to protect endangered species.[9] In this context, the goal of "cultural diversity" took on a distinctly anti-foreign tone and was interpreted as code for keeping out foreign product to preserve locally produced content.

Once established in various reports and meeting summaries, the premise that cultural activities are "special" was in turn used as the rationale for the argument that cultural activities, because of their unique connections with national and community heritage, should not be subject to trade rules imposed on ordinary merchandise. Such activities should instead be carved out of the framework of WTO trade disciplines.[10] This was a straightforward restatement of the cultural exception argument for audiovisual services that France had unsuccessfully advanced during the Uruguay Round of world trade negotiations (1986–94), now expanded to extend beyond

---

8. David Waterman, *Hollywood's Road to Riches* (Cambridge: Harvard University Press, 2005), 155.
9. UNESCO, "Cultural Diversity and Biodiversity for Sustainable Development," (January 2003), accessed May 11, 2016, http://unesdoc.unesco.org/images/0013/001322/132262e.pdf.
10. Michel Guerrin and Emmanuel de Roux, "First victory for the UNESCO cultural exception," *Le Monde* (2005).

audiovisual services (motion pictures, video cassettes, and television programs) to include all cultural goods and services such as music, books, and magazines, among others.

A corollary to the cultural exception argument was the message that adoption of the Convention would ensure something called "cultural sovereignty." While the term "cultural sovereignty" was never defined, it was broadly understood as an enabling clause, guaranteeing states the "sovereign right...to maintain, adopt, and implement policies and measures which they consider suitable for the protection and the promotion of the diversity of cultural expressions on their territory...."[11] By removing cultural activities from trade disciplines, so the argument implied, states would be able to regain control over their cultural activities and impose policies that might be viewed as morally or legally impermissible in other areas of trade.

Canada and France, in seeking support for the Convention, were clearly aided by the absence of any generally accepted understanding of the phrase "cultural diversity," which was only vaguely defined in the Convention.[12] Article 4 of the Convention, which relates to "Definitions," reads that: "'Cultural diversity' refers to the manifold ways in which the cultures of groups and societies find expression. These expressions are passed on within and among groups and societies."[13]

11."Cultural Diversity in Action: A Convention to Promote Diversity," *France Diplomatique* (cited in Balassa, *America's Image Abroad*, http://www.vanderbilt.edu/curbcenter/files/Americas-Image-Abroad-final.pdf: 40, footnote 42).

12. Keith Acheson and Christopher Maule, "Convention on Cultural Diversity," *Carleton Economic Papers*, no. 03-05 (2003): 15.

13. UNESCO, "Convention on the Protection and Promotion of the Diversity of Cultural Expressions."

Credit: ItzaFineDay, Citizens of Canada (September 2008)

By allowing "cultural diversity" a loose and open definition, advocates broadened the Convention's appeal, permitting each UNESCO member to read its own objectives into the Convention's broadly defined goals. Some, for example, looked on the Convention as a means to preserve indigenous artifacts and customs and promote ethnic traditions and minority languages, while others looked to the Convention to protect the rights to express one's culture, carry out domestic cultural policies, and foster the development of local cultural industries, [14] policies that could include the application of quotas and subsidies.

---

14. UNESCO, Executive Board, "Report by the Director-General on the Progress Towards the Draft Convention on the Protection of the Diversity of Cultural Contents and Artistic Expressions," *Annex III*, 171 EX/44, Paris, March 17, 2005.

Financial Incentives

In addition to using emotionally charged, all-things-to-all-people rhetoric, Canada and France sought support for the Convention by combining promises of financial support[15] and preferential market access to developing countries with threats of economic retaliation should a nation fail to support the Convention.

Prominent among inducements offered to developing countries was the promise to create an International Fund for Cultural Diversity in parallel with the Convention, a voluntary fund that would help build capacity in developing countries to produce and distribute their own cultural products and establish their own cultural industries.[16]

Offers of financial assistance to developing countries extended beyond promises of support for the Cultural Diversity Fund. U.S. delegates reported that Canada and the EU also paid the travel expenses of delegates sympathetic to their position so they could participate in Convention negotiations at UNESCO headquarters in Paris. Some of these delegates emerged as highly vocal critics of the United States, strongly echoing the position of their sponsors on the UNESCO negotiating floor.[17]

U.S. delegates reported that Canada and the EU also paid the travel expenses of delegates sympathetic to their position so they could participate in Convention negotiations at UNESCO headquarters in Paris.

---

15. J. P. Singh, "Creative Industries and Competitive Advantage: International Networks and the Political Economy of Representation" (paper presented at the American Political Science Association, Chicago, Illinois, August 31, 2007): 21.

16. Ivan Bernier, "An Important Aspect of the Implementation of the Convention on the Protection and Promotion of the Diversity of Cultural Expressions: The International Fund for Cultural Diversity," *Cultural Diversity News* 17, no. 11 (2007): 2.

17. Author's interview with Jane Cowley, Former Deputy Director for Office of UNESCO Affairs, U.S. Department of State, February 4, 2008.

The U.S. Response

Concerns with the Draft Cultural Diversity Convention

The United States had little opportunity to state publicly its position on the Cultural Diversity Convention until it rejoined UNESCO in October 2003, after a 19-year absence.[18] By that time the initiative, which had already been under discussion informally for several years, had been formally placed on the UNESCO agenda, and a number of delegations, uncertain of U.S. "loyalty" to UNESCO, looked with suspicion on U.S. motives in opposing the Convention.

As expressed in various statements by U.S. officials, U.S. concerns over the Convention's possible impact centered on the Convention's broad and vaguely defined scope, sweeping operational mandates, and ambiguous provisions outlining the relationship between the Convention and other international agreements.[19]

U.S. officials recognized that supporters of the Convention were motivated in large part by the dominant position of American motion picture exports in most markets. They were concerned, however, that because the scope of the Convention was broad and ill-defined, its provisions could be interpreted to extend far beyond motion pictures, touching on any service, good, or agricultural product that might be viewed as being related to cultural expression.[20]

---

18. Under President Reagan in 1983, the United States withdrew from UNESCO in protest over UNESCO's promotion of a New World Information Order, viewed as a threat to freedom of the press, and to express concern over charges of corruption and mismanagement of UNESCO funds.

19. U.S. Department of State, Office of the Spokesman, "The Convention on the Protection and Promotion of the Diversity of Cultural Expressions," *Fact Sheet*, October 11, 2005.

20. Ibid.

Concerns over the broad and undefined scope of the Convention were heightened by the Convention's sweeping provisions concerning implementation. Paragraph 1 of the Convention's Article 6, "Right of parties at the national level," reads that "each Party may adopt measures aimed at protecting and promoting the diversity of cultural expressions within its territory."[21] So broadly cast was this language, some argued, that it could be misread as providing countries with authorization to impose an unlimited range of trade-restrictive measures in the name of "protecting" cultural diversity.

U.S. negotiators were especially concerned by Article 20 of the Convention,[22] a section that conveyed mixed signals about the relationship of the Convention to other international agreements, including the WTO.[23] According to statements by U.S. officials, Article 20's message on the relationship between the Convention and other international agreements could "be misinterpreted as support for...major world markets to shut out goods and services from developing and other markets."[24] To drive home this point, U.S. negotiators compiled a broad listing of goods, services and agricultural products that could be considered to represent "cultural expressions." The listing included textiles, magazines, books written in a foreign language, coffee, and foie gras,[25] New World wines,[26] geographical indications,[27] and a traditional farming way of life.

---

21. UNESCO, "Convention on the Protection and Promotion of the Diversity of Cultural Expressions."

22. Aimee R. Fullman, "Reconcilable Differences: The United States versus the Canadian Perspective Towards UNESCO's Convention on the Protection of the Diversity of Cultural Contents and Artistic Expressions" (Master's thesis, George Mason University, 2005), accessed May 11, 2016, http://www.aimeefullman.com/Reconciliable_Differencespdf.pdf.

23. Tania Voon, "UNESCO and the WTO: A Clash of Cultures," *International and Comparative Law Quarterly* 635, no. 3 (2006): 2.

24. U.S. Department of State, Bureau of International Information Programs, "U.S. Opposes 'Deeply Flawed' U.N. Cultural Diversity Convention," October 21, 2005.

25. "UNESCO Overwhelmingly Approves Cultural Diversity Treaty," *Bridges Weekly Trade News Digest* 9, no. 36 (2005).

26. Janice A. Smith and Helle C. Dale, "Cultural Diversity and Freedom at Risk at UNESCO," Web Memo no. 885, *The Heritage Foundation*, October 17, 2005, accessed May

Stated Position in UNESCO

In the UNESCO setting, the U.S. response to the draft Cultural Diversity Convention focused on the Convention's implications for both human rights and international trade. Negotiations in UNESCO were led by the State Department, which initiated development of talking points on human rights; the Office of the United States Trade Representative (USTR) took the lead in developing talking points on trade.

Whether emphasizing human rights or trade, most U.S. statements on the Convention shared several themes:

First, the United States was careful to avow support for the concept of "cultural diversity," recognizing that the term resonated favorably with most UNESCO delegations. U.S. statements usually began with some variation on the statement that "the United States is among the most culturally diverse countries in the world,"[28] or that the United States is the most "open country in the world [sic] to the diversity of the world's cultures, people, and products."[29]

Second, U.S. statements often included examples of U.S. programs providing support to diverse cultures in the United States, such as the National Heritage Fellowships, one of which was awarded to a

---

11, 2016,
http://www.heritage.org/research/reports/2005/10/cultural-diversity-and-freedom-at-risk-at-unesco.

27. A geographical indication is a sign used on goods that have a specific geographical origin and possess qualities, reputation, or characteristics that are essentially attributable to that place of origin; for example, Bordeaux wine.

28. U.S. Department of State, Bureau of International Information Programs, "United States Opposes Draft U.N. Cultural Diversity Convention: Ambassador Louise Oliver tells UNESCO the draft is defective" (October 17, 2005): 1.

29. U.S. Department of State, Bureau of International Information Programs, "U.S. Opposes 'Deeply Flawed' U.N. Cultural Diversity Convention," 3–4.

Navajo weaver, another of which was awarded to an Italian American who created the San Francisco Opera House.[30]

Third, the United States, wishing to appear "cooperative" in negotiating the Convention, carefully avoided outright criticism of the Convention or its objectives. Instead, U.S. comments focused on requests for specific language changes to the draft, of which there were many.[31]

In addressing the Convention's human rights implications, the United States focused on the possibility that the Convention's vague language could easily justify government-imposed restrictions on freedom of expression, including censorship and limitations on press freedom and suppression of minority rights.

The United States also linked the Convention's potential for human rights abuses to the Convention's unstated trade agenda. In her address to the General Conference Plenary, U.S. Ambassador to UNESCO Louise Oliver referred to "disturbing statements by some government leaders who have indicated a clear intention to use this Convention to control—not facilitate—the flow of goods, services, and ideas...." By attempting "to block the import of agricultural and other products from the developing world and others," said Ambassador Oliver, "those leaders would extend the Convention's reach into trade matters, for which there is no justification....The goal of the United States is to ensure the free flow of diversity in all its forms—cultural, informational, and trade."[32]

---

30. Dana Gioia, "UNESCO Cultural Diversity Convention: The U.S. View" (Foreign Press Center Roundtable, September 27, 2005).

31. Author's interview with Jane Cowley, Former Deputy Director for Office of UNESCO Affairs, U.S. Department of State, February 4, 2008.

32. U.S. Department of State, International Information Programs, "United States Opposes Draft U.N. Cultural Diversity Convention: Ambassador Louise Oliver tells UNESCO the draft is defective."

Absence of Financial Incentives

In contrast to the financial pledges offered by Canada and France to support the Convention's Cultural Diversity Fund, the United States made no effort to counterbalance such offers with incentives of its own, either in the form of direct funding of specific cultural projects to promote cultural diversity or technical training in such areas as preservation of indigenous cultures, marketing, or the use of communication technologies to promote cultural diversity.

The absence of U.S. financial incentives was not the result of a failure to appreciate the financial challenges facing developing countries in the cultural area. The United States, however, was already in the position of funding 22 percent of UNESCO's budget,[33] and was not prepared to devote additional resources to the voluntary Cultural Fund: In 2004 the United States contributed $19 billion in official government assistance to UNESCO, and approximately $50 billion in private grants, remittances, and private investment from U.S. citizens.[34]

Defending the decision not to contribute to the Cultural Fund, the United States took the position that trade, rather than financial support, was the best way to achieve cultural diversity. "In addition to being the largest donor in the world, the United States is also the largest consumer of exports from the developing world with approximately $393 billion last year in net imports, more than 70 percent of the combined G7 balance," Ambassador Oliver stated. Linking trade to economic development as the solution for developing countries, Ambassador Oliver concluded that "Stronger

---

33. Smith and Dale, "Cultural Diversity and Freedom at Risk at UNESCO," 4.

34. U.S. Department of State, Bureau of International Information Programs, "U.S. Seeks Improved Draft Convention on Cultural Diversity" (September 23, 2005): 6.

economies will enable developing countries to nurture and promote their own unique cultures, thereby increasing cultural diversity."[35] Left unaddressed, however, was the plight of developing countries not yet at a level to take advantage of the benefits that trade could offer to their cultural sector.

Behind the official rhetoric and economic justification for the U.S. refusal to offer financial incentives specifically targeted to promote cultural diversity were more fundamental issues. Some U.S. delegates considered that Canada and the EU were engaged in "buying votes" to gain support for the Convention and objected to asking the U.S. delegation to "stoop" to such a tactic.[36] More generally, cultural issues were historically not high-priority issues for the U.S. government, and UNESCO was, at best, considered only a marginal international organization as a forum for representing and advancing U.S. interests.

The U.S. private sector, too, having decided to adopt a low public profile on the Convention, showed no interest in influencing the outcome on the Convention by funding UNESCO cultural projects. Motion Picture Association of America (MPAA) representatives, when approached with the suggestion that they help to fund a UNESCO cultural development program, replied in the negative.

Assessment of U.S. Response

Reception by UNESCO Delegates

Most UNESCO delegates were not trade specialists, but were instead drawn from their respective countries' ministries of culture. These delegates, aware of the difficulties faced by their domestic motion picture producers when attempting to enter the U.S. market, especially resented the dominance of U.S. motion picture imports in

---

35. Ibid.

36. Author's interview with Jane Cowley, Former Deputy Director for Office of UNESCO Affairs, U.S. Department of State, February 4, 2008.

their home market. As such, they were favorably predisposed to the Convention's vague language supporting "cultural diversity," "national identity," and "cultural sovereignty."

Non-U.S. cultural leaders had no reason to be sympathetic to the United States in the matter of trade in media in general, and film in particular. "Since the mid-1990s," writes David Waterman, American films "routinely account[ed] for more than half the box office in ... France, Germany, Italy, the United Kingdom, and Japan,...." while domestic filmmakers in these countries saw "an inverse pattern of decline in the market share of domestically produced movies....a trade pattern repeated in most countries worldwide." [37] In consequence, the United States was a ready target for the cultural aspirations and frustrations of many UNESCO delegates.

In contrast to the broad appeal of the Convention's vaguely defined "cultural diversity" message, the U.S. position on the Convention—often couched in legalistic trade terminology—was of little interest to most UNESCO delegates.[38] Trade arguments did not resonate with cultural leaders, a disconnect that was especially apparent in the legal debate over the importance of the Convention's Article 20, an issue of particular concern to the U.S. delegation.

Although some UNESCO delegations included trade officials who were impressed with trade arguments presented by the United States, these officials were in the minority, and in the UNESCO setting were unable to prevail in disagreements with their colleagues from the culture ministries. Other delegations, including close allies of the United States, discounted the trade implications of the Convention,

---

37. Waterman, 157.
38. Fullman, 40; see discussion based on testimony of delegation members.

believing that U.S. concerns over Article 20 were exaggerated.[39] Still others stood off to the side, having been encouraged to believe that the Cultural Diversity Convention was really only about trade, and so was essentially a French–U.S. issue that had little to do with them.

In addition to the limited appeal of the trade arguments that formed the core of the U.S. position, U.S. introductory remarks avowing support for "cultural diversity" appeared self-serving to countries resentful of the overwhelming presence of American films in their market. Rhetorical examples selected to illustrate U.S. appreciation for minority cultures in the United States failed to address concerns of delegations interested mostly in how the United States might help them foster their own cultural development, not in how the United States was supporting cultural diversity at home. In addition, references to U.S. openness to the diversity of the world's "people" rang hollow in light of visa problems that an increasing number of foreign artists encountered in attempting to come to the United States.

Rather than winning the allegiance of delegations to the U.S. position on the Cultural Diversity Convention, U.S. statements on cultural diversity instead largely served to reinforce the impression that the United States was indifferent to, or incapable of understanding, the pent up frustrations that animated so much of the discussion on the Convention.[40]

In the matter of financial incentives, it is unclear if the U.S. decision to not compete with Canada or the EU in offering financial initiatives for cultural development was justified or prudent;

---

39. International Centre for Trade and Sustainable Development, "UNESCO Overwhelmingly approves cultural diversity treaty," *Bridges Weekly Trade News Digest* 9, no. 36 (2005): 3.

40. The perception of U.S. indifference to the national identity concerns of foreign countries is supported by a 2004 survey showing that most Americans had "scant appreciation of foreign fears about the Americanization of their cultures." See Andrew Kohut and Bruce Stokes, *America Against the World: How We Are Different and Why We Are Disliked* (New York: Times Books, 2006), 85.

Ambassador Oliver's use of trade references and issues in a statement to an audience composed primarily of officials from culture ministries is also of questionable value. And culture ministers, concerned with developing their film sector, might have wondered why the country whose movie industry dominated foreign markets worldwide was unwilling to provide assistance to their film sector at least at the same level as that offered by Canada and France.

Impact on Final Negotiation of the Convention

When it became clear to U.S. negotiators in the summer of 2005 that Cultural Diversity Convention advocates had assembled an irreversible network of supporting delegations, U.S. strategy shifted gears. In the final weeks before the UNESCO General Conference voted in October 2005 to adopt the Cultural Diversity Convention, the United States undertook a series of high-level efforts to persuade member delegations to delay adopting the Convention until its vague and misleading language could be clarified, thereby permitting adoption by consensus. Secretary of State Condoleezza Rice sent a letter to all the Foreign Ministers of the Member States of UNESCO on October 4, urging them to prolong discussion of the draft convention, and expressing concern that it "could be misused by governments to legitimize ...controls over the flow of information, ...suppress minority cultural practices (for example, the wearing of head scarves)" and, if adopted, "could also have a chilling effect on ongoing negotiations at the WTO."[41]

---

41. U.S. Secretary of State Condoleezza Rice letter to UNESCO Foreign Ministers, "UNESCO Member States Adopt Cultural Diversity Convention by Landslide Vote Despite Intense U.S. Opposition; Stage Set for Launch of Ratification Campaign," *Coalition Currents* 3, no. 7 (2005): 4.

Despite such high-level communication, and the strenuous efforts of U.S. negotiators to delay the Convention's adoption, the United States remained almost totally isolated in both its opposition to the Convention and its desire to postpone a final vote. On October 20, by a vote of 148 to 2, the General Conference adopted the Convention. Out of 154 members voting on the Convention, only four—Australia, Nicaragua, Honduras and Liberia abstained from voting, and Israel alone joined the United States in opposition to the Convention.

U.S. Press Coverage

In the United States, adoption of the Convention received only limited press coverage; the few articles on the subject that appeared focused primarily on problems with UNESCO as an institution and Jacques Chirac's vanity.[42] The *New York Times'* Alan Riding, while acknowledging that cultural diversity had become "the buzz phrase for opposition to cultural homogeneity a l'americaine," did not explore the reasons for the near-universal resonance of the term, nor did he probe the attitudes that justified the willingness of 148 countries, including close allies of the United States, to override U.S. objections to the Convention.[43]

The minimal, cursory domestic news coverage of the near-total isolation surrounding U.S. opposition to adoption of the Convention is notable because the vote in October 2005 took place at a time when the declining image of the United States abroad was an issue of growing concern to U.S. policymakers,[44] as well as to the private

---

42. George Will, "Dimwitted Nod to 'Diversity,'" *The Washington Post* (October 12, 2005): A17.

43. Alan Riding, "U.S. Stands Alone on UNESCO Cultural Issue," *The New York Times*, October 13, 2005, accessed May 11, 2016, http://www.nytimes.com/2005/10/13/arts/us-stands-alone-on-unesco-cultural-issue.html.

44. In April 2005, the Government Accountability Office published a report attributing the limited success of U.S. public diplomacy "in responding to growing negative sentiments directed to the United States" to the absence of a national communications strategy. See GAO, "U.S. Public Diplomacy: Interagency Coordination

sector[45] and academics.[46] In 2003, the Pew Global Attitudes Projects had reported that in one poll after another, "the portrayal overseas of American democracy, values, and culture is at an all time low.[47] In July 2005, with considerable fanfare, presidential advisor Karen Hughes assumed the title of Under Secretary of State for Public Diplomacy and Public Affairs. But even as public diplomacy was shifted to a front burner, no link was established between the hostility that U.S. officials encountered in the UNESCO Convention negotiations and the front-page attention accorded to America's declining image abroad, reflecting that, as a policy matter, little serious attention was accorded to cultural issues.

Cultural and Policy Issues Unaddressed in Negotiation of the Cultural Diversity Convention

Questions Raised by the Outcome of the UNESCO Negotiations

The record of the UNESCO negotiations implicitly questions the way the United States engages cultural issues in an international setting: Why did the United States encounter so much difficulty in formulating a message to address effectively the cultural concerns of UNESCO delegations? Does the United States direct sufficient high-level attention to cultural matters, and, if not, which institutions in our society—commercial, non-commercial, or governmental—should be doing more? If cultural matters are

---

Efforts Hampered by the Lack of a National Communication Strategy," GAO-05-323 (Washington, DC, April 2005): 4.

45. See Business for Diplomatic Action, whose mission is to "enlist the U.S. business community in actions to improve the standing of America in the world."

46. Joseph S. Nye, *Soft Power: The Means to Success in World Politics* (Cambridge: Harvard University Press, 2004).

47. The Pew Research Center for the People and the Press, "Views of a Changing World 2003: War With Iraq Further Divides Global Publics," June 3, 2003, accessed May 11, 2016, http://peoplepress.org/reports/display.php3?ReportID=185.

recognized as important policy tools, why were the public diplomacy implications of the Convention accorded so little attention by policymakers at the very moment when other public diplomacy concerns were front-page news?

In the initial period of the Convention's development (1998–2003), efforts by Canada and France to win support for the proposal did not attract high-level attention within the U.S. government. Lacking a Minister of Culture or Secretary of Cultural Affairs, U.S. officials who attended these meetings, including the Chairman of the National Endowment for the Arts (NEA), were granted only observer status. Their meeting reports to the State Department of growing support for the Cultural Diversity Convention were largely ignored.

The Cultural Diversity Convention received high-level political attention only after the UNESCO Intergovernmental Committee meeting in June 2005, when it became apparent that the Convention would be adopted at the October meeting of the UNESCO General Conference. When the Convention did receive high-level attention, with Secretary of State Rice writing (but, significantly, not telephoning) her counterparts to urge delay, her objections focused on trade and human rights implications of the Convention.

MPAA staff had closely followed development of the diversity agenda beginning in 1998. Lacking a representative voice in the early meetings, however, they were not positioned to affect the movement's progress directly, though they maintained regular contacts on the issue with officials at State and the Office of the United States Trade Representative.

While MPAA member companies worried that the Convention could affect their commercial interests, they remained determined to maintain a low profile in debate on the issue to avoid emerging as a rallying point for Convention supporters. Given the power of movies as a symbol of U.S. domination, it would have been far too easy for proponents of the Convention to claim that their case was validated by objections from those they viewed as the very embodiment of "cultural imperialism."[48] The industry's position complemented the U.S. government's decision to focus objections to the Convention on its trade and human rights implications, avoiding any specific mention of motion picture issues.

Reflecting the absence of serious attention to cultural issues that characterized the U.S. position on the Cultural Diversity Convention, neither U.S. government officials nor the U.S. private sector has yet to consider the deeper, underlying issues that galvanized support for the Convention—charges of U.S. "cultural hegemony" and complaints that the U.S. market was unreceptive to foreign films. Although difficult to design and implement, programs that address the deep resentment attendant to the power of U.S. film exports can have positive results that influence perceptions of America vis-à-vis the outside world.

Recommendation: Focus on Film Distribution

American movies owe much of their global success to sophisticated technology and internationally recognized movie stars, combined with stories that possess cross-cultural appeal. But U.S. films also owe much to American film distributors, who possess a worldwide distribution network and well-honed marketing skills that ensure the movies they distribute reach movie theaters worldwide. The role of U.S. film distributors is well understood by foreign filmmakers, many of whom are eager to have their own work distributed by a major U.S. distributor, or the subsidiaries that some U.S. distributors

---

48. Author's interview with Fritz Attaway, Executive Vice President, Motion Picture Association of America, January 14, 2008.

have created for independent and foreign films better suited for the art house circuit.

The issue of foreign filmmakers seeking to obtain distribution by U.S. film distributors is not new. In the 1980s, when motion picture trade issues were first addressed in the nascent General Agreement on Trade in Services, members of the U.S. delegation were queried by the French on why, with American films dominating French movie theaters, it was so difficult for French films to obtain distribution in the United States. The response that Americans are resistant to subtitled or dubbed films, and are unacquainted with most French movie stars (because the French do not spend as much advertising and marketing their films as do their American counterparts) did little to assuage the suspicion that hidden trade barriers were responsible for keeping French films out of the American marketplace.[49]

Effective distribution and marketing of a film is closely tied to both its initial financing and to its commercial and artistic success. Because the economics of the movie business are such that even low-budget films have difficulty in recouping their initial investment if distribution is limited to the domestic market, a wider, even a global, audience provides local movie producers, often heavily dependent on government subsidies, with an increased degree of financial independence. Financial independence in turn affords filmmakers the means to introduce the advanced technology so much admired in American movies.[50] More broadly, assisting producers with maximizing market opportunities will increase the potential for a return on investment and help the film sector to generate employment and revenue for the economy as a whole.

---

49. Author discussion with trade official, 1987.
50. Carol Balassa, "Trade Issues in the Motion Picture Industry," Unpublished Report, Office of the United States Trade Representative, 1981.

A number of current professional development programs for foreign filmmakers focus on the production, or creative, aspects of filmmaking: screenwriting, acting, directing, filming, and editing. Largely unaddressed by public and private sector programs, however, is the distribution and marketing of motion pictures, the very skills necessary to ensure a film's commercial and artistic success. Effective distribution of a film includes developing a marketing strategy to maximize a film's earning potential in different available media and mounting an advertising campaign to support the film's marketing strategy.

Given the importance of film distribution to foreign filmmakers, and the fact that various professional development programs have paid little attention to the issue, a film distribution program, carried out in conjunction with film experts to assist filmmakers in formulating a comprehensive market strategy in the international marketplace, constitutes a programmatic intervention likely to produce significant positive policy outcomes.

The film distribution program envisaged here will adopt a two-pronged approach. It will explain the realities of the international market place to foreign filmmakers, with a special focus on the structure and challenges of the U.S. market, where distribution of a motion picture is costly, and chances of commercial success uncertain. [51] The program will also discuss different distribution options available to filmmakers worldwide, including, but not limited to, distribution in the United States.

To ensure that a U.S.-sponsored film distribution program has a maximum impact in improving foreigners' images of the United

---

51. Author's interview with Bonnie Richardson, Former Vice President for Trade and Federal Affairs, MPAA, February 18, 2008.

States, careful thought needs to be given to how to "brand" the program. To what extent should the film distribution program be presented as an initiative of the U.S. government, as one offered by a partnership between the U.S. government and the U.S. film community, solely by the U.S. film community, or by a quasi-private film organization such as the American Film Institute? It might well be preferable, for instance, that "branding" of such a program concentrate on publicizing participation by the U.S. private sector, whose film production and distribution expertise is the subject of worldwide admiration.

Conclusion: Link between Proposed Film Distribution Program and Public Diplomacy

Beyond the economics of film distribution lie the broader issues of cultural diversity, cultural identity, and cultural sovereignty, as reflected in the UNESCO Convention negotiations. The worldwide popularity of motion pictures has made them an important vehicle to express the filmmaker's story, which often reflects his or her culture, to both domestic and international audiences. "You have to come from somewhere," says Taiwan-born director Ang Lee, speaking of the role his films play in preserving periods of China's history for the next generation."[52]

Ang Lee's statement underscores that when foreigners object to the dominant presence of U.S. films in their market, and question what they suspect are hidden trade barriers keeping their movies out of the United States, they are expressing far more than commercial concerns. They are expressing resentment at being denied the opportunity to express their culture through the medium of movies they have created, as American films are able to do in their country. To many, the issue becomes one of cultural disrespect.

---

52. Emily Parker, "The Weekend Interview with Ang Lee: Man Without a Country," *The Wall Street Journal*, December 1, 2007, A13.

From the public diplomacy perspective, the proposed film distribution program reflects a new approach to the use of U.S. motion picture expertise for public diplomacy purposes. Past programs, such as those sponsored by the United States Information Agency, have relied largely on using selected motion pictures to tell our story as a means of improving foreigners' perceptions of the United States. Such programs have been part of what may be termed an "outreach" approach, aimed at delivering a specific message about the United States to foreigners.

In contrast to public diplomacy programs designed to "send" a message, the film distribution program envisaged here is about listening, offering foreigners the opportunity to tell their story. The approach conveys respect for different cultures and at the same time provides support for local artists and business leaders to take greater control over their cultural policies, an issue whose importance was clearly manifest in references to "cultural sovereignty" that appeared repeatedly during negotiation of the Cultural Diversity Convention.

At a time when so many nations fear a loss of cultural identity, and couple that fear with resentment of what is perceived to be self-serving, unilateral U.S. action, a professional training program in film distribution that provides foreigners the opportunity to make their story known may be a small, but constructive, first step in mitigating the perception that the United States is unconcerned with the views and culture of other nations.

6

Diplomacy and the Efficacy of Transnational Applied Cultural Networks

Robert Albro

Credit: Seventh Fleet Cultural Diplomacy, US naval seamen and students from a school for the blind in Thailand

Lately, it has been suggested that models for creative collaboration could constructively be applied to the work of public diplomacy.[1] This suggestion registers the fact that in recent decades circumstances have changed around the work of diplomacy. Publics are now much less distant, more assertive, and actively engaged participants in the making of their encompassing

---

1. Geoffrey Cowan and Amelia Arsenault, "Moving from Monologue to Dialogue to Collaboration: The Three Layers of Public Diplomacy," *The Annals of the American Academy of Political and Social Science*616, no. 1(2008): 10-30; Ali Fisher, *Collaborative Public Diplomacy: How Transnational Networks Influenced American Studies in Europe* (New York: Palgrave Macmillan, 2013); Tara Sonenshine, "Collaborative Diplomacy," U.S. Department of State, accessed April 10, 2016, http://www.state.gov/r/remarks/-2012/199297.htm; Stephanie Stallings, "Real-Time Diplomacy and Collaborative Creation," accessed April 10, 2016, https://artsdiplomacy.com/2012/10/01/real-time-diplomacy-and-collaborative-creatio n/; Rhonda Zaharna, Amelia Arsenault, and Ali Fisher, eds., *Relational, Networked and Collaborative Approaches to Public Diplomacy: the Connective Mindshift* (New York: Routledge, 2014).

cultural worlds. Embracing this new, often technologically mediated, reality requires rethinking some of the more familiar approaches to diplomacy and perhaps some of its fundamental goals.

There are certainly multiple models for collaborative diplomacy. In different ways, most of these involve the emergence of networks as an increasingly important medium for diplomacy. In many respects, organized cultural exchanges can be considered an earlier generation's systematic experiment with the promotion of networks in diplomacy.[2] It has, however, been challenging to measure the benefits of cultural exchanges in ways other than anecdotal. Despite this, the previous decade has seen a proliferation of new kinds of policy-focused cultural networks, which typically feature attention to cultural content as part of more encompassing humanitarian goals. Here, I explore some of the implications of this newer variety of cultural networks, giving particular attention to how best to understand their effects and potential benefits for public diplomacy.[3]

The Collaborative Turn

The turn to collaborative diplomacy is part of a wider collaboration trend across a range of related activities, from innovation, to science, and the arts. Thomas Friedman is representative of much recent enthusiasm, which can be traced to a zeal for Silicon Valley-style creative problem solving.[4] For Friedman, such problem solving is

---

2. Yale Richmond, *Cultural Exchange and the Cold War: Raising the Iron Curtain* (University Park: The Pennsylvania State University Press, 2014).

3. The ideas developed in this chapter originated in a series of long blog posts, which can be found at my Public Policy Anthropologist blog site: http://robertalbro.com/.

4. Thomas L. Friedman, "Collaborate vs. Collaborate," *The New York Times*, January 12, 2013, accessed May 12, 2016, http://www.nytimes.com/2013/01/13/opinion/sunday/friedman-collaborate-vs-collaborate.html.

epitomized by online platforms like GitHub [5] – the largest open-source computer code-sharing host in the world – or Thingiverse[6] – an online open platform for sharing digital design files through creative commons licensing used by artists, designers, and engineers. In this spirit Friedman also highlights customer-driven, non-zero-sum so-called "co-opetition" networks exemplified by the likes of LinkedIn. His message: innovation today is necessarily and unprecedentedly collaborative.

Likewise, major scientific challenges – whether climate change, biosecurity, or nanotechnology – are transboundary problems requiring CERN [7] -type collaborations in the search for global solutions. Scientific knowledge production is, as a result, now anything but a case of the solitary visionary toiling alone in a lab and, instead, is an increasingly borderless activity. Access to necessary expertise, ideas, samples, funding, equipment and machinery now routinely requires sustained international cooperation. As a result, the number of transnational research networks has risen steeply. Recent years have seen a steady increase, for example, in published papers in physics with more than 1,000 authors.[8] The National Science Foundation's new Science Across Virtual Institutes [9] platform, which fosters global interaction among STEM [10] researchers, exemplifies this turn. One result of this has been the emergence of a new and more multipolar era of science diplomacy.[11] Still nascent biodiplomacy[12] is a case in point, as it promotes "new forms of technology-based international partnerships" with the

---

5. See https://github.com/about.

6. See https://www.thingiverse.com/.

7. CERN is the term commonly used to refer to the Geneva-based European Organization for Nuclear Research.

8. Jonathan Adams, "Collaborations: The Rise of Research Networks," *Nature* 490 (2012): 335-336.

9. See http://www.nsf.gov/news/special_reports/savi/images/savi_factsheet.pdf.

10. STEM is an acronym referring to Science, Technology, Engineering and Math education.

11. USC Center on Public Diplomacy, *Science Diplomacy and the Prevention of Conflict* (Los Angeles: University of Southern California, 2010).

12. See http://www.atdforum.org/IMG/pdf/Biodiplomacy.pdf.

promise to "alter the traditional patterns of international cooperation."[13]

The relatively recent turn to the pursuit of so-called collaborative diplomacy tends to emphasize trust-building through cooperation around shared objectives and values, and, when carried out by government,[14] often encourages more interagency partnerships in projecting the U.S. image abroad. This is in part a practical call: given scarce resources for diplomacy, no one agency can go it alone. And, again, many geopolitical problems are interconnected and cross-cutting in nature, and so require multiple partners if they are to be effectively addressed.

In addition, the power of social networking – as a social media-driven basis for collaboration – promises to vastly expand outreach and engagement as well as improve responsiveness in real time.[15] Key cultural diplomacy actors, such as museums and other public cultural institutions, have experimented with social media as a way to make the cultural experiences they provide more collaborative or participatory and to promote greater audience engagement, community building, and curation.[16] In the context of this collaborative turn, proponents of media- and social media-driven participatory cultural engagement have emphasized

---

13. Calestous Juma, "The New Age of Biodiplomacy," *Georgetown Journal of International Affairs* (2005): 105-114.

14. At least in government and for the case of cultural diplomacy, the turn to collaboration has tended to carry over the perceived virtues of Silicon Valley-derived assumptions about digital social media and innovation. One such example is the U.S. Department of State's Bureau of Educational and Cultural Affairs recent Collaboratory initiative, http://www.state.gov/r/pa/prs/ps/2013/11/216185.htm.

15. Andreas Sandre, Digital Diplomacy: Conversations on Innovation in Foreign Policy (London: Rowman & Littlefield, 2015); Philip Seib, Real-Time Diplomacy: Politics and Power in the Social Media Era (New York: Palgrave Macmillan, 2012).

16. Elisa Giaccardi, *Heritage and Social Media: Understanding Heritage in a Participatory Culture* (New York: Routledge, 2012).

the blurring or disappearance of former distinctions between traditional cultural producers and consumers, or performers and audience members. Now digital museum visitors can help curate new exhibits, online music festival participants are frequently spectators and performers, and online serials engage in crowdsourced storytelling.

Culture and Networks

The collaborative diplomacy of the applied work of arts and culture I have in mind differs from the traditional model, held over from the Cold War, of sending, for example, the New York Philharmonic to North Korea for a one-off concert. Instead, we might look more closely at the efficacy of what I will call transnational applied cultural networks. Rather than promotion of one's own cultural community or national cultural identity, applied cultural networks facilitate relationships of collaborative storytelling and the co-creation of cultural knowledge. Whether as a dimension of humanitarian response, conflict mitigation, or peace-building, these networks apply arts-based activities associated with the theater, heritage conservation, or museum curation, among others, to facilitate skills transfer, enable expressive opportunities, and, most importantly, to help build shared cultural and normative worlds of discourse and practice. These cultural networks have their policy analogues as well, which I explore further below.

The cultural networks I am highlighting here foreground the kinds of expertise, encounters, and negotiations that lead to what urbanist Jane Jacobs, writing about the economic development of cities, identified as "knowledge spillovers": the non-rivalrous cross-fertilization of ideas among individuals that serves to advance neighboring fields. [17] In contrast, U.S. approaches to cultural diplomacy are often preoccupied with zero-sum goals of national self-representation, the importance of message projection, and

---

17. Jane Jacobs, *The Economy of Cities* (New York: Vintage Books, 1969).

identification of common starting points for cooperation, usually articulated as "shared values," in order to advance national interests.[18] However, instead of beginning with sometimes incorrect or superficial perceived shared values or interests as a way to build trust and goodwill, the work of applied cultural networks foregrounds the often negotiated and emergent, if eventually shared, outcomes of collaboration.

Transnational applied cultural networks can create new opportunities for public dialogue. They can, for example, potentially transform how diverse and otherwise disconnected people share in often

Applied cultural networks facilitate relationships of collaborative storytelling and the co-creation of cultural knowledge.

contentious, internally diverse, and variously imagined regional cultural blocs like "Europe." The Europeana[19] project, a cross-border, cross-domain, user-centered service drawing on the collections of over 2000 European libraries, archives, and museums, is one ambitious example of this sort of frame-building. Europeana offers users opportunities to participate in their own shared cultural heritage while creating new ways of doing so by empowering them to generate original cultural content about what "Europe" is or could be.

---

18. Robert Albro, "The Disjunction of Image and Word in US and Chinese Soft Power Projection," *International Journal of Cultural Policy* 21, no. 4 (2015): 382-399; Richard Arndt, *The First Resort of Kings: American Cultural Diplomacy in the Twentieth Century* (Dulles: Potomac Books, 2007).

19. See http://www.europeana.eu/portal/.

Credit: The Europeana Cloud Logo

Networked virtual platforms producing user-generated digital content represent one model for creative cultural collaboration but certainly do not exhaust the possibilities. Over at least the last 50 years, with one foot in the humanities and another in the social sciences, cultural studies have documented the diverse historical sources of cultural expression.[20] With regular attention to the multiple sources of any given expressive form – say, the Japanese influence upon the spaghetti western – practitioners in this field have, in particular, highlighted the hybrid results of cultural engagements, often as these occur along fraught social frontiers, and in ways relevant to the practice of diplomacy.

Applied cultural studies have much to offer the practice of cultural diplomacy, starting with helping to reverse-engineer the fallacy of assuming creative expression to be derived from a unitary

20. Lawrence Grossberg et al., eds., *Cultural Studies* (New York: Routledge, 1991); John Storey, *What is Cultural Studies? A Reader* (London: Arnold, 2010).

cultural source. If we are to further explore possibilities of creative collaboration, greater appreciation for the multiple processes and mechanisms of cross-fertilization informed by the field of cultural studies might help counter a tendency to view cultural exchanges as acts of display in the service of representations of national identity.[21] Too often this tendency mistakenly encourages an understanding of the representational work of cultural diplomacy as universal and self-evident, when such work is more accurately a negotiated expression of particular cultural engagements among counterparts.

Networks and Diplomacy

In the effort to understand the significance of networks for diplomacy, at present we lack a sharper and more grounded appreciation for how influential ideas, values, or cultural meanings travel through social arrangements of people, including applied cultural networks, and how network participants differently relate to network content. A first step toward correcting this is to give more attention to the ways that sustained participation in applied cultural networks is one key resource for building up shared frameworks of interaction, often across hard to cross or polarized geopolitical frontiers.[22] A second step is also to give attention to the variable interpretations accompanying cultural information as it travels through networks, as, among other effects, cultural content is combined, negotiated or hybridized, or genres potentially blurred, in

---

21. A notable result of a survey of cultural diplomacy practitioners I carried out between 2009 and 2011 was identification of the pervasive assumption that a primary purpose for the uses of culture in contexts of diplomacy is as an unproblematic means to represent the nation, an issue I have explore in detail elsewhere: http://uscpublicdiplomacy.org/blog/cultural_diplomacys_representational_conceit/.

22. Margaret Keck and Kathryn Sikkink, *Activists Beyond Borders: Advocacy Networks in International Politics* (Ithaca: Cornell University Press, 1998).

such diverse kinds of interpretive work as bricolage,[23] or more recently, in a culture jam or mash-up.[24]

To better appreciate the efficacy of transnational applied cultural networks, we need to change how we conceive of the role of networks for diplomacy. Particularly in security policy and security studies, there have been a flood of so-called link analyses,[25] where the game is always some variation on the theme of identifying connections between nodes in or across networks, that is, establishing who is connected to whom and how. Analytic priority is given to determining the number of connections, their distribution and shape, within and across networks. The goal of link analyses is typically to identify crucial "information nodes" or "information brokers": in the War on Terror, the "bad guys;" in public diplomacy, desirable "target populations."

Anne-Marie Slaughter's call for more attention from U.S. foreign policy decision-makers to the ubiquity of "network centrality" was timely.[26] But, while she notes in passing network "nutrients" – flows of goods, services, expertise, funding, and political support – she is most interested in the density of connections and positioning of networks. We can point to similar trends among academic researchers. A recent study of how influence spreads through social networks of Facebook users concluded that friend pairs who interact more frequently both on and off line, and so exhibit "strong ties," have a much greater influence on one another's behavior than do

---

23. "Bricolage" is a term used in the scholarship of cultural studies to refer to the creation of something, including a particular cultural meaning, from a diverse range of available sources. See Dick Hebdige, *Subculture: The Meaning of Style* (London: Routledge, 1979).

24. For discussions of culture jams or mashups, consult Henry Jenkins, *Convergence Culture: Where Old and New Media Collide* (New York: NYU Press, 2008); Bruce Grenville et al., eds., *MashUp: The Birth of Modern Culture* (London: Black Dog Publishing, 2016).

25. Karl M. Van Meter, "Terrorists/Liberators: Researching and Dealing with Adversary Social Networks," *Connections* 24, no. 3(2002): 66-78.

26. Anne-Marie Slaughter, "A Grand Strategy of Network Centrality," in *America's Path: Grand Strategy for the Next Administration*, ed. R. Fontaine and K. Lord (Washington, DC: Center for New American Security, 2012), 43-56.

persons who interact only occasionally or only online, and so exhibit "weak ties".[27] In a comparable example, researchers used the computational tools of social network analysis to assess the extent of historical or fictional sources for well-known oral epic narratives such as the *Iliad*.[28] Their analysis predictably privileged connections that were highly assortative – that is, with high frequencies of people associating with people like themselves – as one key "real-life indicator" corroborating an epic's likely historical origin. As with the case of link analyses, in each case researcher attention is upon the frequency, quality and distribution of connections, where behavior is treated as an empirically observable and correlated outcome of connection. How cultural meanings or beliefs might travel through a network is not considered.

To summarize, among researchers and public diplomacy practitioners concerned with networks, more attention has been given to identifying the locations of people, their behavior, their connections, and network nodes, than has been given to how specific cultural information is distributed across networks or what these symbols, values, or stories might mean to network participants. Assortativity is a useful principle in epidemiology because it helps explain the behavior of diseases as they spread through a population. But for the case of human networks we are too prone to use viral metaphors to describe the movements of information, ideas, or beliefs. Despite our fascination with social media technologies, we should not assume that a contagion model best characterizes the relationship of stories or values to networks. Instead, this might be a

---

27. Robert M. Bond et al., "A 61-Million Person Experiment in Social Influence and Political Mobilization," *Nature* 489 (2012): 295-298.

28. Mac Padraig Carron and Ralph Kenna, "If Achilles Used Facebook..." *The New York Times*, September 8, 2012, accessed May 12, 2016, http://www.nytimes.com/2012/09/09/opinion/sunday/the-social-networks-of-myths.html.

case of the "fallacy of misplaced concreteness," to borrow A. N. Whitehead's useful term.[29]

In contrast, significant work has been done on so-called "knowledge-based networks" and their relevance for public diplomacy. One case is Mai'a Cross's analysis of networks of policy decision makers working toward security integration in the European Union.[30] She shows how greater internal network cohesion increases network influence. For the EU case, cohesion does not simply follow from shared participation in a given network. It is, instead, derived from the ways that networks of these decision-makers come to share expertise and common cultural and professional norms through regular participation in the same meetings and other forms of long-term structured communication.

Assortative thinking encourages demonstrations of how like seeks like, while knowledge-based networks depend primarily on the effective development of shared commonalities amid diversity. However, exclusive attention to the facts of connectivity through networks – rather than to the ways people invest network participation with significance – supports an incorrect assumption that the cultural information, knowledge, symbols, or stories that circulate through networks are shared in the same ways and mean the same things. Social solidarity – or shared network participation – does not require cultural consensus. If we want to better understand the efficacy of public diplomacy networks through which specific kinds of cultural content circulate we should, instead, give more attention to the ways different network participants invest such content with significance and how often different investments are negotiated in shared work.

---

29. Alfred North Whitehead, *Science and the Modern World* (New York: Simon & Schuster, 1997 [1925]), 51.
30. Mai'a Cross, Security Integration in Europe: How Knowledge-based Networks Are Transforming the European Union (Ann Arbor: University of Michigan Press, 2011).

Transnational Applied Cultural Networks

An energetic three-day convening dedicated to "Global Performance, Civic Imagination, and Cultural Diplomacy,"[31] in which I participated, was also a step in the ongoing development of a global network linking artists, performers, cultural producers, policymakers, human rights activists, social justice advocates, academics, diplomacy practitioners, and others operating internationally and variously pursuing new intersections of the arts with cultural diplomacy. The several days of conversation sought to further encourage the development of this incipient global network of the "applied arts," in the process asking what it means when the arts are incorporated into the work of other sectors and put to other ends, like diplomacy.

In addition to the opportunity to witness this effort of network building, the meeting served as further evidence of increased attention to partnering, collaboration, and reciprocity as the basis for global outreach by often U.S.-based arts and culture nonprofits and other agencies of non-governmental and citizen diplomacy. Convening a variety of diverse endeavors across the applied humanities and arts, this meeting was an example of the spirit of "mutualism."[32] The goal throughout was less the pursuit of national self-interest and more an effort to build closer inter-relationships among participants of diverse nationalities working in similar arts fields.

---

31. The conference took place at Georgetown University, June 14-16, 2012. Further details can be found here: https://globallab.georgetown.edu/Convening.

32. "Mutualism" is a concept taken up here and there in the policy discussion around cultural diplomacy but, at least so far, not usually pursued in practice. An exception is Bill Ivey and Heather Hurlburt, "Cultural Diplomacy and the National Interest: In Search of a 21st Century Perspective," *The Curb Center for Art, Enterprise and Public Policy at Vanderbilt* (2008), accessed May 12, 2016, http://www. vanderbilt.edu/curbcenter/-culturaldiplomacy.

The organizers set the tone for this meeting by contrasting their efforts with past U.S. programs like the Jazz Ambassadors during the Cold War.[33] Although that program was highly successful then, times have changed. As they pointed out, now it is neither appropriate nor effective simply to represent one's "culture in a monolithic way" in the context of organized cultural exchanges. Nowadays it is necessary, instead, to "work more collaboratively" and to ask, "What story do we want to tell together?" The organizers promoted theater as one such richly expressive avenue for collaborative storytelling. During the meeting their goal was summarized as a "movement away from models of display to imparting agency to others."

As a contribution to cultural policy, the meeting offered "performance" as a methodology available for the purposes of:

- amplifying local voices
- enabling people to find ways to tell their stories
- creating contexts for public dialogue
- enabling social critique
- transforming conflicts
- pursuing reconciliation.

Art was discussed not as a medium of message delivery so much as "a part of the agenda of others," where, along with the transfer of skills such as choreography, a collaborative goal is to better appreciate how other people express themselves and what this might mean for how they currently think about themselves, their circumstances, and their worlds.

This meeting, finally, provided multiple examples of this sort of collaboration, such as Theatre Without Borders,[34] which facilitates

---

33. The organizers, Derek Goldman and Cynthia Schneider, develop this contrast in the course of a radio interview given in conjunction with the meeting, see https://thekojonnamdishow.org/shows/2012-06-13/when-theater-meets-foreign-policy-cultural-diplomacy. All quotes from this event are taken either from the interview transcript or from the author's meeting notes.

34. See http://www.theatrewithoutborders.com/.

global theater exchange among people and institutions. Theatre Without Borders has collaborated with Brandeis University's Peacebuilding and the Arts[35] program to use performance creatively to transform understandings of conflict in chronic conflict zones around the world. Utilizing the tools of community-based performance, their project has sought to restore peoples' expressive capacities as a way to help them address publicly questions of justice, memory, identity, and resistance, but also complicity. In other words, this collaboration has enabled dialogue among the participants in, and victims of, chronic violence, without imposing an agenda on that conversation.

My experience with this emerging network around socially-engaged applied artists now working globally is just one corner of a larger international environment in which cultural producers, workers, and agencies – including nonprofits, museums, archives, and libraries – are pursuing applied cultural and humanitarian work with partners. Applied cultural networks now comprise a growing diversity of creative collaborations leveraging the knowledge, expertise, and creativity of U.S. cultural professionals, in the service of a variety of international partnerships well beyond the traditional work of arts management or expectations for cultural exchange.

By and large these collaborations are not on the radar of decision-makers in international affairs. They include such diverse efforts as:

- participatory curation
- crowdsourced social media
- archival training

---

35. See http://www.brandeis.edu/ethics/peacebuildingarts/.

- oral history and public memory projects
- cultural heritage conservation
- digital game design
- documentary film making
- culture mapping
- the negotiation of cultural copyright and building of cultural commons
- the management and exhibition of antiquities and other national cultural collections.

These diverse forms of expertise and collective activities offer new avenues for cultural diplomacy, though not as we might conventionally understand it.

The Case of Heritage-Based Networks

A striking example of the efficacy of transnational applied cultural networks in the humanitarian context of disaster relief is the Haiti Cultural Recovery Project.[36] Coordinated among many partners and led by the Smithsonian Institution, this project has mobilized applied cultural practitioners from the United States and elsewhere to support the efforts of Haitian cultural professionals to rescue, safeguard, and restore the country's national cultural heritage in the aftermath of the 2010 earthquake. The rescue of key expressions of Haiti's heritage has provided continuity to Haitian cultural identity by saving artifacts of collective cultural memory, helping to maintain a cultural basis for Haiti to address its post-disaster national identity going forward.

Incorporated into the overall disaster relief effort, the Haiti Cultural Recovery Project was primarily composed of museum professionals – conservators and curators – engaged in the work of

---

36. Richard Kurin, *Saving Haiti's Heritage: Cultural Recovery After the Earthquake* (Washington, DC: Smithsonian Institution, 2011), accessed May 12, 2016, http://haiti.si.edu/.

stabilizing, documenting and restoring artwork. Their work encompassed: paintings, murals, artifacts, documents, media, architectural features, and historical and archival items. Smithsonian conservators also helped to train their Haitian counterparts in the skills of conservation and restoration and to build and promote a sustainable Haitian-led center. The work of rescuing Haiti's threatened art evolved into an opportunity to relationship-build, to share "common values" around heritage conservation, and to generate new shared creative cultural expressions. Understood by Haitian counterparts as "arts for survival" that activate the relationship between culture and resilience through connecting art, healing, and community, this work has included considerable media coverage, a website, a documentary film, as well as new museum exhibitions focused on the recovery effort.

Notable is the kind of U.S.-Haitian relationship this project represents. The guiding question of the collaboration was "What do Haitians want to do?" With this as the goal, a cultural recovery base was set up in Haiti, rather than bringing the artworks to the United States for treatment. Capacity-building of Haitian counterparts was one major feature of the project. Cultural conservators from the Smithsonian and other U.S. institutions provided a supporting role in helping Haiti consolidate its own efforts. All decisions about relative cultural value in the work of identifying, inventorying, and prioritizing individual items of cultural heritage were made by Haitians. As such U.S. and Haitian colleagues worked together throughout the project to preserve the ability of the Haitian people "to tell their own story to future generations."

The proliferation of U.S.–China transnational networks is a second example of the kind of collaborative cultural diplomacy I am highlighting here. These networks can be found across a broad range of initiatives, often involving academic institutions and think tanks in the United States. Two notable networks specifically concerned with cultural fields include:

1. an ongoing collaboration between the Getty Conservation Institute (GCI) and China's State Administration for Cultural Heritage, which has resulted in the bilingual "China Principles" for cultural heritage conservation;
2. the China–U.S. Folklore and Intangible Cultural Heritage Project, a cooperative undertaking between U.S.-based folklorists and their Chinese counterparts, which has contributed to the further internationalization of folklore studies.

The partnership initiated by the GCI and China's State Administration for Cultural Heritage offers a snapshot of how such alternative collaborative approaches can promote sustained dialogues about distinct national conceptions of culture. GCI has been working with Chinese counterparts for more than a decade to develop national Chinese guidelines for cultural heritage conservation and management, which are also intended to express specifically Chinese concepts of conservation. This ongoing process has included extensive conversation, information sharing, technical, methodological, and academic cooperation between U.S. and Chinese architects, art historians, archaeologists, local site managers, and others. This cooperation has taken place through organized meetings, workshops, and site visits, including visits to U.S. and Chinese heritage sites.

The resulting bilingual "China Principles"[37] are a product of regular dialogues about the relationship of heritage preservation to relevant challenges in China related to rapid economic development, social mobility, changing values, and increasing tourism. However,

---

37. Further background on the "China Principles" and the Getty Conservation Institute's ongoing collaboration with China's State Administration for Cultural Heritage can be found here:
http://www.getty.edu/conservation/our_projects/field_projects/china/index.html.

they also address potentially controversial issues, such as appropriate secular approaches to the management of sacred sites experiencing renewed religious use. This network relationship, in short, has involved the application of expertise by U.S. cultural professionals in the promotion of Chinese cultural heritage. It has fostered the development of a shared framework of heritage management and a new network of heritage professionals, while helping to promote a Chinese approach to its own heritage. In the process, it has facilitated ongoing transnational dialogue about the meaning of "heritage" among counterparts, as one increasingly prevalent global framework for making sense, in this case, of the relationship of culture to politics and identity.

The China-U.S. Folklore and Intangible Cultural Heritage Project[38] is another example of an incipient applied cultural network with direct implications for cultural diplomacy. This project promotes the internationalization of folklore studies around a commitment to shared cultural policy concepts like "heritage." Scholars, who also share comparable disciplinary backgrounds, are working together to identify, document, present, and safeguard cultural heritage considered to be important for the "national interest and well-being" of the United States and China. Counterparts, have also undertaken "to compare and analyze a wide range of activities in China and the United States," with particular attention given to similarities and differences of their respective national approaches to the study and preservation of intangible cultural heritage.[39]

---

38. See http://www.afsnet.org/?page=FICH.

39. UNESCO is largely responsible for the international adoption of this term. Article 2 of the UN's *Convention for the Safeguarding of the Intangible Cultural Heritage* defines "intangible cultural heritage" to include: "the practices, representations, expressions, knowledge, skills – as well as the instruments, objects, artifacts and cultural

This project has thus served as a U.S.-China platform to develop "habits of cooperation" and to generate shared products with a focus on "tradition-based cultural expressions." U.S. professionals now actively engaging with partners in the Chinese Folklore Society as they work to help establish a "field of folklore studies with Chinese characteristics." Translation of all documents, presentations, and outcomes of meetings into both English and Mandarin serves to juxtapose shared and distinctive discourse, terms of reference, and meanings to encourage more self-reflexive engagement among counterparts throughout the network.[40] This shared set of pursuits actively directs attention among Chinese and American heritage professionals to the often differing policy, theoretical, and practical priorities guiding the work of folklorists in both countries, including the distinct purposes to which heritage has been put in the work of national identity. As an outcome of their collaboration, practitioners from the United States and China have had to articulate and to work out different underlying assumptions and theories that in part determine the scope, meaning, and location of intangible cultural heritage in both countries.

One such issue has been recognition of the different time horizons informing the work of heritage professionals. U.S. practitioners are much more invested in contemporary expressions of popular culture, while their Chinese counterparts express greater interest in the past and in more traditional cultural expression. Recognition of these differences, and the ways they direct the professional development of cultural fields in each country, provides a much more constructive basis for ongoing conversation about culture as a subject of national concern than do competitive national soft power programs that primarily traffic in differences. For project

---

spaces associated therewith – that communities, groups and, in some cases, individuals recognize as part of their cultural heritage."

40. Such a process facilitates the co-construction of what linguists have called "intertexts," referring to points of contact, relationships, mutual referentiality, or overlaps, among otherwise distinct texts. See William F. Hanks, *Intertexts: Writings on Language, Utterance and Context* (London: Rowman & Littlefield, 2000).

co-leader and former National Endowment for the Arts chairman, Bill Ivey, this sustained and topically-focused collaboration has led to the ongoing reassessment of key concepts associated with his work as a folklorist, in particular, the notion of "authenticity" as a point of reference for professional practice in the heritage conservation field in the United States.[41]

Cultural Networks and the Future of Diplomacy

The collaborative work of transnational applied cultural networks highlights how effective cultural diplomacy need not aspire to message control or branding. Effectiveness is not always greatest when closely linked to the priorities of policymakers or defined national interests. Nor is it always desirable for acts of cultural diplomacy to be framed in terms of the goal of the representation of a people or nation. The development of these cultural networks, which feature the collaborative efforts of U.S.-based cultural producers and workers with counterparts elsewhere in the world, suggests another approach, which we can learn from as we rethink conventional wisdom about cultural diplomacy.

This alternate approach prioritizes working through collaboration rather than exchange, ceding authority while bringing skills, promoting the agency of others and pursuing shared creative outcomes while seeking to address the needs of others in humanitarian terms. This approach avoids trying to convert people into receptive audiences for our own story. Instead, it uses diverse forms of networked arts and culture collaboration to generate new cultural knowledge and to help construct shared, if still contested

41. Bill Ivey, "Preliminary Thoughts on the Concept of 'Authenticity' in US Folklore/ICH Work" (paper presented at the Fifth China-US Forum on Intangible Cultural Heritage, Santa Fe, New Mexico, November 11, 2014).

and diversely inhabited, frames of common understanding and action.

Over the past year the destruction of cultural heritage sites in Iraq and Syria has regularly been in the news.[42] To be effective cultural heritage protection efforts in conflict zones have to coordinate a wide range of humanitarian responders and local stakeholders, including militaries, other security forces and government agencies, UN and UNESCO personnel, non-governmental organizations, academic archaeologists and museum professionals. Given a consistent lack of effective coordination among stakeholders, identifying promising collaborative approaches to address the rising geopolitical volatility of heritage, as a dimension of conflict in international affairs, has of late been a major priority for stakeholders in the work of heritage protection.

An important, if underappreciated, part of the challenge for collaboration around heritage protection in conflict zones is the need to better balance a tendency to treat cultural heritage as chiefly tangible – as a set of material artifacts, built structures, or archaeological sites. Heritage is, at least as importantly, intangible context-dependent cultural knowledge, and an expression of collective meaning and memory. Competing cultural traditions and attachments to heritage are themselves often the source of political and military conflict. ISIS knows this well, as it seeks to enforce its own cultural historical narrative of a restored caliphate and to erase rival accounts of regional history by destroying heritage sites.

When we disregard what heritage means and to whom, we often ignore what matters most in conflicts over heritage. We need, therefore, to collaboratively reconnect the intangible to the tangible,

---

42. I am referring primarily to the destruction by the Islamic State of Christian shrines, Shi'a mosques and shrines, and Assyrian archaeological sites, in Mosul, Nineveh, Nimrud, Khorsabad, and Hatra, all in Iraq, and Palmyra, in Syria, during 2014-2015.

as part of the humanitarian response to heritage crises.[43] This has yet to happen, but diverse actors including the International Committee of the Blue Shield, Smithsonian Institution, the U.S. Department of State's Cultural Heritage Center, UNESCO, and others, are beginning to construct the necessary transnational networks of heritage professionals to make it possible.

---

43. This was the conclusion of a report coming out of an April 2015 workshop on "Cultural Heritage: Conflict and Reconciliation" I helped organize, co-sponsored by the University of Chicago's Cultural Policy Center and the Smithsonian Institution. See Cultural Policy Center, *Perspectives on Cultural Heritage: Research, Practice, Policy* (Chicago: University of Chicago, 2015), accessed May 12, 2016, https://culturalpolicy.-uchicago.edu/perspectives-cultural-heritage-research-practice-p olicy.

7

Public Diplomacy Engages Religious Communities, Actors, and Organizations: A Belated and Transformative Marriage
Peter Kovach

Credit: Calvin Wray, I Am Canadian (February 2010)

On August 7, 2013, Secretary of State John Kerry and Melissa Rogers, Director of the White House Office of Faith-Based and Neighborhood Partnerships, announced the creation of the Department of State Office of Faith-Based Community Initiatives at a ceremony that installed Secretary Kerry's trusted friend, Dr. Shaun Casey, to head it.[1] The office's creation culminated a process launched earlier under Secretary Clinton by a State Department-based Religion and Foreign Policy Working Group. Religion is inexorably becoming a factor in our diplomacy and public diplomacy. But that marriage is very much a work in progress. There still is much potential to explore and capacity to train for and otherwise institutionalize.

Speaking during the launch of the new office, Secretary Kerry said, "All these faiths are virtuous and they are in fact ... tied together by the golden rule, as well as fundamental concerns about the human condition, about poverty, about relationships between people, or

---

1. See http://www.state.gov/secretary/remarks/2013/08/212781.htm.

responsibilities to each other. And they all come from the same human heart."[2] The Secretary declared the new office's mission "...to engage more closely with faith communities around the world, with the belief that we need to partner with them to solve global challenges..." Kerry suggested that the potential for partnerships with those communities is "enormous." By way of marching orders, Secretary Kerry admonished Department employees ....

> *to go out and engage religious leaders and faith-based communities in our day-to-day work. Build strong relationships with them and listen to their insights and understand the important contributions that they can make individually and that we can make together... .in doing so ... you will have the great leadership from my friend, Dr. Shaun Casey, who is going to lead the charge to integrate our engagement with faith communities with our diplomacy and with our development.*[3]

At the same August 7, 2013 event, Dr. Casey cautioned against the simplistic view that religion can "save and solve everything," rightly saying that reality lies in a middle ground based on situational discretion. Discerning whether a faith-based organization is the best partner in any given initiative is the essential art of this vehicle for diplomacy.   Additionally, Dr. Casey astutely declared that "our [Department of State] collaboration with my office is not to design and create a new silo that addresses religion in an isolated manner."[4]

In fact, that ceremony was a keystone moment in a welcome development substantively launched in George W. Bush's

---

2. Ibid.
3. Ibid.
4. Ibid.

administration. The bipartisan trend is best described as an intention to effectively engage faith-based civil society in a partnership to fulfill secular policy goals, when appropriate. The revamped structure comes with a supporting legal framework which coupled that intention to a regulatory edifice painstakingly respectful of constitutional boundaries. The various offices in cabinet agencies of Faith-Based and Community Initiatives were established in January 2001 in the early days of the Bush administration, notably before 9/11. Not to be naive, the faith-based and community offices have given the last two administrations a mechanism to mobilize faith communities in support of key legislation.

The establishment of Dr. Casey's office complemented but left separate the Office of International Religious Freedom created by the International Religious Freedom Act of 1998. The Act solidified U.S. government efforts to defend religious freedom internationally, gelling political partnership between the earlier "moral majority" which morphed into the alliance that we now dub 'neoconservatism' in a strange bedfellows partnership with the human rights focused community. There is today a solid non-partisan consensus that government, in appropriate situations and in pursuit of secular goals, should be able to engage faith-based civil society to promote the greater good.

Since its founding, the Department of State Office of Faith-Based Community Initiatives has evolved into a kind of bureaucratic umbrella for offices oriented toward outreach to faith communities—outreach that has engaged public diplomacy assets creatively and regularly. The Special Representative to Muslim Communities, Special Envoy to Monitor and Combat Anti-Semitism, and Special Envoy to the Organization of Islamic Cooperation are affiliated with Dr. Casey's umbrella structure. Sensibly left separate is the apparatus to monitor and advocate religious freedom, the Office of International Religious Freedom headed by the Ambassador at Large for International Religious Freedom, an entity that anomalously operates together under a congressional mandate though located in the Department of State's Bureau of Democracy, Human Rights, and Labor.

There is a consensus that the three areas best suited for diplomatic engagement with religious civil society are: (1) economic and other development issues, including health, the environment, food, the role of women, and youth mobilization; (2) conflict resolution; and (3) garnering support for human rights including, of course, religious freedom; these, in addition to the traditional engagement of political officers with religious leadership. The three areas are largely an elaboration from the "U.S. Strategy on Religious Leader and Faith Community Engagement."[5]

The name of Dr. Casey's office was changed to the Office of Religion and Global Affairs, reflecting his title. Its establishment and growth represent a plateau of accomplishment in the ongoing course, one hopes, of a leap forward. It has huge implications for the breadth of our diplomacy, including our public diplomacy.

For public diplomacy, the added equity of communications partners and influence in and through faith communities cannot be ignored. In most societies, religious leaders have the potential to play a major role in shaping opinion around the initiatives of U.S. policy and the values that underlie our policies. Religious leaders control many channels of communication from the pulpit to mass media.

Many of the approaches to achieving the three goals inherently involve public diplomacy programs and modalities that engage religious civil society as key audiences and in some instances, implementation partners. This is an engagement that requires

---

5. See http://www.state.gov/s/rga/strategy/.

message sensitivity. It requires, too, a new generation of public diplomacy officers who have been trained to recognize and work fully mindful of their own religious/spiritual background and the intellectual/emotional baggage they bring to the work in that light, as well as the legal and bureaucratic obstacles and culture that traditionally have inhibited such engagement.

The institutionalization of religion in diplomacy, however, is still very much a work in progress. Below, I lay out some of the cultural and bureaucratic obstacles to realize the potential of such partnerships. These obstacles include personal and bureaucratic bias and reticence, and training regimes at the State Department's Foreign Service Institute (FSI) that are still in the process of being developed and that are seriously undersubscribed. I also discuss a remarkable body of regulatory reform engineered by the United States Agency for International Development (USAID) General Counsel's office in 2004 that carefully lays out parameters for contractual engagement with faith-based organizations. These parameters, while honoring separation of church and state in the Establishment Clause of the U.S. Constitution, lay out a framework that effectively guides how a federal official in the program field should maneuver in engaging religious leaders and faith-based civil society. Finally, we will look at some specific public diplomacy programs that embodied an openness to engaging religious actors in the service of secular policy goals.

Cultural Impediments To Engagement

As diverse as our diplomatic staffs have become across gender, class, and ethnicity, the foreign and civil service cadre in the federal agencies that comprise the foreign affairs community tends to comprise graduates of the same kind of top state or elite private schools. In these settings, even religion majors (such as myself) set aside their spirituality to view the world through the rational lenses of strategizing and problem solving. These biases are part and parcel of the heritage of the English Enlightenment that our institutions of higher learning and our bureaucracies are predicated upon.

The Foreign Service exam and other elite entry points such as the Presidential Management Fellowship competition stress rationality, objective knowledge, and evidence-based processing to solve problems. We leave our personal spiritual or religious identity at the door when we enter the ranks. On an instinctive level when overseas, we tend to seek out western-style problem solvers on the local scene as our interlocutors and—more important for public diplomacy programming or development work—our program partners.

Taking a look at behaviors rewarded by our diplomatic bureaucracies, it is the same kind of rational problem solving analysis and action that gets one ahead. Faced with a situation in which engagement with faith leaders or their institutions and followers is an option for accomplishing a strategic goal, there still is a tendency to hide behind our cultivated rationality. On top of that, there is a natural caution regarding violations of the Establishment Clause... a state of mind one might dub "First Amendmentitis." It is not rare to hear officers articulate fear of legal scrutiny or worse: public accusation of violating the separation clause by the Christian Right or militant atheist activists. To their credit, Department of State political officers have traditionally interacted with religious leaders in societies where such leaders are clearly influential in the policy debate or policy implementation arenas.

"Engaging Religious Communities Abroad: A New Imperative for U.S. Foreign Policy" had the potential to be a keystone document compiled under the auspices of the Chicago Council on Global

Affairs.[6] Unfortunately, although the bulk of the festschrift was chockablock with cutting-edge ideas about engagement, the book had little to no traction at the Department of State because of its inaccurate and off-putting premise: that State had never engaged religious players. That premise flew in the face of decades of political reporting. Senior officers who had embraced opportunities to engage with faith-based civil society were roundly put off, even offended, by this assertion. As a result, an otherwise excellent piece had little impact in developing our diplomacy with religious actors.

That traditional engagement of reporting and building trust through an exchange of views was interesting to observe from a PD officer's vantage point. In Morocco of the 1970s and 1980s, where urban ghettos of recent immigrants from the rural interior abounded, Salafist imams quickly emerged as great but possibly dangerous influencers. I noticed when I arrived as a public diplomacy officer in the mid-1980s that the political officer charged with engaging and reporting on this growing influence in society approached his meetings with these religious leaders with a palpable sense of unease. His cable drafts reflected that unease and were held back by the Deputy Chief of Mission. He was succeeded in this period by an officer from a minority religious community—one who had made his peace with his own religious and spiritual identity. Within a few months, the newcomer had successfully and comfortably engaged with these Salafist leaders and written a series of insightful cables that earned him a Superior Honor Award.

In 2010, the Pew Forum Center for the Study of Religion issued a report that, among other things, measured how much major American religious groups know about both their own tradition and other faith groups' beliefs.[7] Self-identifying Jews, Mormons, as well as atheists and agnostics came out on top. Interestingly, the

---

6. See https://www.thechicagocouncil.org/publication/engaging-religious-communities-abroad-new-imperative-us-foreign-policy.

7. See http://www.pewforum.org/2010/09/28/u-s-religious-knowledge-survey/.

award-winning officer was an observant Jew, one very much comfortable in his own religious "skin" and open to knowing others.

My overall point is that State has in the context of political reporting been engaging religious leaders throughout its history. The second point is that an officer who brings a thoughtful, comfortable awareness of his or her own religious or philosophical identity is going to be far better equipped for such engagement, whether in the context of reporting, programming, communication, advocacy, or peace-building. Thirdly, training should create the space for officers to develop that kind of self-awareness.

The Training Piece

Given the tremendous potential in engaging religious civil society in the specified arenas of development, conflict resolution, support for human rights and religious freedom as well as in communication leading to mutual understanding, we will look at a training that challenged our rationalist biases and our First Amendmentitis. By way of background, religious engagement in the FSI curriculum was long represented by the one-day course, Appeal of Conscience, a talkfest convened by Rabbi Arthur Schneier. A few years ago, every student in language studies was obliged to sit through this course—an exercise whose essential message of tolerance and building peace through religious engagement, while important, was simplistic in light of current scholarship and practice. Although the Appeal may have been somewhat lacking, the requirement for everyone in language or area studies to sit through the training was admirable.

Credit: Ben Sutherland, Symbols of all religions and faiths (July 2011); Beth Levin, religion_all_front (February 2010)

In 2011, USAID developed a most effective one-day course, Programming in Religious Contexts, and hired contractors to deliver it. This course, written by personnel in USAID's Office of Faith-Based and Community Initiatives, was unfunded after about six iterations over roughly a two-year period, presumably because USAID was deferring to FSI's more extensive offerings on Religion and Foreign Policy. The current iteration of the Religion and Foreign Policy training is a rambling four-day FSI elective course that objectively touches the essential bases through a cast of Washington D.C.–area speakers key to most aspects of religious engagement in today's diplomacy. These bases include religion and politics, a demographic unit highlighting the somewhat contested Pew Forum research that shows an uptake in religious affiliation worldwide,[8] and then a review of the by now impressive array of bureaucratic components mentioned above that address the potential in engaging faith-based civil society.

The course is a work in progress. The review covering relevant offices as of this writing includes:

1. the Office of International Religious Freedom and (also created by the International Religious Freedom Act of 1998) the United States Commission for International Religious Freedom;
2. outreach offices at the White House and at State;
3. DOD religious engagement through the chaplain corps;
4. a consideration of the Establishment Clause and the superb regulations described below to keep officers out of legal trouble;
5. an introduction to religion and women's empowerment; and, finally,
6. a section on religion as it complements democracy and development from a USAID perspective.

The course checks all the right objective boxes, but one wonders if and how the disparate units hung together in the minds of course takers. Missing, significantly, is consideration of the public diplomacy aspect of faith-based engagement.

Missing too is the personal and systematic impact that the now-unfunded USAID course packed to groups of 25 students drawn from a robust range of interagency partners. In that eight-hour course, participants broke into five discussion groups. The first

---

8. Other research shows a trend away from adherence to organized religion, a concomitant rise in spiritualism, as well as an increase in atheism or agnosticism—especially among youth.

module aimed at arriving at a definition of religion in its multiple facets and the potential roles religious actors could play in diplomatic and development work. As a precursor to the core module on the First Amendment and the 2004 rewriting of the regulations governing program engagement with faith-based organizations (known as "the Rule"),[9] the second module delved into the process of developing coherent development objectives—to make sure involvement with faith-based partners refers back to a secular policy objective—a major point of the course. The next module covered the substance of the USAID General Counsel's office legal framework, "the Rule." Perhaps the major problem in both these trainings is that they reached only about 75 students a year. This hardly begins to address what we are describing as a cultural deficit in our cadre.

The main legal markers the 2004 reform set out are worth noting in detail here. Covering programmatic collaboration more than mere engagement, they offer a definitive cure against 'First Amendmentitis' and give program entities, including public affairs sections, comprehensive guidance in the endeavor of engaging religious civil society organizations as program partners. The main points of the Rule are as follows:

- Faith-based organizations are allowed to compete for federal grants on an equal footing with secular organizations to help government officials find the organization best suited to accomplish a secular policy or program objective.
- A faith-based NGO winning a U.S. government grant must separate the grant-subsidized activity from any religious activity in either time or space. This means that the subsidized activity can take place in ritual space but not in proximate time to religious activity.

---

9. "Participation by Religious Organizations in USAID Programs," Final Rule 69 FR 61716, October 20, 2004, accessed July 6, 2016, https://www.usaid.gov/faith-based-and-community-initiatives/usaid-rule-participation.

The NGO may maintain religious art, icons, or symbols in the program space. The federal money, however, may not be used for any inherently religious activity.

- Recipients of services contracted by a U.S. government grant to a faith-based organization cannot be discriminated against for not belonging to the grantee faith community, and religious activity cannot be a condition for receiving the contracted services.
- The faith-based organization may continue to govern itself and hire on a religious basis.
- USG funding dedicated to infrastructure upgrades or construction must not exceed the proportion of the facility used for the funded secular activity. USG money should not be used to construct spaces used principally as places of worship.[10]

A fourth module in the Programming in Religious Contexts course comprised exercises posing examples of discretionary situations. Some of the situations evoked discussion of whether a faith-based partner was best suited for the grant or whether a specific circumstance violated the Rule.

The final module was a keystone of the day—a chance to reflect on and share one's own religious/spiritual/philosophical leanings and narratives, if any, and to reflect on the rationalist bias of federal departments. This module was not offered early in the day because it was felt most students would be far more reticent to share such personal reflections with strangers they have just met.

---

10. Ibid.

By day's end, each group had been working together through exercises and discussions for more than six hours, so they achieved a higher level of interpersonal comfort. The major point, however, is that this reflective element is totally missing from the FSI courses. Self-knowledge and mindfulness of our workplace biases are essential to operating in cross-cultural environments of any sort, especially in an arena as culturally loaded as religious or interfaith engagement.

The interactive component of the former USAID course is essential not only in the portion in which personal and institutional values are concerned, but in the interactive analytical discussion around whether a case conforms to "the Rule" and whether a faith-based partner is the best choice for a given project.

Training a public diplomat should involve case studies of engagement and communication that resulted in attitudinal or behavioral change in any of the three arenas that engagement with faith-based communities rightfully focuses on: peacebuilding, development, and the promotion of human rights and religious freedom.

Peacebuilding and the role of dialogue and narrative exchange among combatants leading to breakthroughs in communication and behaviors should be at the forefront. American faith-based NGOs supported this practice in Nigeria years ago in reconciling Muslims and Christians in an economically neglected region. Starting with the events recorded in the well-known documentary "Imam and the Pastor," the contagion of interfaith reconciliation worked itself up to the senior Sunni imam and Anglican bishop in the country.

Examples of engagement by a PD officer that led to expanded dialogue, mutual understanding, and influence should be presented, as well as examples of where, in the service of development and social change, a PD program possibly undertaken with an interfaith partner could be highlighted. The work of public diplomatists in sync with the Bureau of Conflict and Stabilizations Operations' work with Syrian refugees and faith leaders is a currently unfolding treasure trove of examples. So, too, are recent International Visitor Leadership Program activities bringing together a full variety of faith leaders from conflicted parts of the Middle East.

In sum, there is a rich lore of experience to draw from. How FSI can harvest and selectively incorporate these examples is the real challenge. A partnership among the Association for Diplomatic Studies and Training that compiles oral histories of Foreign Service officers, the public diplomacy training office, and the political training office that organizes the Religion and Foreign Policy courses ideally would collaborate in compiling such a Public Diplomacy unit.

A complementary training in what officers across generations would recognize as 'social mapping' or 'geographic information systems' is another key component for targeting proper program partners, influencers, and the media that influence them or through which they assert influence. Social mapping has been used in counterterrorism communications for several years. The Department of State Humanitarian Information Unit's open mapping project[11] is an example of engagement with volunteers using a software application. Proper mapping can guide officers in assessing whether to conduct public diplomacy through faith community influencers or media in all the spheres they might be called on to initiate or complement complex efforts to build peace, support interfaith cooperation and human rights, achieve communication resonance, and work toward any desirable policy goal.

---

11. See http://mapgive.state.gov/.

All this raises a more fundamental question and challenge in the realm of training. Effective public diplomacy initiatives operating with or through faith-based partners also require significant attitudinal self-examination on both individual and institutional levels.   How do you instill a positive institutional disposition toward the challenges of engaging faith-based communities in the service of foreign policy—not just to the handfuls that take a "Religion and Foreign Policy" course or who took the previous USAID-funded training? Increasing engagement with religious players in the service of foreign policy goals requires incorporating personal and institutional introspection, operationalizing the Rule, and coming to grips with one's own cultural biases.

Public Diplomacy Successes in and through Faith-Based Engagement

Prior to my first assignment with the United States Information Agency (USIA), in Yemen, I did an excellent area studies course at the FSI under the tutelage of Dr. Peter Bechtold. Bechtold was the prototype of an intellectual who—a deeply religious Catholic himself and totally comfortable in his own religious identity—was particularly strong in giving his students a sense of Islam, its history, its theology and doctrine, and its practice on the ground. I arrived in Yemen feeling well prepared to engage. Curiously, I found that many of my senior colleagues, officers with much stronger Arabic than mine, consorted mostly with the few Yemenis who shared a Western outlook from having been educated in the West or in the Soviet Union.

Frustrated by this, and empowered by an encouraging PAO, I ventured to meet some of the more religious among Sanaa's civil society leaders. As a public diplomacy practitioner, one set of encounters was with the editors of weeklies affiliated with the *Ikhwan Muslimeen*, the Muslim Brotherhood; in Yemen, that meant both Sunni and the Shi'a (Zaidi) brotherhoods. My initial visits were greeted with a kind of bemused astonishment. We agreed that the brotherhoods would receive a USIA product known then as the Arabic Wireless File on those days that solar storms and other atmospheric imponderables allowed my office to download it by radio and that they would consider running some of our articles about American life. We both made good on our promises. A stream of articles describing a variety of facets of America, including Islam in America, began to appear. One of the editors eventually allowed that I was the only foreign diplomat to ever call on him.[12]

The payoff? I received a call from the head of TV and radio, a Baathist with little quarter for things American. He and his colleagues had rebuffed my previous attempts to try to place even soft American cultural materials on Yemeni radio and TV. He apparently was intrigued enough by the materials appearing in the brotherhoods' journals or getting pressure from someone higher up to alter his disposition towards accepting our materials. This led to a positive turnaround for our efforts to place Voice of America- or USIA-produced WorldNet TV materials on Yemen Radio and Television. This small and rather symbolic victory for our outreach efforts had a larger impact in my career: I became determined to push the margins in my contacts; to talk to people of influence having less familiarity, greater doubts, or deeper misconceptions about our policies and our society.

A push for broader diplomatic and PD program outreach imbued in my professional soul from the Yemen experience found fertile ground for full expression in Bahrain. Bahrain even today remains a country ruled for over two centuries by a Sunni clan from the Nejd region of Central Saudi Arabia, Sunni leaders presiding over a population that at the time in early 1980's was estimated to be about

12. Peter Kovach, "The Public Diplomat-A First Person Account," in *Handbook of Public Diplomacy*, ed. Nancy Snow and Philip Taylor (New York: Routledge, 2009), 202.

75 percent Shi'a. My arrival coming just three years after the Iranian Revolution, I found myself in an insular city-state whose major communities were newly wary of one another. The Iran–Iraq War was further riling Bahraini wariness of the "other" across sectarian lines. Many Bahraini Shi'a—especially the Shi'a majority of Arab rather than Persian origin—harbored new doubts about the United States' attitude towards them out of a paranoia that we wrongly associated them with Iran in the wake of the Revolution and hostage crisis. The mission had minimal contact with the community other than formal contact with educated, urbanized, somewhat secular leaders in formal office calls and diplomatic social events.

While my early journeys out to the vast swath of Shi'a villages mid-island elicited expression of Shi'a concern over perceived American disapproval of them, from a Shi'a perspective of America, there were some frankly surprising positive images and feelings, especially among the generation over 25 years of age. When an American company took over management of Bahrain's huge Bahrain Petroleum Company (BAPCO) refinery from British predecessors a decade earlier, the Americans found a company segregated in a pattern all too familiar, similar to that of the American South of just two decades earlier: i.e., segregated eateries and toilets, even water fountains. Their first day, the Americans totally desegregated the facility—an act that indelibly put the United States on the positive side of a line of demarcation in the eyes of a majority of Bahrain's citizenry. Second, also in the tumultuous 1970s, Shi'a with their strong doctrines of legitimacy in governance marveled at what they generally viewed as "the peaceful overthrow of a corrupt government," referring to the impeachment and resignation of President Nixon over the Watergate scandal.

My self-appointed task as PAO and as one of only three Arabic-speaking officers in the small embassy was to make sure that America kept an adequate social presence in the village social centers known as Mata'am, attending weddings, funerals, and other ceremonial occasions by indicating my openness to such invites. The other was to make sure that leaders of the Bahraini Shi'a elites as well as the emerging technocracy dominated by a rising Persian Shi'a technocratic middle class were well serviced by USIA programs, particularly exchanges. This was particularly important in a country in which the embassy was without a USAID mission, making it all the more necessary to engage through faith-based and campus civil society and not just in the bureaucratic workspace.

I was particularly concerned about the 60 percent of the Shi'a population under 25 who had neither direct memory of BAPCO desegregation nor of Watergate and whose views of America were colored by suspicions of U.S. collusion with Sunni leadership and identification of them to some degree with the Iranian Revolution. In a small state where sports clubs were a great uniting force in the community, the answer readily suggested itself: sports exchange. In a cable to USIA, I generated the idea of sending out a basketball team to run clinics and scrimmage with club teams. I asked for a team that might legitimately lose a game or two; to wit, a Division III elite school whose players would be sophisticated enough to understand the importance of the exchange experience beyond sport.

In the end, USIA got me exactly what I had requested. The Americans did drop a game to a leading club and the whole thing was drowned in positive press coverage that my colleagues and I arranged, the vital complement guaranteeing resonance of a program effort beyond the immediate social milieu of its direct beneficiaries. The great deliverable was that the Shi'a Mata'am began to reach out to the small embassy with more invitations and a higher comfort level—elements that substantially upped our collective mission access to the majority of citizens in that small country.[13]

In the early 1990s, the Department and USIA were seized with concern about how best to engage "political Islam" in the field. A number of expert panels fretting over the subject were convened under Department auspices. The discussions to my mind reflected our cultural discomfort with engaging faith-based civil society, especially in the Arab world at a time when it was obvious that the road to democratization, a major U.S. strategic goal, led directly through Muslim civil society, if not Islamic political parties.

I brought my ideas to the table, forged through almost nine years in the Arab world and experiences like the two mentioned above in public diplomacy work. Finding myself in a management position in USIA's Near Eastern Affairs bureau, my lingering passion was getting our officers to move in wider circles within the host societies where they served. In the Arab world, that almost exclusively meant an engagement with faith-based civil society. My earlier impulses from contact work with more religious types and organizations suggested a more robust engagement to implement the current policy priority of public diplomats' dealings with political Islam.

One of my great patrons and role models, Ambassador William Rugh, persuaded Department of State Assistant Secretary for North African, Near Eastern, and South Asian Affairs Edward Djerejian to make a major policy speech reflecting my persistent obsession with wider PD outreach to those that neither knew us well or necessarily agreed with us. I was tasked with writing the talking points for speech delivered by Assistant Secretary Djerejian in June 1992. Djerejian called for engagement beyond our normal comfort zone with important leaders and communities that would talk to us and in terms of program support, with a democratically inclined civil society that was not just dedicated to "one man, one vote, one time."

---

13. Kovach, 203.

It was a speech that set a policy direction for our public diplomacy in the Arab world that was to last until September 12, 2001, when engaging the "silent" majority of Muslims became the obvious challenge of the current post- 9/11 epoch.[14]

Another example, almost 20 years later, illustrates the power of working information campaigns through faith leaders in traditional societies due to the far greater credibility they have, especially compared to government officials. The Leaders of Influence program in Bangladesh was spearheaded by USAID and featured judicious application of the 2004 Rule governing program partnership with faith-based organizations. An active Public Affairs Section complemented the work on many levels.

Bangladesh is a country with serious public health deficits in both basic hygienic practice and the credence that citizens in villages and urban slums place in modern health clinics. To complement a huge investment in building new clinics and broaden the outreach of those government clinics, USAID conceived of using faith leaders—Hindu, Buddhist, Christian and Muslim—to convey habits conducive to health, including attendance at clinics. USAID funded a three-day portion of a 45-day Bangladesh government-funded course for imams. The course focused on why and how to influence villagers to make healthier choices. In addition to touting the services in the new clinics, the faith community leaders played a key health communications role passing messages on hygiene, mother and child health, nutrition, and more. USAID further funded a two-day seminar going into greater depth on how clerics could be change agents to improve health and life expectancy in villages, a

---

14. Kovach, 206.

retreat that brought imams together with their Hindu, Buddhist, and Christian counterparts for a capstone training.

A second notable outcome was a collaborative spirit among faith leaders in a country that has had its share of interfaith conflict—especially among the three minority religions (e.g., Hinduism, Buddhism, and Christianity). All clergy seemed unanimous in their determination to combat what they openly acknowledged was the corruption of local officials impeding their new role as health coaches. Regarding the Rule, USAID funding for the imam training was confined to instruction for the three days, including hall rental and instruction, room, and board for the interfaith participants. USAID also supplied collateral materials.

In the realm of exchanges, the Bureau of Educational and Cultural Affairs and a few of our embassies have in recent years broken new ground in establishing exchanges focused on exposing participants to diverse religious life in the United States or involving seminarians and other religious functionaries. Many of these exchanges are the brainchild of Imam Bashar Arafat, a Syrian–American cleric. Imam Arafat, based on his work in Baltimore as a police chaplain, emerged as a pioneering interfaith player on that urban scene. His idea is that by bringing foreign visitors to encounter the American interfaith scene, he can give Americans a more nuanced view of the variety within the Islamic tradition and give Muslim visitors a sense of a new kind of Islamic practice based on interfaith cooperation and other forms of dialogue.

Imam Arafat pioneered Better Understanding for a Better World (BUBW), which three times each year convenes 80 high school exchange students including a smattering of Americans for a five-day intensive interfaith experience, visiting a variety of houses of worship including some outside the trio of Abrahamic traditions. In their evaluations, students—many coming from places a lot less religiously pluralistic than the United States—describe BUBW as a world-view altering experience. The leaders of the different faiths in communities who host BUBW sessions, engaged by this imaginative public diplomacy program, have expanded their interaction and cooperation in other spheres.

Imam Arafat has more recently focused his attention on exposing Muslim seminarians from abroad to American religious diversity and interfaith interaction to enable them to better teach about world religion, lead in finding common values to bridge conflict, and to see Islam thriving in a uniquely American setting engaged in the interplay of American pluralism. Embassies in Cairo, Rabat, and Amman have all directly funded exchanges of seminarians who have travelled to the United States on Arafat's International Observers Programs. They observe BUBW sessions for two days and then are scheduled for another ten days or so of encounters with the people and projects of American mosques and their interfaith partners ... a very powerful tool.

In cooperation with the U.S. Consulate in Milan, Imam Arafat has begun working with both Catholic and Muslim seminarians on a program to create a more enlightened platform from which Europeans can deal with their immigration issues. Imam Arafat believes that public diplomacy helps Americans to better see Islam in an American context, while showing Muslim visitors a robust, moderate American Islam thriving in interfaith and community engagement—a desirable model they can take home.

An interesting example using gender and education as vehicles for peacemaking and reconciliation came from a grant proposal that the Department of State's Bureau of Democracy, Human Rights, and Labor considered giving to an interfaith mothers group united to support educational excellence in Jerusalem. Both Palestinian and

Israeli societies value education as a catapult to success for youth. In Jerusalem, there is an impressive number of groups that engage across faith-based lines for peace and unity but who have little resonance beyond their actual membership.

The mothers group was notable because they incorporated their work into a weekly TV program focused on education, with Palestinian Muslim and Christian women sitting in common cause with their Jewish counterparts and seen in living rooms throughout the country. It was a program that struck at a point of common inflection—education and children—and generated both enthusiasm for sitting in common cause and positive images of engagement in a segregated society whose religious communities subsist largely in reciprocated suspicion of the religious and national "other." This was certainly a public diplomacy initiative in which it hardly mattered that the money and competition for the grant might have come entirely from outside the Department's bureaucracy dedicated to PD.

Finally, a dramatic example of work between the former Special Envoy to Monitor and Combat Anti-Semitism Hannah Rosenthal and the former Special Representative to Muslim Communities Farah Pandith. Shortly after they were introduced (their offices were not under the same umbrella as they now are in Dr. Casey's structure), they journeyed together to Astana, Kazakhstan, for the Organization for Security and Cooperation in Europe Conference on Tolerance and Non-discrimination, held June 29, 2010. At dinner together the evening before scheduled speeches to Kazakhstan's varied faith communities, they decided to deliver one another's speeches the next day—so Ms. Rosenthal spoke to a Muslim audience on Islamophobia and Ms. Pandith spoke to a gathering of Jews on combatting anti-Semitism. They both ended their speeches with the words, "Jews cannot fight anti-Semitism alone. Muslims cannot fight 'Islamophobia' alone. Roma cannot fight—alone. The LGBT community cannot fight—alone. And the list goes on. Hate is hate, but we can overcome it together." Their dramatic gesture was noted by the wire services with significant international news pick up.

Spurred on by the positive reaction of the youth contingent there in Astana, they followed up by spawning a largely Web-based campaign, 2011 Hours Against Hate, which aimed to get young people more involved in donating at least an hour of their time to groups or organizations that don't look like them, pray like them, or live like them. This effort was supported throughout the PD regional bureaus.

Conclusion

Once officers have come to grips with their personal religiosity or philosophical orientation and considered the rationalist cultural biases inherent in and rewarded by our bureaucracy, they have taken the first step toward planning and implementing a diplomacy and public diplomacy that more readily engages religious audiences taking on partnership with faith-based civil society. But this training has to be made available for the majority of officers, not solely for the 75 or so that take a single course in a year at FSI.

Introduction to the regulatory Rule, an exercise that shouldn't even take an hour, would liberate even the most secular and skittish of our colleagues from any lingering First Amendmentitis. Solid area studies offerings exploring the dimensions of religion and society in a culture such as that I experienced 34 years ago are another essential piece of the puzzle.

Finally, rather than falling all over religious engagement as a new "in" thing, evoking in a course some exercises that test collective judgment on when a faith-based partnership is the best avenue to achieve a program or communications goal and when not will put the current generation of public diplomatists in great position to engage faith-based leaders and communities wisely and effectively.

8

Nontraditional Public Diplomacy in the Iraq-Afghan Wars
Or The Ups and Downs of Strategic Communicators

Helle C. Dale

Credit: DVIDSHUB/Akbar Kheyl Activity, 2010

With a brief memo for the Commanders of Combatant Commands, issued on November 28, 2012, Assistant Secretary of Defense for Public Affairs George Little banished the term "strategic communication" from the Pentagon's vocabulary and ended one of the Pentagon's more controversial programs associated with the wars in Afghanistan and Iraq.[1] Strategic communication—a term used by the Department of Defense and ranging from pure, locally contextualized public diplomacy, to propaganda, to psychological operations (psy-ops)—had been part of the U.S. government's attempt to win "hearts and minds" in the two countries where the U.S. military had found itself engaged on unfamiliar terrain for a

1. See http://www.usatoday.com/story/news/nation/2012/12/03/pentagon-trims-strategic-communication/1743485/. For George Little memorandum to which it refers, see https://foreignpolicymag.files.wordpress.com/2015/01/121206_brooksmemo.pdf.

decade, following the terrorist attacks on New York and Washington on September 11, 2001.[2]

The Department of Defense (DOD) had recognized that everything it does communicates a message, from having soldiers distribute soccer balls in conflict zones to scheduling joint exercises off the coasts of foreign nations. However, DOD had struggled for several years to align its actions with the messages it intended to communicate to foreign audiences. For instance, communicating with village elders in an Afghan village might prevent a misinterpretation of U.S. military action by the local population. With the growth of global communications, these messages were (and obviously still are) quickly transmitted around the world and affect not only military operations, but also perceptions of the United States by foreign audiences. In this new role for the Pentagon, expanding its traditional war-fighting capacities to include nation-building activities and communication, it had come into interagency competition with the Department of State and other agencies that also directly engage foreign audiences.

The reasons cited for Little's announcement were bureaucratic, but the fact is that this nontraditional variety of public diplomacy had shifted power and resources from State to DOD under the two deployments, and this shift had had its critics. Under Secretary of State Hillary Clinton, and Secretary of Defense Robert Gates, the push had been to return outreach activities in the two countries to State. It had been surrounded by controversy almost from Day One.[3]

---

2. Rosa Brooks, "Confessions of a Strategic Communicator: Tales from Inside the Pentagon's Message Machine," *Foreign Policy*, December 6, 2012, accessed June 11, 2016, http://foreignpolicy.com/2012/12/06/confessions-of-a-strategic-communicator/.
3. George Little memorandum,
https://foreignpolicymag.files.wordpress.com/2015/01/121206_brooksmemo.pdf.

According to the DOD memo, the military would be phasing out use of the term "strategic communication" due to a number of issues associated with the various Office of Strategic Communication programs. For one, while attempting to streamline interagency communications by creating unified and understandable messages from the U.S. leadership, the office had created multiple levels of bureaucracy and duplication of programs. Many already existed in the sphere of public affairs or diplomacy or both. As further detailed in the memo:

> SC was viewed as a means to synchronize communication efforts across the department, however, over the last six years we learned that it actually added a layer of staffing and planning that blurred the roles and functions of traditional staff elements and resulted in confusion and inefficiencies.[4]

Costs relating to DOD's Strategic Communication programs were also reported to have spiraled out of control, reaching almost $1 billion in the budget year 2009.[5] Many lawmakers, including those from the House and Senate Armed Services committees and the House Appropriations Committee, believed SC programs were growing too quickly and consuming ever greater financial resources. Aside from these issues, strategic communication had a number of high-level critics in the media and academia, from former Secretary of State Richard Holbrooke to former chairman of the Joint Chiefs of Staff, Adm. Michael Mullen. Strategic communication programs were viewed at best as ineffective and worst as bordering on psychological operations. Some charged strategic communication programs with restricting media freedom and generating propaganda. Noted former National Security Advisor Zbigniew Brzezinski in 2004, "In our entire

---

4. Ibid.
5. Walter Pincus, "Fine Print: Panels Raise Concerns Over Pentagon's Strategic Communications," *The Washington Post*, July 28, 2009, accessed June 11, 2016, http://www.washingtonpost.com/wp-dyn/content/article/2009/07/27/AR200907270 1896.html.

history as a nation, world opinion has never been as hostile towards the United States as it is today."[6]

Needless to say, strategic communication programs will likely continue in some capacity, even if the term is no longer used by the DOD, particularly used in the challenge posed by information warfare conducted through social media. The use of strategic communication and similar programs was set to be reduced by the U.S. government, until the rise of a new brand of terrorism with ISIS (the Islamic State in Iraq and Syria) in 2014. ISIS has occasioned a whole new push by State and DOD to counter the avalanche of Internet propaganda. In a sense a new U.S. communication cycle has begun.

Public diplomacy in the first decade of the twenty-first century faced great new challenges. Following the devastating terrorist attacks on September 11, 2001, and the resulting military actions in Afghanistan and Iraq, the State Department as well as the DOD scrambled to improve their outreach in these nations. The sheer number of different communication programs involved suggests the urgency in trying to reach publics for whom a U.S. presence was alien—and not always wanted.

To some, strategic communication meant public diplomacy strategically marketed to certain audiences for a certain effect, thus bordering on psychological operations; to others, it meant a strategic synchronization of the messaging of U.S. government agencies, thus bordering on totalitarian propaganda. For those who practiced it,

---

6. Christopher Paul, "Whither Strategic Communication? A Survey of Current Proposals and Recommendations," *Occasional Papers* (RAND Corporation, 2009): 1, accessed June 11, 2016, http://www.rand.org/pubs/occasional_papers/OP250.html, citing Zbigniew Brzezinski, "Hostility to America has never been so great," *New Perspective Quarterly* 21(4), Summer 2004.

however, strategic communication meant specifically tailored outreach informed by cultural understanding.

2001–2002 State Department Intensifies Outreach to Muslim Countries

The first post-9/11 public diplomacy efforts came from the State Department's Bureau of Educational and Cultural Affairs, along with other organizations within the State Department, and focused on building connections between American citizens and those of other countries, particularly those within Arab Muslim world. In 2002, State launched the "Shared Values Initiative" to highlight the common values and beliefs shared by Muslims in the countries of the Middle East and in the U.S., to demonstrate that America is not at war with Islam, and stimulate dialogue between the United States and the Muslim world. The $15 million initiative centered on a paid television campaign, which was developed by a private sector advertising firm and attempted to illustrate the daily lives of Muslim Americans. This multimedia campaign also included a booklet on "Muslim life in America," speaker tours, an interactive website to promote dialogue between Muslims in the United States and abroad, and other information programs.[7]

Also in 2002, the Bureau of Educational and Cultural Affairs developed an exchange initiative specifically for youth from Muslim communities called "Partnerships for Learning," which provided an organizing theme to help guide the department's exchange investments. Designed to reach a "younger, broader, deeper" audience in the Muslim world, one senior State official called

7. United States Government Accountability Office, "GAO-06-535 U.S. Public Diplomacy: State Department Efforts to Engage Muslim Audiences Lack Certain Communication Elements and Face Significant Challenges," *Report to the Chairman, Subcommittee on Science, the Departments of State, Justice, and Commerce, and Related Agencies, Committee on Appropriations, House of Representatives* (2006): 11, accessed June 11, 2016, http://pdf.usaid.gov/pdf_docs/pcaab427.pdf.

Partnerships for Learning "the heart of our extensive engagement with the Arab and Muslim world."[8]

The State Department also launched the Arabic-language *Hi* magazine in July 2003, which had an annual budget of $4.5 million. Designed to highlight American culture, values, and lifestyles, *Hi* targeted youth in the Middle East and North Africa and was expected to generate a more positive perception of the United States among Arab youth. The magazine was also distributed through U.S. embassies. In December 2005, State suspended publication of *Hi* pending the results of an internal evaluation, which was prompted by concerns over the magazine's cost, reach, and impact, according to State officials.[9]

Another example of a traditional public diplomacy program was the State Department's Iraq Cultural Heritage Initiative, established in 2009 to protect and preserve Iraqi historical sites by engaging American institutional partners to collaborate with the Iraq State Board of Antiquities and Heritage. Collaborations included "infrastructure upgrades at the Iraq Museum in Baghdad, site management planning and architectural conservation in Babylon, and training Iraqi professionals in the conservation of objects, sites, and monuments at a specialized institute in Erbil." As further described on the State Department website, the project was meant to demonstrate the American people's respect for the people of Iraq as heirs to one of the world's oldest civilizations.[10]

---

8. Ibid., 13.
9. Ibid., 12.
10. See http://eca.state.gov/cultural-heritage-center/iraq-cultural-heritage-initiative.

Credit: DVIDSHUB/Route clearance mission, 2013

The Pentagon Gets into the Action: Media Program (2011)

It was clear, however, that military engagements brought a whole new level of challenges, far beyond the scope of State's traditional approach of listening to, informing, engaging, and through those processes, influencing global publics. Then-Secretary of Defense Donald Rumsfeld keenly perceived the need for a more targeted, direct, and positive approach to public opinion in this new environment. From his perspective, U.S. troops had the more intense challenge of engaging populations who had a minimal understanding of what the United States was doing in their countries. They were often influenced strongly by enemy inaccurate, severely tainted propaganda. As Rumsfeld stated in a March 2006 speech at the Army War College, Carlisle Barracks, Pennsylvania: "If I were rating, I would say we probably deserve a D or D+ as a country as how well we're doing in the battle of ideas that's taking place. I'm not going to suggest that it's easy, but we have not found the formula as a country."[11]

And it was not a struggle made any easier by the critical attitudes at home towards any efforts by the Pentagon to communicate its actions or intentions. Rumsfeld again, at Carlisle:

> We're conducting a war today [when] for the first time in the history of the world, in the 21st century, [sic] all of these new realities—video cameras and digital cameras and 24 hour talk shows and bloggers and the internet and e-mails and all of these things [sic] have changed how people communicate. And as a result, everything anyone says goes to multiple audiences.   Every time the United States tries to do anything that would communicate something positive about what we're doing in the world we're criticized in the press and in the Congress, and we have a reappraisal and say oh, my goodness, is that something we should be doing? How do we do it in a way that is considered acceptable in our society?[12]

One of Rumsfeld's first efforts was standing up the Office of Strategic Influence at the Pentagon, dating from 2001, a small operation which was tasked with creating content favorable to the United States (and unfavorable to its enemies) and planting it in local Iraqi media without the fingerprints of the U.S. government. While there was no indication that disinformation was being peddled, once discovered, the covert nature of the operation was quickly

---

11. Remarks by Secretary of Defense Donald H. Rumsfeld (Army War College, Carlisle Barracks, Pennsylvania, March 27, 2006), accessed June 11, 2016, http://www.au.af.mil/au/awc/awcgate/dod/tr20060327-12710.htm.
    12. Ibid.

denounced in the U.S. media. The office was closed down after just one year of operation.[13]

Also, there was frequent friction between State and the Pentagon over which approach to take and over who would control the funding. The more Pentagon funding grew for its strategic communication programs, the more it was resented by State Department officials concerned with bureaucratic turf invasion. A fierce interagency rivalry that developed between Donald Rumsfeld's Pentagon and Gen. Colin Powell's State Department in part had strategic communication as a focal point.[14]

Another of the Pentagon's first efforts was also a most successful one: the Embedded Media program. Throughout the Iraq war, roughly 700 journalists were allowed close access to military units via a strategic communication initiative, the Embedded Media program. The program was unique and, generally, was positively received by the American public. A similar program occurred in the Afghan war.[15]

From a military perspective, giving reporters an eyewitness perspective on the action provided a very different and more positive coverage than that of reporters writing their copy from the vantage point of a military commend far from the frontlines. Needless to say, this was not without its critics, particularly from the European media which accused American journalists of being in bed with U.S. military and serving as its propagandists. The charge both from Europe and

---

13. Eric Schmitt, "Rumsfeld Formally Disbands Office of Strategic Influence," *New York Times*, February 26, 2002, accessed June 11, 2016, http://www.nytimes.com/2002/02/26/national/26CND-PENTAG.html.

14. Col. Jeryl Ludowese, "Strategic Communications: Who Should Lead the Long War of Ideas" (U.S. Army War College, Carlisle Barracks, Pennsylvania, 2006), accessed June 11, 2016, http://www.au.af.mil/au/awc/awcgate/army-usawc/long_war_of_ideas.pdf.

15. Hannah Debenham, "The Pros and Cons of Embedded Journalism," *Media Ethics and Society*, October 22, 2014, accessed June 11, 2016, http://scrippsmediaethics.blogspot.com/2014/10/pros-and-cons-of-embedded-journalism.html.

from the American left was that American journalists were allowing themselves to be co-opted by their closeness to the soldiers on the ground.[16]

Abu Ghraib and its Consequences

The Abu Ghraib prisoner-abuse scandal came to light in late 2003. Photographs revealing that U.S. troops had subjected prisoners in this U.S.-run military prison in Iraq to humiliating treatment spread around world via the Internet, and repercussions were widespread. The U.S. deployment in Iraq was already highly unpopular internationally, so the Pentagon tried to tackle the debacle through a number of strategic communication efforts. Several of these backfired, such as the U.S. military's hire of a number of public relations firms to assist with damage control and future strategic communication initiatives. "All the News that is Fit to Slant," read a *Seattle Times* headline, fairly typical of the domestic and international reaction.[17]

Other Pentagon initiatives, which came closer to traditional public affairs and public diplomacy, included the *Joint Hometown News Service*, previously the *Army & Air Force Hometown News Service*, which merged with the *Defense Media Activity*, a new organization created by the 2005 Defense Base Realignment and

---

16. Eric Green, "U.S. Newsman Sees Pros and Cons for 'Embedded' Reporters," *IIP Digital*, September 7, 2007, accessed June 11, 2016, http://iipdigital.usembassy.gov/st/english/article/2007/09/200709071508561xeneerg 0.3741114.html#axzz3ELyNJL62; Michael Pasquarett, "Reporters on the Ground: The Military and the Media's Joint Experience during Operation Iraqi Freedom," *Center for Strategic Leadership: Issue Paper*, vol. 08-03 (October2003), accessed June 11, 2016, http://www.iwar.org.uk/news-archive/iraq/oif-reporters.pdf.

17. Ernest Londono, "Baghdad Now: All the news that's fit to slant," *The Seattle Times*, June 8, 2009, accessed June 11, 2016, http://www.seattletimes.com/nation-world/baghdad-now-all-the-news-thats-fit-to-slant/.

Closure Commission Report. Representing a domestic media-wing of the Pentagon's strategic communication program, the organization planned to put out 5,400 press releases, 3,000 television releases, and 1,600 radio interviews in 2009.[18]

Also in 2005, the 1st Armored Division launched *Baghdad Now* to inform the Iraqi people of the coalition forces' intentions. The newspaper was disseminated by what was then the U.S. Army Psychological Operations teams (later renamed Military Information Support Operations in an effort to minimize controversy) and highlights the accomplishments of coalition and Iraqi community members in the rebuilding of the country, while also promoting democracy and human rights.

Again, the Pentagon's attempt with *Baghdad Now*, a more traditional public diplomacy campaign, was borne out of frustration that no other U.S. government department was taking the lead producing positive news. The publication, though, did not exactly convince Iraqis that their prospects were improving day by day, running counter to their own perceptions.[19]

The "America Supports You" program was set up in 2004 to keep troops informed about volunteer donations; however, the military awarded $11.8 million in contracts to a public relations firm to advertise donations to the public and garner support for the military at a time when public opinion was turning against the Iraq war. Military officials severed their contract with the firm in question, the Rendon Group, a strategic communication firm, which reportedly

---

18. Fox News, "Pentagon Spending Billions on PR to Sway World Opinion," *Politics*, February 5, 2009, accessed June 11, 2016, http://www.foxnews.com/politics/2009/02/05/pentagon-spending-billions-pr-sway-world-opinion/.
19. See Londono, http://www.seattletimes.com/nation-world/baghdad-now-all-the-news-thats-fit-to-slant/.

was profiling reporters seeking to cover the ongoing war in Afghanistan.[20]

Military Information Support Teams (MIST)

Additional controversy was aroused by the Military Information Support Teams (MIST), a detachment of psychological operators who employ military information support at tactical, operational and strategic levels. Some of the operators were from academia—historians, anthropologists, sociologists—who could help bridge the gap between Americans and the Afghans and Iraqis among whom they were deployed. Among their missions were providing commanders with additional tools for positively influencing foreign populations, countering misleading information and perceptions, and countering the efforts of violent extremist organizations. Yet, with with mounting opposition to the Afghan and Iraqi deployments at home, opposition on university campuses quickly galvanized against the program.[21]

From about 2006 (there likely were other earlier operations) onward, MIST made visits to foreign embassies under the direction of Unified Combatant Command. The nature of these visits varied based on the immediate needs of the region. MIST played a role in various strategic communication initiatives throughout Africa and the Middle East.[22]

---

20. Military Ends Contract With Rendon Group, Firm That Profiled Reporters, *The Huffington Post*, October 16, 2009,
http://www.cbsnews.com/news/military-ends-contract-for-profiling-media/.
21. Russell Rumbaugh and Matthew Leatherman, "The Pentagon as Pitchman: Perception and Reality as Public Diplomacy," *Stimson* (September 2012), accessed June 11, 2016,
http://www.stimson.org/images/uploads/research-pdfs/Pentagon_as_pitchman.pdf.
22. Brian Carlson, "Pentagon Abandons Strategic Communication?" *Public Diplomacy Council*, December 18, 2012, accessed June 11, 2016,

New Guidelines for Public Diplomacy and Strategic Communication

In June, 2007, the National Security Council produced a comprehensive set of new guidelines for directing Public Diplomacy and Strategic Communication, in an effort to produce a better coordinated communications effort by the U.S. government's various actors. These new guidelines covered, but were not limited to, the Afghan and Iraq wars; specifically the guidelines focused on streamlining interagency coordination, reviewing existing policies, confronting extremist ideologies, highlighting certain efforts by the U.S. military (i.e., humanitarian response), and media outreach.[23]

By 2007, Secretary of Defense Rumsfeld had been replaced by Robert Gates, who had a very different view of how to communicate the rationale for U.S. military engagement and who should do it. In Gates's view, strategic communication as it had evolved under his predecessor had its limitations and was best returned to the State Department. At the National Defense University in September, 2008, Gates stated:

> *The Quadrennial Defense Review highlighted the importance of strategic communications as a vital capability, and good work has been done since. However, we can't lapse into using communications as a crutch for shortcomings in policy or execution. As Admiral Mullen has noted, in the broader battle for hearts and minds abroad, we have to be as good at listening to others as we are at telling them our story. And when it comes to perceptions at home, when all is said and done, the best way to convince the American people we're*

---

http://publicdiplomacycouncil.org/commentaries/12-18-12/pentagon-abandons-strategic-communication.

23. Policy Coordinating Committee, "U.S. National Strategy for Public Diplomacy and Strategic Communication," *Strategic Communication and Public Diplomacy* (June 2007), accessed June 11, 2016, http://www.au.af.mil/au/awc/awcgate/state/natstrat_strat_comm.pdf.

winning a war is through credible and demonstrable results, as we have done in Iraq.[24]

A Department for Strategic Communication

Meanwhile, back in Washington, a lack of coordination between government departments and the interagency rivalry over strategic communication resulted for the first time since 1999 (when the United States Information Agency was abolished) in legislation to constitute a new agency to communicate the U.S. government's intentions. Among the problems created by the interagency rivalry in Washngton was a total inability to agreee on the fundamental American values to be conveyed by strategic communication, making U.S. efforts seem far more tepid that the strident propaganda presented by our adversaries.[25] The quest for more effective and streamlined communication in May of 2008 resulted in The Smith-Thornberry amendment (H.A. 5) to the National Defense Authorization Act for Fiscal Year 2009. The bill sought to bolster strategic communication by requiring the creation of a comprehensive interagency strategy for strategic communication and public diplomacy, a description of the specific roles of the State and Defense departments, and a detailed assessment of the viability of a new Center for Strategic Communication.[26]

---

24. Secretary of Defense Robert Gates (speech at the National Defense University, Washington, DC, September 29, 2008), accessed June 11, 2016, http://www.defense.gov/speeches/speech.aspx?speechid=1279.

25. William Darley, "The Missing Component of U.S. Strategic Communication," *Joint Force Quarterly* 47, 4th quarter (2007): 109-113.

26. Tony Blankley and Oliver Horn, "Strategizing Strategic Communication," *WebMemo#1939 on National Security and Defense*, May 29, 2008, accessed June 11, 2016, http://www.heritage.org/research/reports/2008/05/strategizing-strategic-communication.

The Department of State and Bureau of Public Affairs also countered al Qaeda and Taliban propaganda by establishing a Rapid Response Unit, which is able to address urgent issues by providing approved strategic messages that military leaders can use to develop military oriented strategic communication products.[27]

In a town hall meeting with Robert Gates in October, 2009, Secretary of State Hillary Clinton described what the rapid reaction team was up against and justified the move to place the State Department again in the lead role:

> *The Taliban and their allies use cell phones to intimidate people. We found out that they were running FM—illegal FM stations literally off the back of motorcycles, and they were telling people "We're going to behead this person," and "We're going to do that." So we are competing in that space. And obviously, we have to work together, but we have the lead on it because it needs to stand for more than just our military might; it needs to represent all of our national interests and values.*[28]

U.S. Broadcasting as Part of the Strategic Communications Effort

Just as the State Department had moved to reassert control over strategic communication, the Broadcasting Board of Governors (BBG) released a strategic plan for 2008–2013 that focused on combating extremism and authoritarianism while protecting freedom and democracy. The plan included a review of existing strategies and resources. Focus was placed on critical priority countries for U.S. foreign policy. Means of signal delivery, such as television, FM radio, and the Internet, should vary according to audience demographics, media habits, trends, and other factors.

---

27. U.S. Joint Forces Command, *Commander's Handbook for Strategic Communication and Communication Strategy* (June 24, 2010): 21, accessed June 11, 2016, http://www.dtic.mil/doctrine/doctrine/jwfc/sc_hbk10.pdf.

28. Town Hall with Secretary of Defense Gates on American Power and Persuasion, October 5, 2009, accessed June 11, 2016, http://www.state.gov/secretary/20092013clinton/rm/2009a/10/130315.htm.

Decisions should be based on thorough audience research and U.S. national priorities. Likewise, interfaith dialogue, modernity, and democracy should be pushed in news gathering, reporting, and programming by the U.S. government-funded broadcasters responsible for reaching the Arab states.[29]

Alhurra

Aspects of this plan went back to 2004 when the BBG oversaw the launch of Alhurra, a United States-based Arabic-language satellite TV channel. Like other efforts to influence public opinion in the Middle East, however, Alhurra[30] has seen its share of critics, for having too little audience reach, and lack of quality programming.[31]

Obama White House Call for Overhaul of Strategic Communication

With the transition from the Bush to the Obama administration came a new strategy "to improve the image of the United States and its allies" and "to counter the propaganda that is key to the enemy's terror campaign" in the Afghan war. Ambassador Richard Holbrooke referred to strategic communication as "[a] major gap to be filled."[32] Given all the initiatives that had gone before in the eight years of U.S. deployments, this gap existed not for want of effort. Yet, Rosa Brooks, former counselor in the office of the Undersecretary of

---

29. Broadcasting Board of Governors, *2008-2013 Strategic Plan* (2008), accessed June 11, 2016,
http://www.bbg.gov/wp-content/media/2011/12/bbg_strategic_plan_2008-2013.pdf.
    30. Alhurra, "About Us,"
"http://www.alhurra.com/info/about-us/112.html#ixzz3ES0ahVmB.
    31. Helene Cooper, "Unfriendly Views on U.S. Backed Arabic TV," *The New York Times*, May 17, 2007, accessed June 11, 2016,
http://www.nytimes.com/2007/05/17/washington/17hurra.html?_r=0.
    32. Walter Pincus, "Fine Print: Panels Raise Concerns over Pentagon's Strategic Communications."

Defense for Policy, wrote in *Foreign Policy* magazine about the total confusion she experienced on taking office at the Pentagon and being made responsible for figuring out what the agency's Strategic Communications programs added up to.[33]   Clearly the Obama administration was not inclined to follow the Bush/Rumsfeld model.[34]

At the State Department, meanwhile, one of the most successful initiatives in Strategic Communication was taking form, a new experimental program to counter propaganda from the Taliban and al Qaeda while more fully engaging the local populations of Afghanistan and Pakistan. Starting small in 2009, the Center for Strategic Counterterrorism Communications[35] at State in the office of the Undersecretary for Public Diplomacy and Public Affairs under Bush appointee James Glassman, the CSCC had remained at the core of the U.S. government's efforts to reach potentially radicalized Muslim youth.[36]

The State Department Back in the Drivers' Seat

It is an unfortunate fact that President Obama's campaign promise to drawdown   troops from Iraq and Afghanistan produced a power vacuum readily filled by a brand of terrorism that makes al Qaeda pale by comparison,and has necessitated an official reversal that will keep 5,500 troops deployed in Afghanistan indefinitely, and the

---

33. Rosa Brooks, "Confessions of a Strategic Communicator: Tales from Inside the Pentagon's Message Machine."

34. Press Briefing by Bruce Riedel, Ambassador Richard Holbrooke, and Michelle Flournoy on the New Strategy for Afghanistan and Pakistan (The White House, March 27, 2009), accessed June 11, 2016, http://www.whitehouse.gov/the_press_office /Press-Briefing-by-Bruce-Riedel-Ambassador-Richard-Holbrooke-and-Michelle-Flourno y-on-the-New-Strategy-for-Afghanistan-and-Pakistan/.

35. Hayes Brown, "Meet The State Department Team Trying To Troll ISIS Into Oblivion," *Think Progress*, September 18, 2014, accessed June 11, 2016, http://thinkprogress.org/world/2014/09/18/3568366/think-again-turn-away/.

36. Thom Shanker, "U.S. Plans a Mission Against Taliban's Propaganda," *The New York Times*, August 15, 2009, accessed June 11, 2016, http://www.nytimes.com/2009/08/16/world/asia/16policy.html?gwh=13DAD1DBF1E 94E397AF913D99DDFDA99&gwt=pay.

reinsertion of U.S. special forces in Iraq.[37] The Islamic State in Iraq and Syria (ISIS) has borrowed the al Qaeda communication method, but ISIS, far more adept at social media manipulation, has produced an even greater challenge than the one the Pentagon was attempting to deal with under Rumsfeld.

The bureaucratic battle over strategic communication, however, had been lost by the Pentagon. The White House, the National Security Council, and the State Department were all uneasy with the expanded role undertaken by DOD. In the Spring of 2016, the Obama administration decided to reorganize its efforts to counter the information warfare waged by ISIS, al Qaeda and other terrorist groups. The Center for Strategic Counterterrorism Communications at the State Department was renamed the Global Engagement Center and given two main tasks: The first, to foster cooperation with other countries to counter terrorist propaganda mainly through exposing the reality of life in Iraq and Syria under terrorist control and through offering a more positive vision. Secondly, the Center was tasked with coordinating the efforts of the multitude of U.S. federal government departments that have a slice of counterterrorist policy in some form. While the thinking behind the change makes sense success remains elusive and at best has to be seen in a very long-term perspective.[38]

Today, the United States and its allies have been drawn into a confrontation with yet another foe in Iraq and Syria, one far more

---

37. Fox News, "Obama to Keep 5,500 Troops in Afghanistan Beyond 2016," *Politics*, October 15, 2015, accessed June 11, 2016, http://www.foxnews.com/politics/2015/10/15/obama-to-keep-5500-us-troops-in-afghanistan-beyond-2016.html.

38. For example, see http://docs.house.gov/meetings/FA/FA00/20160713/105223/HHRG-114-FA00-MState-R000487-20160713.pdf.

radical than any we have dealt with before. The Taliban in Afghanistan are resurging and increasingly emboldened in their attacks. Is the State Department prepared to deal with this threat, which requires even sharper tools in the U.S. strategic communications tool kit? In the absence of a massive military engagement, the Pentagon is relieved not to be the lead agency anymore. Yet, if there was ever a time for a massive synchronized Strategic Communication effort to reach Muslim populations, it surely is now.

9

Cultural Diplomacy Partnerships: Cracking the Credibility Nut with Inclusive Participation

Deborah L. Trent

Credit: USA Pavilion at Shanghai Expo

Modern and contemporary dance are unique in a way that we can reach into rarely discussed political and social issues through the inviting use of the universal language of movement. These may be things that the government, or to be more specific the State Department, won't have such easy access to or comfortable discussions about. Through our State Department-funded trips, one of the great things that we've been able to do in the scheduled master classes and through performing in places that are more remote and away from the capitals, is that we can talk about these issues. I think that's one of the things that's been the most rewarding for us.[1]

---

1. Kathryn Sydell Pilkington, "Cultural Diplomacy and Partnerships" (discussion at the Public Diplomacy Council Fall Forum, Washington, DC, November 12, 2013). [Fall Forum transcripts are unpublished to maintain confidentiality of identified speakers other than those permitting identification here.]

Above, the co-artistic director of ballet Company E provides a sense of the relationships and mutual understanding in an effective cultural diplomacy program. Government-sponsored cultural diplomacy is "the exchange of ideas, information, art, and other aspects of culture among nations and their peoples in order to foster mutual understanding."[2] The United States Department of State's Bureau of Educational and Cultural Affairs (ECA) manages many of these exchanges through grants and partnerships with non-governmental organizations (NGOs), both non-profit and for-profit.[3]

Since the mid-20th century, cultural diplomacy through public-private partnerships (PPPs), has been generating lasting people-to-people relationships such as the one with Company E. Especially after the 9/11 attacks, the ability of PPPs to leverage funding while engaging diverse audiences and top cultural artists has received increased recognition.[4]

Nevertheless, three key questions need answers: Would engaging more stakeholders and participants increase mutual understanding among global publics? Would this approach also improve the U.S. government's credibility globally? How can more socially inclusive and participatory PPPs increase impact and support non-governmental advocacy for cultural diplomacy programs? Answers are crucial, because the success of cultural diplomacy

2. Milton C. Cummings, "Cultural Diplomacy and the United States Government: A Survey," *Cultural Diplomacy Research Series* (2009): 1, accessed March 5, 2016, http://www.americansforthearts.org/by-program/reports-and-data/legislation-policy/naappd/cultural-diplomacy-and-the-united-states-government-a-survey.

3. See http://eca.state.gov/about-bureau-0/organizational-structure/office-citizen-exchanges.

4. U.S. Department of State, "Cultural Diplomacy: The Linchpin of Public Diplomacy," *Report of the Advisory Committee on Cultural Diplomacy* (September, 2005): 1-2.

depends on the perceived credibility of its governmental purveyor as perceived among audiences, participants, and taxpayers.[5]

It has been argued that a firewall is needed between U.S. cultural diplomacy programs and foreign policy in order to maximize the credibility of the United States.[6]   In contrast, this chapter considers a bridge – PPP – to link the United States with global publics.

In considering PPPs as a bridge, this chapter addresses the challenge of audience outreach and engagement resulting from the proliferation of information and communication technologies and static or decreased funding with which public diplomats administer programs. This policy dialogue about programmatic quality, scale, and scope is intended for policy and implementation stakeholders inside and beyond ECA.

The chapter also reviews the 2013 Public Diplomacy Council (PDC) Fall Forum session at the Department of State on cultural diplomacy and partnerships.[7] It draws on other literature regarding cost-shared cultural diplomacy programs in the performing arts of dance and music, as well as writing, museum and archaeological studies, and their impacts on people-to-people engagements among diverse cultures.

Additionally, the chapter draws on the experience of the neighboring fields of peacebuilding and development. It argues that

---

5. Robert H. Gass and John S. Seiter, "Credibility and Public Diplomacy," in *Routledge Handbook of Public Diplomacy,* ed. Nancy Snow and Philip M. Taylor (New York: Routledge, 2009), 155-156; Matthew Wallin, "What Constitutes Credibility in US Public Diplomacy," *American Security Project*, November 9, 2015, accessed March 5, 2016, http://www.americansecurityproject.org/what-constitutes-credibility-in-us-public-diplomacy/. See also http://www.state.gov/documents/organization/249770.pdf#120, cited in http://www.state.gov/documents/organization/251971.pdf.
6. Nicholas J. Cull, *The National Theatre of Scotland's Black Watch: Theatre as Cultural Diplomacy* (Los Angeles: USC Center on Public Diplomacy, 2007): 12, accessed March 5, 2016, http://uscpublicdiplomacy.org/sites/uscpublicdiplomacy.org/files/legacy/media/Black_Watch_Publication_010808.pdf.
7. See http://publicdiplomacycouncil.org/2013-fall-forum.

credible cultural diplomacy PPPs and their future funding could benefit from applying the inclusion and participation techniques and experience of these fields.[8] It concludes that this approach supports mutual understanding and helps sustain adequately funded programs.

Framing Cultural Diplomacy as Public-Private Partnership

Cultural diplomacy is situated under the umbrella of U.S. public diplomacy, whose purpose is to inform, influence, and understand global publics, and, increasingly, to engage with them in relationships that promote national interests.[9] In people-to-people exchanges to foster mutual understanding, cultural diplomacy takes one or more of four "forms,"[10] which are:

1. The "prestige gift";
2. "Cultural information" that is lesser known and broadens perceptions of the United States;
3. Two-way and multi-party "dialogue and collaboration";
4. Building "institutional capacity."[11]

For example, sending jazz great Duke Ellington and his band overseas is a prestige gift. Online and touring exhibits of the Smithsonian Institution's Asian Pacific American Center[12] transmit lesser known, perspective-widening cultural information. Multi-directional dialogue and collaboration are fostered through

---

8. See http://www.dmeforpeace.org/; http://www.inclusivesecurity.org/webinar-what-matters-most-measuring-plans-for-inclusive-security/.

9. Public and cultural diplomacy are conducted by the U.S. Department of State, other federal agencies, and subnationally, but this chapter primarily concerns State's programs.

10. Nick Cull, "Jamming for Uncle Sam: Getting the Best from Cultural Diplomacy," *The Huffington Post Blog*, July 26, 2010, accessed March 5, 2016, http://www.huffingtonpost.com/nick-cull/jamming-for-uncle-sam-get_b_659850.html.

11. Ibid.

12. http://smithsonianapa.org/

mural arts instruction in Latin American locales[13] to facilitate engagement on communal conflicts due to discrimination, public health problems, and other issues. Institutional capacity is built with grants through the Ambassadors Fund for Cultural Preservation.[14]

Generally, cultural diplomacy partnerships link closest to the third and fourth forms, and the first or second may also be in play, as with the U.S.A. Pavilion at the 2010 Shanghai Expo. Over seven million visitors to the pavilion – from provincial Chinese to national leaders to global citizens and leaders – offered unprecedented outreach opportunity for dialogue.[15] Also on a grand scale were: collaboration, with 68 U.S. commercial sponsors and 16 suppliers; capacity-building for the U.S. consulate in Shanghai, the country mission, and businesses headquartered in many states; scores of top-flight, world-renowned American artists and performers; and the sharing of U.S. cultural diversity and information facilitated by 160 Student Ambassadors whose Mandarin language skills and unstoppable enthusiasm were key to broadening perceptions.[16]

Ellington's larger than life presence overseas, engagement between U.S.-based diasporas and global publics, American muralists working with Central and South American communities, citizens abroad preserving their antiquities, and the U.S.A. Pavilion showcasing a society's achievements, all demonstrate respect for international interlocutors and support foreign policy goals. They are credible image-builders when they are made: at "arm's length," without excessive self-promotion, in a mutually collaborative and

---

13. http://exchanges.state.gov/us/program/community-engagement -through-arts.

14. http://eca.state.gov/cultural-heritage-center/ambassadors-fund -cultural-preservation.

15. Beatrice Camp, "How I Came to Love the Shanghai Expo," in *The Last Three Feet: Case Studies in Public Diplomacy*, ed. William Kiehl (Washington, DC: Public Diplomacy Council, 2012), 8-18.

16. Ibid.

locally contextualized way, and with patience that allows the time needed for constructive relationships to unfold.[17]

PPP is a collaborative, cross-sector management process for providing services that address citizen demands effectively and use resources, including time, efficiently. Diplomacy and development efforts are increasingly experimenting with PPPs to innovate programs and diversify audience reach and stakeholder participation.[18] The PPP process assumes an appreciation for the value of the financial, institutional, and reputational resources that each stakeholder organization brings to the table, as well as recognition of both their common and divergent interests.

Much of U.S. popular and high culture is generated through profit-making enterprises.[19] Cultural diplomacy that partners across three sectors can lead to more complex, costly, and risky public diplomacy programs, requiring additional regulatory mechanisms than the more typical cultural and educational exchange grants and contracts with NGOs.

The U.S.A. Pavilion in Shanghai was an ultimately successful cultural and trade diplomacy PPP, despite myriad fundraising, contractual, and time pressures, along with media coverage concerns.[20] Its experience demonstrates that the PPP approach needs careful consideration,[21] as does the negotiation process

---

17. Cull, "Jamming for Uncle Sam."
18. See:
http://betterevaluation.org/blog/four_reflections_on_participation_in_evaluation.
19. Patricia M. Goff, "Cultural Diplomacy," in *The Oxford Handbook of Modern Diplomacy*, ed. Andrew F. Cooper et al. (Oxford: Oxford University Press, 2014), 5.
20. Camp, "How I Came to Love the Shanghai Expo."
21. Derick W. Brinkerhoff and Jennifer M. Brinkerhoff, "Public–Private Partnerships: Perspectives on Purposes, Publicness, and Good Governance," *Public*

during design and implementation. [22] Conflict usually arises in negotiating multi-stakeholder interests and identities, and mediation and sharing power are both key for sustained collaboration.[23]

Trust, commitment, and responsibility are demonstrated in PPPs by core-to-peripheral stakeholders through social inclusion and freely expressive, deliberative dialogue, along with hands-on project collaboration to establish enterprises. [24] For example, the commitment to social inclusion in future PPPs in the Department of State's Tech Women is achieved by selecting participants of varying socioeconomic backgrounds and physical abilities.[25] Inclusive design in cultural PPPs strengthens trust and credibility, leads to new sources of funding and other material resources, and stakeholder buy-in.[26]

Administration and Development 31 (2011): 2–14, accessed March 5, 2015, doi: 10.1002/pad.584.

22. Taylor Craig, "International Cultural Exchange Programs: The Curious Relationship of Program Design and Impact" (M.A. thesis, American University, 2015), accessed March 5, 2016, http://auislandora.wrlc.org/islandora/object/auislandora%3A10432/datastream/PDF/view; Will Critchley, Miranda Verburg, and Laurens van Veldhuizen, *Facilitating Multi-stakeholder Partnerships: Lessons from PROLINNOVA* (Silang, Cavite: IIRR/Leusden, December 2006), accessed January 28, 2016, http://www.mspguide.org/resource/facilitating-multi-stakeholder-partnerships-lessons-prolinnova.

23. Critchley, Verburg, and van Veldhuizen, *Facilitating Multi-stakeholder Partnerships: Lessons from PROLINNOV*; Rosemary O'Leary, Yujin Choi, and Catherine M. Gerard, "The Skill Set of the Successful Collaborator," *Public Administration Review* 72 (2012): S70-S83.

24. Deborah Lee Trent, "Transnational, Trans-Sectarian Engagement: A Revised Approach to U.S. Public Diplomacy toward Lebanon"(Ph.D. diss., The George Washington University, 2012), ProQuest3524305, accessed March 1, 2016, http://pqdtopen.proquest.com/doc/1038836409.html?FMT=AI; http://www.inclusivesecurity.org/webinar-what-matters-most-measuring-plans-for-inclusive-security/.

25. See https://www.techwomen.org/press-release/silicon-valley-leaders-to-mentor-technical-women-from-the-middle-east-and-north-africa-through-new-public-private-partnership.

26. For example, http://www.state.gov/s/partnerships/index.htm; https://www.usaid.gov/partnerships; Brinkerhoff and Brinkerhoff, "Public–Private Partnerships: Perspectives on Purposes, Publicness, and Good Governance"; Erin McCandless et al., eds., *Peace Dividends and Beyond: Contributions to Administrative and Social Services to Peacebuilding* (New York: United Nations Peacebuilding Support Office, 2012), accessed March 5, 2016, http://www.un.org/en/peacebuilding/pbso/pdf/peace_dividends.pdf; Yongheng Yang,

Strategically, the NGO partners of PPPs – e.g., colleges, universities, research institutions, and implementing organizations in the United States and abroad – have long kept cultural ties going during times of rocky official bilateral relations.[27] Attendees at the 2013 PDC Fall Forum session on cultural diplomacy and partnerships raised examples of these ties, which illustrate how 'exchange and arts organizations foster intercultural understanding and professional enrichment among PPP participants'[28] at an arm's length. Session discussant Dr. Sherry Mueller noted that exchangees "learn more about us by the way the program unfolds and is organized than they do by what anybody tells them about our political system or about what we believe."[29]

NGO and commercial partner organizations provide strategic value in other ways. They are crucial for selecting PPP stakeholders, from the most influential leaders (e.g., mayors and chamber of commerce presidents) to grassroots publics (e.g., multi-faith groups and their leadership) whose perceptions about the U.S. government range from supportive to adversarial. When conflicts arise – whether due to overarching political issues or internal partnership challenges – the NGO and commercial partners help mediate them.[30]

Yilin Hou, and Youqiang Yang, "On the Development of Public-Private Partnerships in Transitional Economies: An Explanatory Framework," *Public Administration Review* 73, no. 2 (2013): 301-310.

27. For example, http://www.arce.org/main/about/historyandmission; Michael McCarry, "Public-Private Partnerships and the American Exchange Programs: A View from the Field," *The Journal of Arts Management, Law and Society* 29, no. 1 (1999): 63-69.

28. Kristie Conserve, Greta Morris, and Deborah Trent, "2013 Forum: Cultural Diplomacy and Partnerships," *Public Diplomacy Council*, December 13, 2013, accessed May 26, 2016, http://www.publicdiplomacycouncil.org/commentaries/12-13-13/2013-forum-cultural -diplomacy-and-partnerships.

29. Ibid.

30. R. S. Zaharna, "The Public Diplomacy Challenges of Strategic Stakeholder Engagement," in *Trials of Engagement: The Future of US Public Diplomacy*, ed. Ali Fisher and Scott Lucas (Boston: Martinus Nijhoff, 2011), 201-230.

Building Street Cred

At the 2013 PDC Fall Forum session on cultural diplomacy and partnerships, Dr. Mueller listed four reasons why PPPs, adding diverse voices and programmatic flexibility, have long been central to U.S. public diplomacy. First, they reflect American culture, especially the "primacy of the private sector." Second, they allow for credibility and organizational distance between participants and the U.S. government, or a "bridge," as a session co-moderator observed, rather than a firewall. Third, Mueller continued, private-sector partners offer expertise. Fourth, NGOs can perform exchanges more economically than government.

Despite the bridging effect of PPP, growing networks of non-state actors – who often challenge governmental surveillance and regulation – create difficulty for diplomats to connect with, establish, and build sufficient relationships for significant impact on behavior.[31] We may be intuitively aware that a sister-city partnership deepens mutual understanding and bolsters the U.S. image globally, but we usually can only offer anecdotes. "Partnership" has varied, although positive, connotations in diplomacy, although it sometimes lacks credibility because it is hard to sustain commitment to rhetorically stated goodwill.[32] When a PPP's unique added value appears to diminish, its credibility is further weakened.[33]

The current five-year plan of the U.S. Institute of Peace prioritizes the integration of institute-wide planning, programming,

---

31. Bruce Gregory, "American Public Diplomacy: Enduring Characteristics, Elusive Transformation," *The Hague Journal of Diplomacy* 6, no. 3–4 (2011): 351–372, doi: 10.1163/187119111X583941; John Robert Kelley, *Agency Change: Diplomatic Action beyond the State* (Lanham: Rowman and Littlefield, 2014).

32. Trent, "Transnational, Trans-Sectarian Engagement: A Revised Approach to U.S. Public Diplomacy toward Lebanon," 278, citing Jennifer Marie Brinkerhoff, *Partnership for International Development: Rhetoric or Results?* (Boulder: Lynne Rienner, 2002), 2.

33. Brinkerhoff, Partnership for International Development: Rhetoric or Results?

and impact assessment with decision-making.[34] The plan engages inclusively with participants, implementers, policy makers and donors to explore narratives and experience of core-to-peripheral stakeholders. The participatory nature of the internal review process should help shape, ground, and legitimize PPPs and other cross-sector partnerships undertaken by the institute to reduce violent conflict,[35] narrowing the credibility gap between policy rhetoric and program results.

Stepped-up recruiting of urban and rural dwellers, economically disadvantaged and ethnically- or gender-diverse participants and including them as stakeholders in programs can be an effective strategy in development. [36] As efforts continue to coordinate diplomacy, development, defense, and peacebuilding, practitioners in these fields should share strategies, tools, and processes.[37] The diplomatic goals of cross-cultural dialogue and trust-building and the peacebuilding goal of core-to-peripheral stakeholder conflict management are mutually reinforcing, as experience mediating "the Troubles" in Northern Ireland has shown.[38]

34. United States Institute of Peace, *Strategic Plan: 2014-2019*, accessed May 20, 2016,
http://www.usip.org/sites/default/files/page/pdf/USIP-2014-2019-Strategic-Plan.pdf.
35. Ibid., 6.
36. Will Critchley, Miranda Verburg, and Laurens van Veldhuizen, *Facilitating Multi-stakeholder Partnerships: Lessons from PROLINNOVA;* David L. Brown and Darcy Ashman, "Participation, Social Capital, and Intersectoral Problem Solving: African and Asian cases," *World Development* 24, no. 9 (1996): 1467-79; Khaldoun AbouAssi and Deborah L. Trent, "Understanding Local Participation amidst Challenges: Evidence from Lebanon in the Global South," *Voluntas: International Journal of Voluntary and Nonprofit Organizations* 24, no. 4 (2013): 1113-37.
37. U.S. Department of State, *Enduring Leadership in a Dynamic World: Quadrennial Diplomacy and Development Review 2015*, accessed March 6, 2016,
http://www.state.gov/documents/organization/241429.pdf.
38. Joseph J. Popiolkowski and Nicholas J. Cull, eds., *Public Diplomacy, Cultural Interventions & the Peace Process in Northern Ireland Track Two to Peace?* (Los Angeles: Figueroa Press, 2009), accessed March 6, 2016,

Identity, Interests, and Images

Mutual understanding and strategic communication in cultural diplomacy PPPs hinge on dialogue and exchanges and depend on partners becoming acquainted with each other's organizational identities as well as recognizing their shared and divergent interests.[39] For PPP stakeholders who are artists or performers, the focus is their shared interest in improving their art and marketing it, developing their professional identities, and fulfilling their interests.

In three ways mentioned at the outset of this chapter,[40] the governmental PPP stakeholders also share this interest: first, in the process of spreading lesser known – but prestigious and/or popular – cultural information and goods that favorably influence audience and participant perceptions; second, by creating new methods for dialogical engagement and multi-party collaboration; and third, by building institutional capacity, starting with the PPPs themselves and potentially evolving into spin-off ventures.

These dialogical, collaborative, and institutional products of the PPP increase the credibility accorded by each stakeholder group to the others.[41] Indicators of credible perceptions – space for free expression, deliberation, mutually created enterprise, and additional sources of funding – can be incorporated into the design of the PPP and monitored to assess overall value to mutual understanding and U.S. interests. Doing so through inclusive programming,[42] with participants engaged in determining goals and activities, advances

---

http://uscpublicdiplomacy.org/sites/uscpublicdiplomacy.org/files/legacy/media/Track%20Two%20to%20Peace%20FINAL.pdf.

39. Goff, "Cultural Diplomacy"; Deborah L. Trent, "American Diaspora Diplomacy: U.S. Foreign Policy and Lebanese Americans," *Discussion Papers in Diplomacy*, no. 125 (The Hague: Clingendael, Netherlands Institute of International Relations, 2012), accessed March 6, 2016, http://www.clingendael.nl/publications/2012/20121206_discussionpaperindiplomacy_125_trent_beveiligd.pdf.

40. Cull, "Jamming for Uncle Sam: Getting the Best from Cultural Diplomacy."

41. Gass and Seiter, "Credibility and Public Diplomacy," 155-6.

42. http://www.participatorymethods.org/.

the role of cultural diplomacy in administering policy in a moral, "socially-conscious," and targeted way, as is needed in the United States and across the globe.[43]

The soft-power imagery that cultural PPPs generate is also fostered by diplomats and other implementers who engage core-to-peripheral stakeholders in deliberating their cultural sharing, collaboration, and capacity-building processes. Diplomats and other implementers can encourage effective practices, such as inclusive stakeholder dialogues about:

1. Distinctions between the national identities of the host and home countries involved;
2. "[B]ottom-up understanding of their cultures;
3. "[T]actility," or hands-on experience, of the audience;
4. The priority to be assigned to personal and institutional "relationship-building";
5. "[D]iaspora engagement" as a relatively "low-cost" and "high potential impact" source of local credibility, due to their cross-cultural competencies.[44]

Demonstrating Impact

The 2013 PDC Fall Forum session, "Cultural Diplomacy and Partnerships," involved discussions among two modern dance Company E principals and two managers in the Department of State's Office of Citizen Exchanges. Their discussion, along with my

43. Kathy R. Fitzpatrick, *U.S. Public Diplomacy in a Post-9/11 World: From Messaging to Mutuality* (Los Angeles: Figueroa Press, 2011), 41, accessed March 6, 2016, http://uscpublicdiplomacy.org/sites/uscpublicdiplomacy.org/files/legacy/publications/perspectives/CPDPerspectives_Mutuality.pdf.

44. USC Center on Public Diplomacy, "A New Era in Cultural Diplomacy: Rising Soft Power in Emerging Markets" (CPD Annual Research Conference Report, Los Angeles, California, 2014): 6-13, accessed March 6, 2016, http://uscpublicdiplomacy.org/sites/uscpublicdiplomacy.org/files/useruploads/u2015 0/EmergingMarketsPD.pdf.

2015 interview with one of the dancers and attendance at a Company E performance in the D.C. area, suggest how this relational PPP exemplifies mutual understanding and strategic communication and holds potential to boost advocacy for cultural diplomacy.

The analysis here uses narrative inquiry to discuss excerpts of the dialogue.[45]   Narrative inquiry seeks to reconstruct and interpret events, roles, and other experiences of individuals and groups as they make meaning of them through their stories.[46] Credibility is one standard of rigor in narrative inquiry, because it is perceptual, and in socially inclusive, participatory programming we want to compare core-to-peripheral stakeholders' perceptions in order to measure impact and inform future programs and policy.[47]

Company E's co-founder Paul Emerson has sparked innovation in modern dance around the world, fueled by his professional experience and connections in government and the media.[48]   This network of collaborators has addressed the cross-national interests of embassies, and partner organizations and countries. In five years of partnership with ECA's Arts Envoy Program, Company E exchanges have taken place in Russia, Central Asia, China, South America, the Middle East, and Cuba.

Explaining at the 2013 PDC Fall Forum how this PPP has been successful, co-artistic director Kathryn Pilkington cited the example of a tour through Kazakhstan in 2010. She reflected that it was:

---

45. A narrative is a story, with a recognizable opening and closing, about the culture, society, or history of the narrator. See Sonia M. Ospina and Jennifer Dodge, "It's about Time: Catching Method up to Meaning: The Usefulness of Narrative Inquiry in Public Administration Research," *Public Administration Review* 65, no. 2 (2005): 143-157, accessed May 26, 2016, http://www.jstor.org/stable/3542549; and Jennifer Dodge, Sonia M. Ospina, and Erica Gabrielle Foldy, "Integrating Rigor and Relevance in Public Administration Scholarship: The Contribution of Narrative Inquiry," *Public Administration Review* 65, no. 3 (2005): 286-300, accessed May 26, 2016, http://www.jstor.org/stable/3542505.

46. Ibid.

47. Dodge, Ospina, and Foldy, "Integrating Rigor and Relevance in Public Administration Scholarship: The Contribution of Narrative Inquiry," 295.

48. See http://www.companye.org/Artists/artists.emerson.html.

...mostly a selfish tour... for us to go and perform on large stages. But what we found [was that] the best relationships and the most rewarding parts of the tours came from the master classes that were kind of thrown in along the way.... [T]he State Department has said, 'come out to this place outside of the capital and teach a master class.' And we found that that was the best way for us to connect with the local youth and to – and that kind of started building our relationship – to continue to go back to some of these places.[49]

This narrative reflects a sense of the evolving, unpredictable, and improvised multiplier effects of collaboration. To Ms. Pilkington, these collaborations have strategic value for both governmental and private sector stakeholders. The collaborations inform the cross-cultural perceptions and understandings of the dancers and audiences, and hold potential for future constructive impact.

The remarks of Kathryn Pilkington and colleague, dancer-choreographer Robert Priore, at the Fall Forum reflect that changes also occurred in their attitudes as well as their behavior as a result of the tours overseas.

For example, they recounted their introduction, in Israel, to "Gaga"—the movement language created by Ohad Naharin at the Batsheva Ensemble.[50] As a personalized process of self-discovery, learning Gaga was very difficult even for these two highly trained artists. Mr. Priore recalled being

completely immersed in the Israeli technique.... it's truthfully changed my life, not just as a dancer, but [also] as a human,

---

49. This and subsequent quotations and paraphrasing (unless otherwise noted) are taken from the 2013 PDC Fall Forum transcript, with permission of the speakers.

50. https://www.youtube.com/watch?v=OGPG1QL1vJc.

because it forces you to think in ways you would never think your body would move. And that has not just translated through my dancing but also through my ideology as a person.

Ms. Pilkington described how, at Batsheva, they were instructed to "move through a jar of peanut butter, or discover lines in space, or... think about your body in a much different dimension than just where you are at that point." Learning to dance more naturally, using all the senses, was for Pilkington and Priore an unexpected experience in cross-cultural communication – certainly an example of lesser-known cultural information – that led Company E to integrate Gaga into their teaching curriculum. The school offers it to teens and older students, with the help of visiting Israeli dance instructors.

Below, as Ms. Pilkington reflected, although the collaborative cross-cultural process is at times interpersonally awkward, it offers gratifying opportunities for openness and learning about areas of disagreement:

Modern and contemporary dance are unique in a way that we can reach into rarely discussed political and social issues through the inviting use of the universal language of movement. These may be things that the government, or to be more specific the State Department, won't have such easy access to or comfortable discussions about. Through our State Department-funded trips, one of the great things that we've been able to do in the scheduled master classes and through performing in places that are more remote and away from the capitals, is that we can talk about these issues. I think that's one of the things that's been the most rewarding for us.

More recently, restoration of diplomatic relations between Cuba and the United States has offered gratifying and historic moments of cross-cultural engagement. A Company E video[51] records a hastily

---

51. https://vimeo.com/128155610.

arranged street event in a Havana, Cuba neighborhood in April, 2015. It features core stakeholders, including U.S. diplomats, dancers, and local cultural program implementers, plus local onlookers (not-so-peripheral audience members). Some are asked to share their perspectives on the new opportunities for communication, understanding, and artistic development. The video reveals expressions of enthusiasm and surprise about the performance, which reflect the power of cultural diplomacy and its impact on the individual. In our October 19, 2015 interview, I asked Ms. Pilkington about any preconceptions or images that she held about the many cultures she experienced for the first time in the ECA-sponsored travels. Were her perceptions about Kazakhs, Tajiks, Kyrgyz, Russians, Chinese, Peruvians, Israelis, or Arabs transformed through her experiences? She said that her perceptions did change, despite familiarizing herself with these peoples before travelling. In addition, she said that her counterparts were "hungry to learn" and were "open" to "genuine exchange." To her, the audiences felt like a "breath of fresh air" compared to some in the United States.

Ms. Pilkington's changed perceptions and personal experience abroad transformed her approach to teaching, choreography, and performance. These rewarding personal relationships gained through her cross-cultural experiences have not interfered with Pilkington's artistic and capacity-building goals. She commented on her concern that Palestinian dancers in Ramallah might feel alienated by her work with Israelis, and vice versa. She said that she did not want to "close doors" on collaborating with any partner.

The 2013 PDC Fall Forum also reported on the collaboration between ECA grantees Company E and the International Writing

Program[52] (IWP), described by a cultural program manager as one of ECA's longest-running grantees. The Company E-IWP pairing demonstrates evidence of relational partnership and potential for perceptual and behavioral change.

About one occasion for collaboration, dancer-choreographer Mr. Priore recounted at the Fall Forum:

> *I still keep in touch with the writer...I worked with... he had written a poem. It was not very long, and I choreographed a piece on it, a dance piece, and at the final performance, he was one of the writers – there were, I think, 10 or 12 writers.... and only five came, but – five or six. But he was one of the ones that did come.... Not only is this through a writing exchange but also then we as dancers took those stories that these artists from abroad wrote and created them into movement, and we used music and our bodies ...*

A second occasion was the November 4-5, 2015 program[53] by Company E and IWP at the Cultural Arts Center of Montgomery College outside Washington, D.C. Entitled "Refuge," the program featured an essay and poems by IWP participants from Afghanistan, Estonia, Pakistan, Saudi Arabia, and South Korea. Paul Emerson and a team of choreographers, dancers, musicians, and filmmakers interpreted these writings.

I attended on November 5th, posting to Facebook that it was difficult leaving for another appointment during such a captivating performance. It mirrored the notion in Emerson's welcome in the playbill, that the bonding among the writers and artists is an experience of word and movement around "distant cultures and universal experiences."

---

52. http://iwp.uiowa.edu/.
53. https://twitter.com/uiiwp/status/661996371482820609.

This presentation involved at least 17 people, plus the college faculty and students, the implementers at the University of Iowa, and ECA and embassy staff. Its impact was further widened and deepened by the audience of MC students and faculty, whose ethnic diversity reflected the transnational mosaic that defines the college. With over 3,000 "likes" on Facebook and 190 followers on Twitter, Company E's social media platforms draw many of us into the artistry across time and space.

The interaction of free expression, changing interests, identity-making and image-making, and cultural exchange are difficult to trace using only survey response data, as they emerge from fluid, iterative dialogue, learning, teaching, and performing that change perceptions on the individual level. They have not been easily or credibly measured, and more resources would be required to do so; it is recommended that future methods be agreed to and applied in a systematic way across all stakeholder groups.[54]

Some cultural and public affairs officers may prefer not to poll or interview participants, audiences, and other stakeholders about their exchange experiences, perhaps because they do not want to objectify, or worse, alienate these stakeholders or expend precious time and other resources for little benefit.

Research provides other cautions about polling and interviewing.[55] Yet, the impressions of millions of alumni and other

---

54. Taylor Craig, International Cultural Exchange Programs: The Curious Relationship of Program Design and Impact, 31-32, citing Public and Private Cultural Exchange-Based Diplomacy: New Models for the 21st Century (Salzburg: The Salzburg Global Seminar and The Robert Sterling Clark Foundation, 2012): 2-21; Craig, citing Michael Sikes, The Appreciative Journey: A Guide to Developing International Cultural Exchanges (Columbus: Ohio Arts Council, 2006); see also http://www.dmeforpeace.org/.

55. In evaluating cultural/public diplomacy programs, relying just on polls and surveys can bias results when leading questions are asked and interpreted in culturally

stakeholders – including Ms. Pilkington and Mr. Priore, the Cubans at that impromptu dance in Havana who appeared in the video, and students here and abroad partnering to internationalize dance and writing – provide evidence of increased mutual understanding and credibility.

Likewise, the vignettes above suggest opportunities for diplomats and implementers to engage with the Company E-IWP partnership's core-to-peripheral stakeholders – on four of the five topics mentioned earlier – to explore and assess new commercial and social markets and soft power for cross-cultural collaboration.[56] Informative discussions with these college students, celebrities, and civil society activists could take place on how to:

1. Address the need for greater voicing of and mutual respect for differing cultural identities in the global south and north;
2. Spread the wisdom of "bottom-up stories" from the target audiences and beneficiaries of official diplomacy and development;
3. Document the effects of culturally distinctive experiences of audiences and participants;
4. Elevate the importance of one-to-one relationships across stakeholder groups, up and down age groups and hierarchies, and in both urban and rural locales.[57]

A 2013 PDC Fall Forum discussant from the State Department's Office of Citizen Exchanges noted that engagements that connect policy and programs do happen across the Office of Citizen Exchanges four divisions for sports, culture and arts, youth, and professional fellows.

---

biased ways. Social network analysis may better capture the increasing relational approaches to public diplomacy. See R. S. Zaharna, *The Cultural Awakening in Public Diplomacy* (Los Angeles: Figueroa Press, 2012), 51.

56. USC Center on Public Diplomacy, "A New Era in Cultural Diplomacy: Rising Soft Power in Emerging Market," 6-13.

57. Ibid.

PPPs often make these engagements possible. They counter violent extremism and promote socioeconomic opportunity through virtual and in-person exchanges, and sometimes through alumni and other spin-off activities. For example, a State Department discussant at the Fall Forum said that the International Convention of Disability Rights is advanced through the participation of "mixed-ability groups" in the office's sports and arts programs.

Credit: Meridian/Mural Arts Exchange: Colombia, May 26 – June 16, 2015

Ms. Pilkington commented in the interview that Company E founder Paul Emerson appreciates the importance of grantee reports. He usually writes them on the return flight from a program. She admits to a learning process that is partly trial and error, and once involved dipping into company funds to pay for rebooked tickets due to political instability in the host country. They strive to improve and better inform future engagements.

The foregoing analysis attempts to demonstrate the benefits of inclusive programming in cultural PPPs and across public diplomacy. It suggests that broad, continuous participation of stakeholders increases the potential for free expression, deliberative policy dialogue, and shared identity and interests needed for relational partnering and sustainable enterprise development. The analysis also emphasizes how the one-to-one and many-to-many relationships of PPPs extend outreach capacity and the possibility for societal impact. Finally, it suggests that increased participation can generate more advocates and external sources of funding.

In these partnerships, the perceptions of a handful of individuals in a handful of stakeholder groups changed. Two core stakeholders say that they have transformed their attitudes and their art. These are promising although limited results. On a larger and cross-national scale, baseline, mid-term, and end-of-project measurement is needed to trace identity, interests, images, and behavioral change.

Moving Forward

It is neither desirable nor possible for U.S. cultural diplomacy to crack the tough nut of credibility across all global publics, but with inclusive participation and advocacy, we can soften its shell.

First, how can ECA engage a more youthful, diverse array of partners, stakeholders, and audiences in an era of static staffing and program resource levels?

Public-private partnering, brokered both from overseas posts and the Department, is key for multiplier effect. For relevant project ideas, governmental and non-governmental implementers can reach out to organizations for the humanities, arts, humanitarian issues, and marginalized population groups. They can conduct training in PPP management and participatory methods. [58] They can also inquire about the ECA Evaluation Division's internal Performance Measurement surveying, with data collected from 60,000 to 70,000 participants, many of these in Citizen Exchanges programs.[59]

Second, evidence of credibility and mutual understanding among core-to-peripheral stakeholders of PPPs and their audiences can and should be gathered more systematically.

Systemizing inclusive, participatory program evaluation means monitoring activities as they commence and progress, and evaluating them soon after completion.

Along with ECA, the other bureaus within the office of the Under Secretary of Public Diplomacy and Public Affairs recognize that monitoring and evaluation are critical:

> *In 2015, the Under Secretary instituted a new evaluation policy for public diplomacy to help ensure the impact of PD in advancing U.S. foreign policy is properly assessed. The policy establishes the role of a new evaluation unit in coordinating evaluation efforts for PD initiatives and processes for PD,*

---

58. For example, see Craig, 2015; Will Critchley, Miranda Verburg, and Laurens van Veldhuizen, "Thirty lessons in building effective partnerships," *Facilitating Multi-stakeholder Partnerships: Lessons from PROLINNOVA* (Silang, Cavite: IIRR/Leusden, December 2006), accessed March 6, 2016, http://www.prolinnova.net/sites/default/files/documents/resources/publications/200 7/chapter_6.pdf; http://www.participatorymethods.org/.

59. See http://eca.state.gov/impact/evaluation-eca.

including with regional and functional bureaus, field posts, and PD programs that cross bureaus and/or agencies.[60]

Even so, more independent studies are also needed to be able to generalize about and improve on the impacts of cultural diplomacy. To date, the ECA Evaluation Division has commissioned one evaluation of a cultural PPP – the Jazz Ambassadors/American Music Abroad program – and many other major independent evaluations of Citizen Exchanges programs.[61] The return on investment to taxpayers and other stakeholders needs to be reported quantitatively, qualitatively, rapidly, and widely.

Third, more leadership development and "coalition-building" are needed to increase recognition and funding of cultural PPPs, as Fall Forum discussant Sherry Mueller asserted. They are needed for exchanges, generally, as is promoting social inclusion and participant engagement in program implementation and evaluation.

At the cultural diplomacy and partnerships session of the 2013 PDC Fall Forum, audience members expressed concern over PPP budget allocations.[62] Session discussants suggested that advocates need to leverage a variety of organizational resources, from introducing private international arts groups to community-based cultural organizations to informing local and state lawmakers.[63] It

---

60. The 2015 evaluation policy and infrastructure were explained in a personal communication with staff on April 26, 2016. Staff provided further details:

"The evaluation unit will provide technical guidance and tools for the field that draw on best practices and take into account PD's unique contexts, including setting benchmarks and milestones that measure short-term gains and longer-term success in achieving U.S. foreign policy goals. The unit has already conducted evaluations of several single-country and multi-country programs and also conducts audience research to assist posts in designing and targeting programs to enhance their potential impact. Ultimately the evaluation unit seeks to work with posts around the world to develop a body of data that will shape PD practitioners' understanding of how public diplomacy tools and resources are best applied to support foreign policy objectives."

61. See http://eca.state.gov/impact/evaluation-eca/evaluation-initiative/completed-evaluations.

62. Conserve, Morris & Trent, "2013 Forum: Cultural Diplomacy and Partnerships."

63. Ibid.

was clear from the session that advocacy is critical for promoting cultural diplomacy PPPs.

For example, cultural diplomacy advocates can take mutual advantage of new, bipartisan interest indicated in the new Congressional International Exchange and Study Caucus.[64] It was formed in October, 2015, by Co-chairs Representative Steve Pearce (New Mexico) and Representative Jim Himes (Connecticut).

The first Caucus focusing on international exchanges, it is the result of an initiative of the AFS-USA[65] Government Relations Advisory Group and cooperation with the Alliance for International Exchange. The January 27, 2016 public gathering[66] of exchange advocates included videoed remarks by the Co-chairs of the Caucus, who, along with other speakers at the proceedings, asserted that social inclusion and government/non-profit/private sector partnering promote cross-cultural understanding.

One speaker stressed that engaging more 'non-elites' in exchanges fits with the priorities of the Caucus' founding members.[67] Another, a Foreign Service Officer seconded to the National Security Council as Director of Global Engagement, noted that PPPs sometimes have an advantage over standard grants and contracts because the private sector tolerates risk better.[68]

64.
https://pearce.house.gov/press-release/representatives-pearce-and-himes-announce-creation-international-exchange-and-study.
65. http://www.afsusa.org/.
66.
http://www.globaltiesus.org/news/exchangematters/353-watch-exchanges-matter.
67. https://www.youtube.com/watch?v=mr1WenMn46c.
68. https://www.youtube.com/watch?v=CCKNTigKG8k.

The same administration official also pointed to new programs that "empower" civil society leaders in Russia and other countries, illustrating the arm's length capacity of non-governmental actors to convey locally contextualized, convincing messages. Also important for government and private sector partner credibility is evaluation of program impact, as identified by several speakers. These are two arguments for cultural and other kinds of PPPs to be monitored and evaluated among core and peripheral stakeholders.

Diverse participation leads to better program evaluation to inform and support policy. More credible evidence of program and policy impact facilitates advocacy by non-governmental and private sector partners.

Conclusion

The programs discussed here make a case for the effectiveness of the public-private partnering approach in cultural diplomacy. This potential increases with the benefits of engaging more diverse stakeholders and participants throughout the program cycle.

Multi-stakeholder participation strengthens ownership of and commitment to PPPs and the ability of the combined resources of the public and private partners to expand and enhance cultural diplomacy. The availability of outreach and participatory methods and their successful use in the fields of peacebuilding and development further suggest their potential benefits for effective and efficient application in cultural diplomacy as well, particularly for improving U.S. credibility and image-making at home and abroad.

Providing seed funding to the Company E-Batsheva and -University of Iowa IWP partners has built bridges among both organizations and individual members of the global public, reducing the need for a firewall between their collaborations and policy. Nevertheless, there are no guarantees that a cultural diplomacy PPP will support mutual understanding and other policy goals to the extent envisioned. Each PPP is driven as much by people and organizations outside government as inside.

The increasing number and diversity of non-state actors, including traditional media outlets, social media, and extremists, both expand audiences for these PPPs and compound the constraints involved in their implementation. Still, including more participant, audience, and peripheral stakeholders in the monitoring and evaluation phases of the program cycle empowers them to voice their perceptions, interests, differences, stories, and dreams among core partners.

As with any shared experience, be they classes in cinematography or new media production, learning is reciprocal and, both immediately and over the longer term, reflects favorably on the images of all stakeholders, including those inside government. To measure and sustain these impacts involves a combination of training, intra-organizational and cross-stakeholder buy-in, advocacy, and some risk-taking.

Emphasis on the challenges of impact measurement within the State Department and across the wider exchanges community is promising. In addition, if the trend in partnering across sectors continues, added attention will be needed to the regulation and accountability of PPPs.

Diplomats and analysts often talk about transformational diplomacy. Transformation is behavioral change. Greater governmental investment in program funds and staff to analyze and document perceptual and behavioral changes resulting from cultural diplomacy PPPs would increase capacity for transformational diplomacy. Increased capacity could also generate stronger justifications for additional funding.

Further questions remain. How do PPPs figure into ECA's evaluation priorities? Is the exchanges advocacy community going to include the topic of PPP credibility and funding in its engagements with the Congressional International Exchange and Study Caucus? Strengthening both mutual understanding across nations and accountability to taxpayers and stakeholders would seem to be part of a public diplomacy policy that is socially responsible and politically neutral.

10

International Education and Public Diplomacy: Technology, MOOCs, and Transforming Engagement

Craig Hayden

Credit: Scott McLeod, January 20, 2013

This chapter explores the U.S. Department of State's recent turn to technological platforms for education and cultural diplomacy activities to demonstrate how perceptions of technological capacity within the organization result in new forms of public diplomacy practice and strategy. In particular, the chapter examines the work of the State Department's Education and Cultural Affairs (ECA) bureau's "Collaboratory" unit, which offers pilot programs in collaborative technologies that leverage social media and video platforms for new and hybrid programs, such as the MOOC (massive online open course) Camp initiative, Google Hangouts and the rise of a human-centered design ethos behind public diplomacy program design.

The purpose of the chapter is to elucidate how some logics of public diplomacy are transformed by the material context of technology, while others endure. New and social media technology is argued to extend the relationship-building aspects of educational and cultural diplomacy, though integrating such technology into the overarching strategy of public diplomacy remains a work in progress.

International education has long been a tradition of public diplomacy and a time-tested tool for governments to facilitate understanding across cultural and political boundaries. This chapter explores issues at stake in educational diplomacy that take advantage of information and communication technologies (ICTs), and how these may challenge traditional thinking on the broader subject of public diplomacy.

The idea of educational exchange as an aspect of public diplomacy may not be new, yet the use of social media for educational exchange has prompted new and innovative practices that provide both opportunities and challenges for policymakers and planners of public diplomacy. ECA is discussed here as a representative case and illustrates how the intersection of technology and educational diplomacy yields (with some caveats) new capacities for measurement and evaluation, critical-theoretical implications for researchers, and opportunities for new forms of practice.

This chapter first introduces the public diplomacy concept and the related notion of "soft power" and describes how educational exchange represents a significant (and undertheorized) component of public diplomacy research and theorization. The chapter then covers ways in which conceptual developments within media studies and communication theory can provide new insight into how technology is changing institutional norms and practices surrounding public diplomacy. The chapter describes aspects of U.S. educational exchange programs that utilize new and social media technology and lays out key opportunities and challenges that have since emerged for public diplomacy policymakers and practitioners.

Setting the Context for Technology, Exchange, and Public Diplomacy

Public diplomacy is a term that describes the practices and programs employed by governments to communicate with foreign publics in order to support foreign policy objectives. It is a broad concept, which covers a number of differing practices. Public diplomacy has been described as including educational diplomacy, cultural diplomacy, international broadcasting, as well as strategic communication and cognate concepts such as nation branding.[1]

While public diplomacy encompasses a broad array of practices by governments to leverage communication methods to reach foreign publics, it remains largely concerned with two primary objectives: the promotion of information through amplification of messages or stories, and the cultivation of relationships that may yield forms of trust or credibility.[2] These objectives are realized within observable impacts in attitude, behavior, and measures of trust. Public diplomacy involves both short-term episodes of mediated advocacy (strategic communication) as well as long-term investments in relationship-building through cultural and educational exchange.[3]

---

1. Nicholas J. Cull, Public Diplomacy: Lessons from the Past (Los Angeles: Figueroa Press, 2009); Bruce Gregory, "Public Diplomacy: Sunrise of an Academic Field," The Annals of the American Academy of Political and Social Science 616, no. 1 (2008): 274–290; Matthew Wallin, The New Public Diplomacy Imperative: America's Vital Need to Communicate Strategically (Washington, DC: American Security Project, 2012).

2. G. Mallone, *Organizing the Nation's Public Diplomacy* (Lanham: University Press of America, 1988); Giles Scott-Smith, "Mapping the Undefinable: Some Thoughts on the Relevance of Exchange Programs within International Relations Theory," *The Annals of the American Academy of Political and Social Science* 616 (2008): 173–195.

3. R.S. Zaharna, "The Soft Power Differential: Network Communication and Mass Communication in Public Diplomacy," *The Hague Journal of Diplomacy* 2, no. 3 (2007): 213–228.

Public diplomacy is, however, ultimately a tool of statecraft, an aspect of diplomatic practice that increasingly is justified as being tied to the demands and objectives of foreign policy strategy.[4] Not surprisingly, public diplomacy is often conflated with the term soft power.[5] The soft power concept describes how states may turn to their soft power resources (culture, values, and foreign policy legitimacy), in order to influence other international actors without coercive means. According to Joseph Nye, public diplomacy is a method by which states can develop the resources required to wield soft power.[6] Soft power is not the same thing as public diplomacy, but the soft power concept serves as a convenient justification for investment in public diplomacy.[7]

Yet soft power is not a readily available concept for evaluation, and there are few analytically demonstrated examples of how something like "soft power" is generated through international education programs or across the broader range of public diplomacy activity. This is not to say that public diplomacy is not effective; rather, it suggests that the soft power concept does not offer obvious measures for foreign policy planners and decision-makers to assess how public diplomacy connects its practices to outcomes.[8]

This problem has weighed upon the practice of public diplomacy in the United States for decades, in part, because the imperatives of public diplomacy are often at cross-purposes. When

---

4. Craig Hayden, "Logics of Narrative and Networks in U.S. Public Diplomacy: Communication Power and U.S. Strategic Engagement," *Journal of International Communication* (2013): 196-218.

5. Nancy Snow, "Rethinking Public Diplomacy," in *Routledge Handbook of Public Diplomacy*, ed. Nancy Snow and Phillip Taylor (New York: Routledge, 2009), 3–11.

6. Joseph S. Nye, Jr., *The Future of Power*, 1st ed. (New York: Public Affairs, 2011).

7. Snow, "Rethinking Public Diplomacy."

8. B. Goldsmith and Y. Horiuchi, "In Search of Soft Power: Does Foreign Public Opinion Matter for U.S. Foreign Policy?" *World Politics* 64, no. 3 (2012): 555–585.

governments seek to influence behavior or mindsets through communicative practices of relationship-building or advocacy, they run the risk of politicizing programs and diminishing perceptions of credibility. Likewise, analyzing participants directly invites perceptions about the intentions of a program, which could diminish the impact of public diplomacy, or even alienate its participants.

Nevertheless, the United States continues to rely on programs based upon path-dependent expectations that established forms of public diplomacy such as educational, cultural, and informational forms of engagement "work."[9] This suggests that unpacking the underlying justificatory arguments behind public diplomacy is an important initial move toward devising and improving practices.

One of the problems with existing research on public diplomacy, however, is that many of the previous studies have focused on the U.S. historical experience.[10] Similarly, much of the typological treatments of public diplomacy suggest room for unpacking the processes and actions that define public diplomacy's subcategories, from international broadcasting to international education. While historical studies have shed light on important continuities in practice, to grasp the significance of the so-called "new public diplomacy" moment, it may be necessary to understand the intersection of practice with organizational comprehension of technological tools, the context for new forms of public diplomacy strategy and programs.

Recent studies have indeed explored public diplomacy through comparative analysis and have allowed for new perspectives on how the concept has proliferated in new institutional, cultural, and

---

9. Katherine Brown and Chris Hensman, eds. (2014 Comprehensive Annual Report on Public Diplomacy and International Broadcasting): 12, accessed June 18, 2016, http://www.state.gov/documents/organization/235159.pdf.

10. J. Melissen, "Between Theory and Practice," in *The New Public Diplomacy: Soft Power in International Relations*, ed. J. Melissen (New York: Palgrave Macmillan, 2005), 6-9.

strategic contexts.[11] One framework for analysis, the "soft power differential" proposed by R.S. Zaharna, focuses attention on the translation of cultural resources through localized and culturally defined understandings of communication and influence.[12]

For Zaharna, since soft power is ultimately a "communication based activity," different communication strategies can produce different outcomes. Zaharna's approach invites consideration of how soft power is more than simply a strategic template but also reflects the concatenation of cultural and ideational attitudes toward persuasive communication that is built into activities like public diplomacy designed to cultivate soft power. Comparative research can rehabilitate the notion of soft power to understand public diplomacy as something more than an "analytical construct" (to borrow Nye's qualification of the term), and also as a reflection of the tools, biases, and contexts at stake in public diplomacy.

The comparative perspective is important, because it invites analysis of what aspects of public diplomacy remain constant across state contexts, and it provides the basis for questions regarding the links between practice and impact, thereby helping to inform understanding of how public diplomacy contributes to goals, objectives, and outcomes. It may also illuminate how notions of engagement and influence among practitioners have changed in light of perceptions about the role of technology in the process of engagement.

---

11. James Pamment, New Public Diplomacy in the 21st Century: A Comparative Study of Policy and Practice (New York: Routledge, 2012); Craig Hayden, The Rhetoric of Soft Power: Public Diplomacy in Global Contexts (Lanham: Rowman and Littlefield/Lexington Books, 2011); Jing Sun, Japan and China as Charm Rivals (Ann Arbor: University of Michigan Press, 2012).
12. Zaharna, "Soft Power Differential."

Outside of academia, however, public concern for public diplomacy (at least in the United States) is often reactive and episodic, rather than consistent. As Bruce Gregory has noted, the shifting status of strategic importance for public diplomacy contributes to the ambivalent relationship between traditional diplomacy and public diplomacy in the United States, though some of this has been rectified in policy strategy introduced by Secretary of State Hillary Clinton in 2010.[13]

Yet, recent developments in geopolitical conflict, such as the growth of Russian propaganda online and the rise of religious extremist organizations using technological platforms, have prompted renewed interest (and criticism) of U.S. public diplomacy and its level of investment in new and social media platforms.[14] The rise of adversaries and potential geostrategic rivals turning to technological means of public diplomacy has created new interest in competing in these venues, to be "present" in important conversations online.[15]

But what does this mean for practice and research, especially when much of U.S. public diplomacy has not fully migrated online? How the United States has adapted its own educational exchange programs to newly available tools represents a promising field of inquiry that may instigate new forms of research questions and theoretical frameworks for public diplomacy writ large. Educational exchange is arguably underexplored as a dimension of public

---

13. Bruce Gregory, "American Public Diplomacy: Enduring Characteristics, Elusive Transformation," *The Hague Journal of Diplomacy* 6, no. 3–4 (2011): 351–372, accessed July 24, 2015,doi: 10.1163/187119111X583941; Hillary Clinton, "Leading through Civilian Power: Redefining American Diplomacy and Development," *Foreign Affairs* (December 2010), accessed May 12, 2016, https://www.foreignaffairs.com/articles/north-america/2010-11-01/leading-through-ci vilian-power.

14. M. Bayles, "Putin's Propaganda Highlights Need for Public Diplomacy," *Boston Globe*, July 28, 2014, accessed May 12, 2016, http://www.bostonglobe.com/opinion/2014/07/28/putin-propaganda-highlights-need-for-public-diplomacy/9tyuKdtfqG2YqjR5mTd3IM/story.html.

15. Dawn McCall, Coordinator of U.S. International Information Programs (presentation to the Public Diplomacy Council, Washington, DC, February 4, 2013).

diplomacy research, with some prominent exceptions.[16] Although intercultural and international communication research has long focused on the context of exchange, much of this research has focused on cultural and psychological experience, on the impact on pedagogy, and on how the experience of exchange manifests in attitudes toward culture, difference, and future actions.

This kind of research sounds promising for public diplomacy, yet it is rarely situated within the ongoing scholarly discussion on public diplomacy strategy and its connection to foreign policy objectives. Put differently, the strategic dimension of public diplomacy to educational exchange is rarely the focus of such intercultural communication and educational research, yet the context of policymaker interest in technology may bring these fields more closely into alignment.

Generally speaking, educational exchange offers a number of opportunities to directly engage research questions that remain uncovered in public diplomacy research and to explore methodological and theoretical frameworks that can advance the practice of measurement and evaluation both within academia and among practitioners. Much of the contemporary public discourse about public diplomacy tends to downplay the viability of refined measures of effectiveness because the impact of programs such as cultural and educational diplomacy is perceived as long-term.[17]

---

16. Giles Scott-Smith, "The Heineken Factor? Using Exchanges to Extend the Reach of U.S. Soft Power," *American Diplomacy* (2011), accessed June 18, 2016, http://www.unc.edu/depts/diplomat/item/2011/0104/comm/scottsmith_heineken.ht ml; Ali Fisher, *Collaborative Public Diplomacy: How Transnational Networks Influenced American Studies in Europe* (New York: Palgrave Macmillan, 2013); C. Atkinson, "Does Soft Power Matter? A Comparative Analysis of Student Exchange Programs 1980-2006," *Foreign Policy Analysis* 6, no. 1 (2010): 1–22.

17. James Pamment, "What Became of the New Public Diplomacy? Recent Developments in British, U.S. and Swedish Public Diplomacy Policy and Evaluation

Understandably, measures of opinion and contact effects may be difficult to discern over extended periods of time. However, educational exchange may offer unique opportunities to apply studies that strive to uncover the mechanisms that drive social capital, which is arguably the key strategic outcome of educational exchange in the service of public diplomacy.

Some have gone so far as to note that such forms of public diplomacy function as an act of faith, where there is an accepted intuition that these programs work, despite the lack of systematic data collection to inform longitudinal perspectives or panel studies over time. [18]

What may be more pressing is understanding how technology shapes and indeed reconciles, within the public diplomacy context, educational exchange and international education.

Although there are certainly methodological opportunities that arise in the field of educational exchange, what may be more pressing is understanding how technology shapes and indeed reconciles, within the public diplomacy context, educational exchange and international education. Put directly, how does the context of newly available modes of communication technology result in differing forms of public diplomacy practice and organizational thinking?

Methods," *The Hague Journal of Diplomacy* 7, no. 3 (2012): 313–336, accessed July 24, 2015,doi: 10.1163/187119112X635177.

18. James Glassman (remarks at Public Diplomacy in the Next Four Years event at George Washington University, Washington, DC, November 13, 2012), accessed June 18, 2016, https://ipdgc.gwu.edu/public-diplomacy-next-four-years and, https://vimeo.com/53454705.

Credit: U.S. Army RDECOM, May 24, 2012

The Context of Technology, Affordance, and Implications

The practice of educational exchange calls for more refined theoretical and, indeed, methodological attention to public diplomacy than what has been typical in previous studies. As this chapter has argued, one of the potentially insightful contributions that educational exchange can make to the understanding of public diplomacy is through its capacity to cultivate social capital, the forms of trust, legitimacy, and identification that can be engendered through the experiences provided by such programs. Yet these measures are complicated by public diplomacy imperatives that are often yoked to larger strategic objectives. This creates distinct challenges to the cultivation of credibility and understanding.[19]

Likewise, educational exchanges historically have been practices of public diplomacy that do not lend themselves to quick persuasion or influence outcomes. However, ministries of foreign affairs such as the U.S. Department of State are under increasing pressure to demonstrate that their public diplomacy programs are both contributing to foreign policy objectives and creating discernible impact. As public diplomacy programs are facing more intense fiscal pressures and scrutiny, methods of demonstrating the returns of collaborative or facilitative programs may be shaping program design and strategy.[20]

What does the use of *technology* represent for educational exchange, international education, and language instruction affiliated with such programs? While there is certainly an expanding opportunity for educational exchange to serve as a site for research on public diplomacy impact, an important initial step is to understand the way in which technology factors into the logics of program design, creates opportunities, and otherwise mitigates the fact that these programs serve public diplomacy objectives. It may also be tempting simply to argue that the use of ICTs represents a more dramatic transformation in both practice and thinking—where social media and new streaming opportunities have opened up new strategies of engagement through their international reach. Although some programs, such as the public–private partnership between the U.S. State Department and the *Soliya* organization's virtual classroom experience with Middle East countries, seem to embody a so-called "exchange 2.0" moment, the advent of such technological interventions merits further analysis of institutional strategy.[21] At some level, communication technologies have always been

---

19. Cull, *Public Diplomacy*; Scott-Smith, "The Heineken Factor?"
20. Pamment, "What Became of the New Public Diplomacy?"
21. D. Roberts, L. Welch, and K. Al-Khanji, "Preparing Global Citizens," *Journal of College and Character* 14, no. 1 (2013): 85–92.

implicated in the communication processes of conducting international education programs, whether in establishing the cultural context of beliefs through media representations or in enabling means of interaction both with home and with new connections abroad.[22] The question here, however, focuses more on how the idea of exchange itself may be transformed by the technological context, and, how the technological context serves a role framing public diplomacy as a strategic intention. This question is warranted, not only because platforms like social media are being used to extend and expand exchange programs, but also because these programs reflect thinking about "lengthening the arc of engagement."[23]

Rather than suggest a deterministic explanation, wherein media technologies play a distinct causal role in shaping or defining exchange programs, this chapter proposes understanding exchange and technology for public diplomacy through institutional logics influenced by the *availability* of technology, as much as how organizational strategies are a reflection of the *expectations* of technology. There has been ample criticism of the State Department's usage of new and social media technologies, articulated in ways that highlight what technology skeptic Evgeny Morozov has termed "solutionism."[24] From plans to distribute Amazon Kindle e-book readers to the use of hashtags and purchasing "likes" on Facebook to promote embassy social media posts, the U.S. Department of State has been the frequent target of complaints about the use of

---

22. W. Roberts, "What is Public Diplomacy? Past Practices, Present Conduct, Possible Future," *Mediterranean Quarterly* 18, no. 4 (2007): 26-52.
23. Author's interview with member of ECA personnel, February 17, 2015.
24. Evgeny Morozov, *To Save Everything, Click Here: The Folly of Technological Solutionism* (New York: Public Affairs, 2013).

technology in the service of statecraft.[25] These criticisms, however, miss the larger question of how the presence of these technologies is changing strategic frameworks about both the practice and purpose of engagement.

By focusing on "practice" and the meaning derived from practice, scholars in media studies and in science and technology studies have avoided deterministic accounts of media technology's influence. For example, Tarlton Gillespie has explored how the idea of "media platform" is itself actively constructed by policy discourse that reflects organizational needs and political biases of companies that have a stake in how they are governed.[26] Others point to the emergence of political strategies that are derived from how media are used, but are not necessarily a product of the technology itself.[27]

In the case of educational exchange, however, the concept most relevant to how educational diplomacy may be transformed is that of *affordance*. This term refers to how the *meaning* of technology is both a product of its functional capacity and the (socially constructed) ways in which it is or may be actually put to use.[28] Put simply, we should direct our attention to how a technology invites public diplomacy planners and strategists to link such technology to the broader objectives of diplomacy. Media technology's informational, connective, and quantitative affordances have increased demands for impact measures, and it is clear that the growth of technological

25. John Hudson, "OMG! State Department Dropped $630,000 on Facebook 'Likes,'" *The Cable Blog*, July 2, 2013, accessed May 12, 2016, http://thecable.foreignpolicy.com/posts/2013/07/02/omg_state_department_dropped_630000_on_facebook_likes.

26. Tarleton Gillespie, "The Politics of 'Platforms,'" *New Media and Society* 12, no. 3 (2010): 347–364, accessed July 24, 2015,doi: 10.1177/1461444809342738.

27. Nick Couldry and Andreas Hepp, "Conceptualizing Mediatization: Contexts, Traditions, Arguments," *Communication Theory* 23, no. 3 (2013): 191-202, accessed July 24, 2015, doi: 10.1111/comt.12019.

28. Lucas Graves, "The Affordances of Blogging: A Case Study in Culture and Technological Effects," *Journal of Communication Inquiry* 31, no. 4 (2007): 331–346, accessed July 24, 2015, doi: 10.1177/0196859907305446.

platforms for educational exchange address a number of competing needs.

Thinking about technological affordances means analyzing how technologies including social media become associated with certain uses over others and reveals more fundamental tensions in how this form of public diplomacy is rationalized and implemented. Technology, in other words, does not so much drive the agenda of public diplomacy planning as much as reveal salient justifications, strategies, and practices.

The United States has arguably been a leader in promoting new and social media for the purpose of public diplomacy. In particular, its earliest adopters were within ECA. As early as 2007, ECA was developing new online portals and web forums, including social media groups, to engage current students and program alumni. ECA developed the State Department's first social media network, Exchanges Connect, and was also the first to use virtual chatrooms and hangouts. Other strategies followed, including the virtual world platform Second Life, followed by an aggressive roll out of embassy Facebook and Twitter accounts to be managed by the Bureau of International Information Programs.

One of the more recent programs that take advantage of available technological platforms is the State Department's MOOC Camp initiative.[29] MOOCs (massive online open courses), a rapidly emerging educational phenomenon, are courses offered over the Internet to large numbers of students, though often without granting formal college credits. MOOCs have been promoted through partnerships with both public and private U.S. universities by a number of companies, including Coursera, EdX, and Udacity. The

29. See http://eca.state.gov/programs-initiatives/mooc-camp.

international exposure that MOOCs provide can be beneficial to U.S. universities, while expanding access to students outside of existing application and revenue models.

The State Department MOOC Camp program was launched in August 2013, representing a partnership between U.S. universities and U.S. companies that design MOOC programs. Unlike traditional MOOCs offered through U.S. universities, the MOOC Camp effort utilized the distinct capacity of U.S. embassies to facilitate participation in MOOC, providing opportunities for students to experience the course together in offline environs such as through embassy spaces, Information Resource Centers, and other facilities operated or funded by the U.S. mission. This hybrid version of the MOOC experience has allowed students from over 60 countries to take courses in English-language instruction, entrepreneurship, business, and other topics.

As of late 2014, the MOOC Camp program has offered more than 200 courses and has achieved a comparatively high level of success in terms of course completion. The State Department's approach of providing MOOCs with an in-person facilitator and group experience has led to significantly higher completion rates than usual. As State Department technological advisor Paul Kruchoski claims, MOOC Camp participants have a 40 percent to 50 percent completion rate, which is notable given that the average MOOC completion rate is well under 10 percent, even from prestigious U.S. universities.[30] More than 4,000 students have participated, and ECA boasts that "[c]amps in Kolkata, Kinshasa, Jakarta, and many other locations had more than 80 percent of their participants complete their courses."[31]

---

30. Charlie Tyson, "From MOOC to Shining MOOC" *Inside Higher Ed*, June 25, 2014, accessed September 24, 2014,
https://www.insidehighered.com/news/2014/06/25/can-moocs-lure-international-stu dents-us-colleges-and-universities.
31. U.S. Department of State, "MOOC Camp,"
http://eca.state.gov/programs-initiatives/mooc-camp.

The program also addresses the reality of potential students who seek higher education opportunities in areas without significant broadband infrastructure that MOOCs require. The U.S. embassy in Benin, for example, used their own connections to download materials from the courses offered, and burned these to DVDs to enable access to content.[32]

MOOC Camp is part of a larger push toward international education programs, and builds upon the State Department's "Education USA" network, which places academic advisors in U.S. embassies and consulates. Through its public–private partnerships, the MOOC Camp and Education USA networks collaborate with teachers, technology providers, and U.S. State Department personnel to create "learning hubs" around the world. These partnerships provide access to education, and they leverage both online and offline communication through weekly meetings with instructors and facilitators.

How does MOOC Camp represent a *strategic* development in public diplomacy? The State Department claims that this program allows students to "test drive" a U.S. higher education experience.[33] This fits within a larger strategic mandate. Meghann Curtis, former Deputy Assistant Secretary for Academic Programs, claimed that "the State Department and USAID promote a more peaceful, prosperous world, and we all know one of the best ways to get there is to ensure that all people have access to high-quality education."[34] Evan Ryan,

---

32. Devon Haynie, "State Department Hosts 'MOOC Camp' for Online Learners," *U.S. News and World Report* (January 20, 2014).

33. U.S. Department of State, "MOOC Camp."

34. Anya Kamenetz, "The State Department Partners with Coursera to Support Free Education in Over 30 Countries," *Fast Company*, October 31, 2013, accessed June 19, 2016,
http://www.fastcompany.com/3020942/generation-flux/the-state-department-partners-with-coursera-to-support-free-education-in-ove.

the Assistant Secretary of State for Educational and Cultural Affairs, argues that

> *Around the world, young people share a common desire for*
> *educational and economic opportunities...This program*
> *allows young people in particular to improve their English*
> *language skills and learn the basics of entrepreneurship.*
> *Both are vital in today's global economy. We also think that*
> *by experiencing U.S. higher education, they may become*
> *interested in studying in the United States.*[35]

But there are other implications to these kinds of interventions, which reflect not only the inherent capacity of the technology to deliver educational content, but the kinds of relations they encourage or cultivate.

Technological platforms provide new routes of access to populations that might not otherwise be available, and they serve to encourage interest in U.S. academic institutions. Every participant in the program is matched with an EducationUSA advisor who will provide counseling on opportunities to go to college in the United States. As Anya Kamenetz observes, this program "isn't all altruistic."[36] The technological environs for international education are increasingly competitive at an international level, and MOOCs provide a means to jockey for attention and capital within global educational flows. New MOOC providers, such as Iversity (Germany) and Veduca (Brazil) compete with American MOOC developers and the universities they support.[37] MOOCs, at some level, are more than a facilitative exercise in empowerment or other form of development

---

35. Haynie, "State Department Hosts 'MOOC Camp' for Online Learners."
36. Kamenetz, "The State Department Partners with Coursera to Support Free Education in Over 30 Countries."
37. Tamar Lewin, "U.S. Teams up with Operator of Online Courses to Plan a Global Network," *The New York Times*, October 31, 2013, accessed June 18, 2016, http://www.nytimes.com/2013/11/01/education/us-plans-global-network-of-free-online-courses.html.

assistance—they are a means to attract foreign students to U.S. universities.[38]

Attracting international students to the United States does more than facilitate long-term relations contributing to social capital and identification. International students contribute to U.S. economic welfare. By some measures, in 2012–2013 international students brought $24 billion to the U.S. economy. Such figures fuel observations that MOOC Camp public–private partnerships are tantamount to a renewed form of "cultural imperialism."[39] The promotional aspect of MOOCs may be unavoidable—but it does highlight some of the critical dimensions of technology when deployed in the service of public diplomacy objectives.

One of the clear implications of the turn to virtual delivery platforms for exchange programs is that they may elide or at least reframe the strategic nature of public diplomacy. As public diplomacy scholar Giles Scott-Smith has observed, attempts to deploy international education programs to more directly influence opinions or attitudes tend not to succeed, while those that facilitate an *empowerment* agenda have demonstrated returns for the facilitating country.[40] The ubiquity of MOOCs and the inherent open source nature of the technologies that carry them have the symbolic potential of diminishing the marked nature of these programs as sponsored by the U.S. government. Technologies like new and social media already carry cultural connotations among potential users, while the flexibility of such programs symbolically conveys attention to the needs of the potential audience. Yet the *material* aspect of

---

38. Tyson, "From MOOC to Shining MOOC."
39. Kamenetz, "The State Department Partners with Coursera to Support Free Education in Over 30 Countries."
40. Scott-Smith, "The Heineken Factor?"

these programs also matters because technology is not a neutral concept.

As Hamilton Bean and Edward Comor have argued, the United States' turn to platforms for strategic engagement—including virtual exchanges, social media messaging online, and the facilitation of discussion through social media—still reflects power asymmetries, all while intervening in socially significant spaces for communication and meaning-creation.[41] The critical implication, therefore, is that MOOC technologies, or, for that matter other public diplomacy efforts that leverage popular means of access (such as the Trace Effects English language video game program[42]), work to reframe the strategic nature of the intervention for public diplomacy by eliding their strategic or instrumental intent.[43]

This is not to suggest that public diplomacy is inherently circumspect from an ethical perspective, or that states should not engage in communication or the provision of resources to foreign publics in order to achieve a form of influence. The question remains, however, as to how these kinds of programs work to embody the kind of "open source" values seemingly embedded in MOOC platforms, and how they may in fact create incentives for future programs that draw resources from offline exchange experiences. These are two separate issues: first, how the technology works to frame the nature of the relationship it creates with students (its transparency, its intentions/purposes, etc.) and, second, how the availability of a tool that promises scalability and readily quantifiable output measures may diminish the use or perceived significance of public diplomacy programs that are not technology-dependent.

---

41. Edward Comor and Hamilton Bean, "America's 'engagement' delusion: Critiquing a public diplomacy consensus," *International Communication Gazette* 74, no. 3 (2012): 203-220, accessed July 24, 2015, doi: 10.1177/1748048511432603
42. See http://www.gamesforchange.org/play/trace-effects/.
43. See http://americanenglish.state.gov/trace-effects.

Given the rise of international education as a global economic phenomenon as much as an aspect of public diplomacy and development, such questions are valid. International education promotion as "industrial policy" for higher education may be facilitated by the expansion of MOOCs for state-sponsored programs. Technology, when viewed as a means of gaining access to populations, can gloss over the instrumental nature of public diplomacy.

The increasingly competitive field of international education and the way in which it can become politicized (as in U.S. public criticism of China's Confucius Institutes) suggest further investigation of the *mediatization* of exchange itself. The affordances of technology may be shaping the norms, values, and expectations for evaluation embedded in planning educational programs.[44] In these cases, the competitive logics of practice associated with other forms of media are potentially transposed into public diplomacy.

Yet at the same time, it should be noted that these same platforms do offer legitimate cost-savings and potentially more inclusive forms of outreach to publics, and that overall they embody an overarching ethic of open access. Public diplomacy, for many countries, is operating under times of strict fiscal scrutiny. MOOCs may thus serve dual duty as both facilitators of educational access and strategic tools for competing in an increasingly crowded market for attention among students seeking education abroad.

---

44. James Pamment, "The Mediatization of Diplomacy," *Hague Journal of Diplomacy* 9, no. 3 (2014): 253-280.

The Collaboratory: Mediatization and Design-Thinking at State

The MOOC Camp case, however, provides a more instructive example of how public diplomacy may be changing in ways that transcend existing arguments about the prevalence of measurement problems or skepticism about technology's idealized role in public diplomacy.[45] "Mediatization" may represent a shift in reasoning that does not follow the competitive logics of other forms of media, as in the case of how political communication has become driven by such logic. The MOOC Camp case, rather, provides a grounded view of how communication technology is challenging the logics of public diplomacy program design and reasoning in ways that suggest a transformation in how the institution constructs its role in relation to foreign publics and sees technologies as resources, and in how information from the field informs shared reasoning about public diplomacy best practices. Mediatization in this view suggests that the gradual acceptance of technology signals positive developments in conceptualizing methods to reach foreign audiences.

The State Department's MOOC Camp initiative is a product of ECA's Collaboratory group, which is tasked with developing new models of public diplomacy programming and support for posts around the world. The Collaboratory is a kind of "skunkworks" within the State Department to bring together best practices and technologies. The MOOC Camp was originally developed by the U.S. Embassy in South Korea but became one of the Collaboratory's most prominent initiatives. MOOC Camp represents, as one of its members observed, an "iteration" in an ongoing process of rethinking concepts such as "reach," exchange, and social media in order to provide a toolkit of new approaches to public diplomacy for posts.[46]

Rather than assert new paradigms, programs like MOOC Camp reflect the Collaboratory's hybrid approach to public diplomacy

---

45. Nicholas J. Cull, "The Long Road to Public Diplomacy 2.0: The Internet in U.S. Public Diplomacy," *International Studies Review* 15 (2013): 123-139.
46. Author's interview with member of ECA personnel, October 14, 2014.

practice that draws upon the social implications associated with communication technology. This means combining the content-providing aspects of platforms with the distinct relational networks associated with field personnel. These kinds of programs draw together technological assets in ways that "spread" rather than "scale."

The Collaboratory draws upon a "human-centered design" approach to devising, evaluating, and implementing public diplomacy programming.[47] Instead of beginning with specific policy mandates or imperatives, programs like MOOC Camp are post-driven and reflect the distinct preferences of audiences for U.S. content and communication in each local context. MOOC Camp is not seen as a technologically determinist solution, but as a combination of established interpersonal public diplomacy methods carried over from decades of cultural relations and education efforts, with the capacity of platforms to sustain network relations of significance over time and distance.

The more subtle effect of the technology is therefore not its overt connective capacity, but the way in which the participatory ethos of platforms including social media inform program design for international education programs like MOOC Camp. This is a departure from other recent interventions, such as ECA's attempts to use SMS text services to deliver English language instruction in Tunisia, which relied on a more transmission-oriented model. Although that approach acknowledged the material reality of how important publics relied on mobile phones, it nonetheless did not fully account for how this technology was already embedded and indeed paid for by its target publics.[48]

---

47. Author's interview with member of ECA personnel, November 6, 2014.
48. Author's interview with member of ECA personnel, October 14, 2014.

In contrast, the "design thinking" approach embodied in programs like MOOC Camp reflects recognition of the need for a "social aspect" to public diplomacy, which relies heavily on field-driven needs and perspectives. It also reflects an iterative approach to public diplomacy program design, allowing for adaptability across different contexts. While considered a successful program, the MOOC Camp initiative was also launched without funds, and it relies totally on volunteers and available MOOC platforms. Communication technology, in this case, extends the insights of education diplomacy already established offline.

The State Department's turn toward social media and other Internet-based platforms for public diplomacy suggests that the implications of technological context are more evolutionary than revolutionary, and that they highlight enduring expectations and practices associated with U.S. public diplomacy. As one ECA official explained, the challenge for new virtual programs is to retain the elements that have traditionally made exchange and education programs work. ECA is attempting to figure out how to incorporate the "human being to human being part" and "how to get the hospitality element in virtual." One consequence is application of a hybrid approach that combines technological platforms with traditional practices that extend the experience of educational exchange. "With this way you can keep that impact going."[49]

More broadly, the adoption of new technological platforms for exchange and virtual encounter suggests a shift away from the basic expectation that these programs foster understanding and toward a more strategic attitude regarding how technology allows ECA programs to serve a catalytic or facilitative role. As an ECA official explains, "technology is just a tool. Exchange is about community. Exchange is about belonging. Belonging to another culture." Although technologies like social media or other online platforms can help by

---

49. Author's interview with member of ECA personnel, November 6, 2014.

enhancing and extending opportunities for belonging, "it is not something that can be controlled from Washington."[50]

Rather than promote a particular message through exchange, the implication here is that the State Department can facilitate and empower actors and networks more effectively creating the change sought through exchange programs. Likewise, new public diplomacy programs built around technological platforms can "create autonomy for participants," recognizing the need for a minimal government footprint. For example, alumni of MOOC Camps can host their own MOOC Camps. Technology adds "different stages to the educational exchange life-cycle."[51]

In subsequent programs, such as the P2P Challenging Extremism contest, teams from universities around the world competed to design public campaigns to address the root causes of extremist recruitment and promote awareness of cross-cultural issues that drive intercultural conflict.[52] This program relied on collaborative technologies, and the solutions solicited through the contest incorporated elements of online and mobile technology in ways that reflect the social and cultural realities of public diplomacy's stakeholders. These kinds of programs suggest a nascent decentralized approach to public diplomacy promoted by ECA's Collaboratory that builds on the recognized benefits of public-private partnerships (and a diminished government "presence" in engagement) as well as technologically-inspired concern with the "end-user" of public diplomacy as a way to begin strategizing how to design and implement effective public diplomacy.

---

50. Author's interview with member of ECA personnel, February 17, 2015.
51. Ibid.
52. N. Arnold, "'Everyday' Students Challenge Extremism," *Dipnote: U.S. State Department Official Blog,* June 10, 2015, accessed May 12, 2016, http://blogs.state.gov/stories/2015/06/10/everyday-students-challenge-extremism.

Conclusion

Although there are certainly critical implications for MOOCs, especially in the study of public diplomacy, the growth of MOOC Camp and Google Hangouts likely signal the rise of hybrid programs that draw on the strengths of both forms of interaction and that deal effectively with environments where exchange programs may be too cost-prohibitive for participants or program planners. Other programs, like the Collaboratory's Virtual Engagement Toolkits used to facilitate the Mandela Washington Fellowship in U.S. embassies across 20 sub-Saharan countries, pave the way for future efforts at education diplomacy that are both cost effective and reflect a localized approach to integrating technology into public diplomacy programs.

The purpose of this chapter is to draw attention to how the affordances of technology both (a) reframe or defer attention to the strategic nature of public diplomacy and (b) begin to serve as a proxy or stand-in for a strategy of engagement. This second point implies that the technology works not only as a tactic of public diplomacy, but also as a template for strategic thinking. This may be especially important in the context of education diplomacy. As Caitlin Byrne and Rebecca Hall claim, "When leveraged successfully, international education is a prime vehicle to contribute to a nation's foreign policy priorities and interests, including its soft power profile."[53] The case of MOOC Camps and the Collaboratory suggests a more nuanced understanding both of how the availability of new forms of communication may challenge the strategic utilization of technology and of its conceptualization as a tool of statecraft.

The way in which MOOC Camp programs reveal shifting organizational reasoning and design practices suggests a cultural

---

53. Caitlin Byrne and Rebecca Hall, "International Education as Public Diplomacy," *IEAA Research Digest 3* (2014), accessed June 19, 2016, http://www.ieaa.org.au/documents/item/258.

impact *within* the State Department on the role and purpose of public diplomacy as a means to facilitate mutual understanding. It is less clear, however, whether developments such as "design thinking" reconcile the existing tensions between what Giles Scott-Smith calls the "public face" of public diplomacy's mission to promote understanding, with its charge to achieve strategic objectives.[54] A sampling of the policy rhetoric surrounding MOOC Camp and other programs suggests that this previous tension between understanding and advocacy is now joined by a new one, between an overt intent to facilitate relationship-building and the commercial implications of promoting the United States in a complicated global economy of higher education.

Historically, much of the public understanding around the term "public diplomacy" is marked by connotations of message management and propaganda. This is unfortunate, since so much of the practice involves the work of education. Importantly, the context of technology for international education within public diplomacy studies is a largely untapped field that could contribute to the building of theory and research questions.

International education as public diplomacy requires more attention, and this convergence of trends (the use of ICTs for program delivery) within a growing array of strategic justifications linking education to diplomacy suggests promising routes for further inquiry. As pressure mounts for programs that demonstrate the value of short-term, virtually-delivered public diplomacy exchange efforts, more research is clearly necessary. In the case of the United States, such trends will likely continue. As the State Department's Kruchoski

---

54. Scott-Smith, "Mapping the Undefinable."

claimed about MOOC Camp, "We're going to keep running it until we see a reason not to."[55]

---

55. Tyson, "From MOOC to Shining MOOC."

11

Funding International Scientific Research Activities as Opportunities for Public Diplomacy

Jong-on Hahm

Credit: Virginia Sea Grant, 2012

Public diplomacy encompasses many spheres of public and private works, which can be enhanced and facilitated by investment in programs that promote cooperation between the United States and other nations. One approach to public diplomacy that warrants closer attention is through the science, technology, engineering, and mathematics (STEM) fields.[1] Science has often played a critical, if understated, role in public diplomacy. In some instances, scientific collaborations have served as conduits for communications in situations where usual channels are not possible. In tenuous relationships, scientific communication can quietly underscore areas of mutual interest. Innovative ways to support scientific

---

1. Throughout this chapter, the terms "STEM" and "science" will be used interchangeably.

collaboration can advance diplomacy, even when diplomacy is at most an oblique goal of the collaborative research.

In spite of the stereotype of scientists toiling alone in laboratories, science is an extraordinarily collaborative endeavor. Research takes place in teams, in laboratories, and in field sites, with many scientists collaborating with colleagues at institutions both local and global. Certain research topics by nature require international collaboration because the subjects cross borders. Examples include space, geologic, atmospheric, and ocean research, as well as biological and ecological studies. Disciplines such as astronomy and physics require resource-intensive facilities that one country cannot support on its own. Examples of these facilities include the Large Hadron Collider at CERN[2] in Switzerland and the Atacama Large Millimeter/submillimeter Array[3] telescope in Chile.

Because scientific disciplines share common principles, language, and standards, science already has a base upon which to build relationships. Similarly, common interests in eradicating disease, reducing hunger, improving living standards, and protecting the environment often inspire collaborative scientific approaches to solving chronic problems. Science is thus a natural ground for cultivating public diplomacy.

One factor that contributes to science as a global medium for diplomacy lies in the U.S. dominance in training the global scientific workforce. For many years, the United States has been the premier destination for students wishing to attain graduate training in STEM fields.[4] In some disciplines, it is estimated that more than 70 percent of graduate students in STEM fields are foreign students.[5] While

---

2. See http://home.cern/topics/large-hadron-collider.
3. See http://www.almaobservatory.org.
4. National Science Board, *Science and Engineering Indicators 2014*, *NSB 14-01* (Arlington: National Science Foundation, 2014).
5. Stuart Anderson, *The Importance of International Students to America* (Washington, DC: National Foundation for American Policy, 2013), accessed May 13, 2016,

some of these foreign graduate students stay in the United States, many return to their countries of origin and continue to collaborate with their mentors and U.S. colleagues. These connections lead to future collaborations and continued cooperation between the individuals and the institutions. In effect, the foreign students form a diaspora of U.S.-trained researchers in the global scientific community.

In addition, STEM research and development (R&D) plays a critical role in catalyzing innovation and economic development. The Organization for Economic Cooperation and Development[6] (OECD) has conducted numerous analyses that highlight STEM research as a key driver of innovation. Such research has spurred many countries to invest in STEM R&D.

A prime example is Singapore. In the past 15 years, Singapore has significantly increased its investment in STEM research and education,[7] and its universities have directly partnered with U.S. institutions, including Yale University and Duke University, as well as the Massachusetts Institute of Technology.

Although satellite campuses of U.S. universities have had mixed success with profitability, enrollment, and degree completion, with some institutions opting for closure or reduced operations,[8] overall, they have served as gateways for U.S. higher education to connect with global populations.

---

http://nfap.com/pdf/New%20NFAP%20Policy%20Brief%20The%20Importance%20of%20International%20Students%20to%20America,%20July%202013.pdf.

6. See http://www.oecd.org.

7. OECD, "Structural Policy Country Notes: Singapore," in *Southeast Asian Economic Outlook 2013: With Perspectives on China and India* (Paris: OECD, 2013), accessed May 13, 2016, http://www.oecd.org/dev/asia-pacific/Singapore.pdf.

8. Elizabeth Redden, "Throwing in the Towel," *Inside Higher Ed*, July 7, 2010, accessed May 13, 2016, https://www.insidehighered.com/news/2010/07/07/msu.

Thus STEM, as a foundation on which innovation is built, is an incentive to form partnerships that provide mutual benefits.

The Role of Federal Agencies

Federal agencies play a pivotal role in promoting public diplomacy by supporting efforts that enhance international collaboration. The Department of State has long viewed science and technology cooperation as a vehicle for diplomacy, including agricultural or engineering support in diplomatic missions.[9] Currently, the State Department has more than 50 bilateral and multilateral Science and Technology Agreements in place to shape cooperation,[10] and their use in diplomatic efforts has been well demonstrated.[11]

Science, technology, and health initiatives play critical roles in foreign policy,[12] and in 2000, the State Department established the Office of the Science and Technology Advisor to the Secretary at the recommendation of the National Academies. The State Department can encourage diplomacy through science; however, it does not provide grants or direct funding support for research collaboration that may enhance science diplomacy.

The U.S. Agency for International Development (USAID) has incorporated science and technology in aid and development initiatives since its inception in 1961. By funding development projects, USAID complements the State Department's efforts in

9. Vaughan C. Turekian and Norman P. Neureiter, "Science and Diplomacy: The Past as Prologue," *Science and Diplomacy*, March 2012, accessed May 13, 2016, http://www.sciencediplomacy.org/editorial/2012/science-and-diplomacy.

10. See http://www.state.gov/e/oes/stc/.

11. Bridget M. Dolan, "Science and Technology Agreements as Tools for Science Diplomacy: A U.S. Case Study," *Science and Diplomacy*, December 2012, accessed May 13, 2016, http://www.sciencediplomacy.org/article/2012/science-and-technology-agreements-tools-for-science-diplomacy.

12. National Research Council, *Pervasive Role of Science, Technology, and Health in Foreign Policy: Imperatives for the Department of State* (Washington, DC: National Academies Press, 1999), accessed May 13, 2016, http://www.nap.edu/catalog.php?record_id=9688.

science diplomacy. Increased focus on science culminated in the creation of the Office of Science and Technology in 2010, directed by its first Chief Scientist. The Office of Science and Technology underscored the importance of science by greatly expanding programs that increased scientific collaboration and by working with science agencies to develop joint programs. Similarly, the Fogarty International Center of the National Institutes of Health (NIH), established in 1968, supports global health and infectious disease research, providing resources to U.S. and foreign investigators in developing countries.

As a research-funding agency, the National Science Foundation (NSF) is tasked with supporting the best in basic research across a broad swath of science, engineering, and mathematics disciplines. International collaboration is not specifically called out in its mission. Nonetheless, for some time, the National Science Board (NSB), NSF's advisory body, has focused on international research collaboration, underscoring the increasing globalization of science and engineering research.[13] In addition to noting the rising R&D capabilities and investments of other countries, the NSB noted the value of collaborating with research partners as they built large state-of-the-art research infrastructures.[14] In the next decade, China is poised to become the global leader in R&D investment by

13. National Science Board, *International Science and Engineering Partnerships: A Priority for U.S. Foreign Policy and Our Nation's Innovation Enterprise* (Arlington: National Science Foundation, 2008), accessed May 13, 2016, http://www.nsf.gov/pubs/2008/nsb084/index.jsp?org=NSF. See also National Science Board, *Globalization of Science and Engineering Research. A Companion to Science and Engineering Indicators 2010* (Arlington: National Science Foundation, 2010), accessed May 13, 2016, http://www.nsf.gov/statistics/nsb1003/?org=NSF.
14. See http://sites.nationalacademies.org/PGA/PEER/PGA_147204.

increasing its expenditures, while other countries have held steady or reduced their R&D expenditures.[15]

As interest in international collaboration grew in the U.S. research community, NSF offered various programs for international research cooperation. Some examples are International Collaborations in Chemistry and the Materials World Network, large programs with many international partners focused on a specific scientific discipline. Other research disciplines were also supported through NSF's regular basic research programs in geosciences and biological sciences. Increasingly, however, interest grew in a program specifically highlighting international collaboration unrestricted by disciplinary focus.

Partnerships for International Research and Education

In 2004, NSF launched Partnerships for International Research and Education (PIRE) to support research and education in international projects in any discipline supported by NSF. The objectives of the PIRE program as detailed in the most recent program description are:

1. Support excellence in science and engineering research and education through international collaboration.
2. Promote opportunities where international collaboration can provide unique advantages of scope, scale, flexibility, expertise, facilities, or access to phenomena, enabling advances that could not occur otherwise.
3. Engage and share resources and research infrastructure within and across institutions to build strong international partnerships.

---

15. Battelle and R&D Magazine, *2014 Global Funding Forecast* (December 2013), accessed July 6, 2016,
http://www.battelle.org/docs/tpp/2014_global_rd_funding_forecast.pdf.

4. Create and promote opportunities for students and early career researchers to participate in substantive international research experiences.[16]

Credit: Steve Jurvetson, 2015

The PIRE program brought to the attention of U.S. universities the potential for funding international research collaborations. Before PIRE, although many U.S. academic institutions had robust study abroad programs, formal programs to conduct scientific research abroad were not known. PIRE assured a high level of interest from universities by awarding four-year grants of up to $2.5 million. The significant award size encouraged universities to consider international collaboration in an institutional manner, rather than the informal manner led by individual faculty members.

---

16. See http://www.nsf.gov/pubs/2016/nsf16571/nsf16571.pdf, 5.

PIRE Projects

PIRE awards provide a glimpse into the breadth and depth of international science research. They also show the commonality of challenges around the world and illustrate the wide distribution of scientific expertise.

PIRE funding has changed significantly since the program began in 2005.[17] The first 12 projects funded ranged from bilateral projects (one U.S. university collaborating with one foreign university) to a group of five universities across the United States working with universities in five different countries. Most projects were focused in one global region, such as Asia or Europe. The projects ranged from social sciences to computer sciences, and geosciences to engineering, representing the different disciplines supported by the agency. In 2007, PIRE increased the number of awards to 20. The majority of projects involved fewer than three countries, and fewer than three world regions.

In the third PIRE competition held in 2010, the program departed significantly from the previous versions of the program. The most important change was the elimination of the budget limit. This change brought considerably more interest in the program from the U.S. research university community. However, as the program's overall budget was not significantly increased, fewer awards were made.

As might be expected, as a whole the awards were larger in size, along with the number of institutions, countries, and world regions. Fifteen awards were made in 2010, the largest of which was more than $6.5 million. That award was made to a group of 12 members collaborating across seven countries in two world regions. In contrast to earlier rounds of the competition, the majority of awardees had projects that comprised more than one country and

---

17. See http://www.nsf.gov/od/iia/ise/pire-2005-list.jsp.

more than one world region. In addition, more projects had institutional partners that were not universities. For instance, more large facilities at government laboratories partnered with U.S. universities. This was partly due to the subject area of the projects, which required access to large-scale facilities such as astronomical observatories.

In 2012, the PIRE program took a different approach. At that time, NSF was in the midst of an agency-wide initiative focused on sustainability, called Science, Engineering, and Education for Sustainability (SEES). For the 2012 PIRE competition, all proposals were required to have a SEES focus. This requirement resulted in a group of awards that featured research on renewable energy, water resources and management, and impacts of climate change. Additionally, the SEES focus threw into relief the increasing universality of challenges across the world, and the need to look beyond U.S. borders for solutions to global problems.

---

1. NSF>PIRE>SEES
Project Example
Water and Commerce

Duke University; North Carolina Central University; Michigan State. This project examines technological development and international aspects of sustainability in water resources in global commerce. It will develop technologies to enable environmental sustainability in global markets. The project involves five universities in France, Turkey, Singapore, and international companies with substantial U.S. presence.

(See http://pire.pratt.duke.edu.)

With dual goals of research and education, each of these projects provided top quality research training to the U.S. students involved and offered an opportunity for public diplomacy at foreign locations. U.S. students were afforded the chance to work in teams with foreign students. For example, in the biodiversity hotspot research project in the Indo-Malay-Philippine Archipelago, U.S. students and local scientists worked together in workshops that provided molecular ecology training. In the PIRE project on bioenergy development in the Americas, U.S. students and faculty participated in immersive exchanges, joint graduate courses, and certificate programs. Many of these projects have continued with support from other sources, including from foreign agencies.

Mismatched Resources

For PIRE researchers collaborating with partners in less developed countries, a mismatch of resources and capacity between the United States and partner research teams created operational challenges. In particular, U.S. research teams enjoyed access to sophisticated equipment and abundant supplies that foreign peers often lacked. In some instances, the lack of supporting infrastructure for laboratory facilities, particularly in remote locations, might require the U.S. researchers to bring an entire portable lab to the research site. In addition, the U.S. researchers, who are frequently also educators, often wanted to provide access to resources to their foreign colleagues and to mentor foreign students and junior researchers. However, NSF funds only U.S. institutions and individuals officially affiliated with U.S. institutions. This restriction was a source of considerable frustration to both U.S. and foreign researchers, as sometimes foreign counterparts did not have the resources to work on equal footing with U.S. scientists.

Additionally, in developing countries, the contrast in policy between NSF and agencies such as USAID and Fogarty International

Center was also challenging. USAID has a wide network of offices located throughout many developing countries with a long history of providing direct aid to foreign organizations. Fogarty also has a long history of providing support for research in foreign countries, support that facilitates access to foreign locales and specialized resources such as health and demographic databases. For U.S. researchers whose work benefits from access to these resources, the ability to offer support to foreign counterparts can provide flexibility in project planning, particularly if services require local knowledge or skills not present in their own teams. Thus, the NSF's prohibition on providing support to foreign researchers was a challenge to forming projects.

For some time, NSF and USAID had formally cooperated on projects of mutual interest. Through formal agreements, these agencies found an apt vehicle for addressing the challenge of mismatched resources.

Partnerships for Enhanced Engagement in Research

In July 2011, USAID and NSF jointly announced[18] a new program called Partnerships for Enhanced Engagement in Research (PEER). Through PEER, the USAID would provide support to the foreign research partners of U.S. researchers. Since PEER's launch, 205 projects have been awarded.[19]

USAID partnered with the National Research Council, the administrative arm of the National Academies, to manage the program. USAID designated which countries would be included in

---

18. See
https://nsf.gov/news/news_summ.jsp?cntn_id=121003&org=IIA&from=news.
19. See http://sites.nationalacademies.org/PGA/PEER/pga_167039.

the PEER program, and foreign researchers could partner only with U.S. researchers holding active NSF awards. There was much enthusiasm for the program, and in 2012, PEER awarded 41 grants in all global regions.

Notably, because PEER was not restricted to researchers with PIRE awards only, but open to any NSF-funded researchers with active grants, the program effectively opened the entire cohort of active NSF awards to international collaboration. This resulted in an extraordinary set of awards highlighting the reach of U.S. scientists and their collaborations, as well as the breadth and depth of scientific research capacity worldwide in research areas beyond the scope of NSF.

The PEER projects included a study of viruses affecting food crops such as cassava in Tanzania, genetic assessment of fish species in Indonesia, the reclamation of nutrients and water from sewage in Bolivia, the use of low-quality water for halophytic forage and renewable energy production, and landslide hazard in Lebanon. The size of the awards was much smaller than the PIRE awards, and many more awards were made.

---

2. USAID-NSF>PEER Project Example

Utilization of Low Quality Water

Using low-quality water for halophytic forage and renewable energy production. Foreign institution: International Center for Biosaline Agriculture.   Research Locale: Uzbekistan. U.S. partner institution: University of Nevada. This project studies the use of saline-loving plants to remove salt from water and saline lands to increase lands and water usable for agriculture. (See http://sites.nationalacademies.org/pga/peer/pga_069267.)

The success of the first round led to interest from other U.S. agencies in participating in the PEER program. In both principle and operation, PEER was attractive to U.S. funding agencies. Because the awards would support collaborators of currently active U.S. researchers, it was likely that the U.S. project would benefit, leading to better research outcomes. Additionally, the National Academies' rigorous review process assured that proposals would be handled in a scientifically valid manner. All partners in the collaborative project, including the funding agency, would be assured that the peer review process would be the same as conducted by the U.S. funding agencies.

The success of the PEER program garnered additional attention from U.S. agencies, and NIH joined the second year of competition. In 2014, National Aeronautics and Space Administration, the Department of Agriculture, Agricultural Research Service, the U.S. Geological Survey, and the Smithsonian Institution formed a partnership. Each agency brought its cadre of grant-supported researchers and trained experts into an ever-widening cohort of researchers working together on globally relevant, collective problems.[20]

The Challenge: Collaborative Research with Contiguous Funding

The example of the PEER program throws into bold relief the complexities of funding international research. Collaborative research requires mutual effort from all partners and a joint commitment and investment, even if the resource burden is not equal. U.S. researchers desiring to collaborate with foreign scientists

---

20. The complete list of funded awards, with links to project descriptions, is on the National Academies PEER website,
http://sites.nationalacademies.org/PGA/PEER/PGA_147204.

may encounter uneven funding that prevents a project from going forward or significantly impairs its progress. For example, to support a collaborative project, U.S. investigators might submit proposals to U.S. funding agencies, while foreign investigators appeal to funding agencies in their respective countries. One side might be funded and the other not. The probability for the project moving forward is then significantly reduced as adjustments must be made to compensate for difference in resources.

Failed attempts to form collaborations can have long-lasting, negative impacts on the scientific relationship and also on the diplomatic relationship. Failures may discourage researchers from attempting to develop new collaborations and agencies from developing efforts to spur collaborative research. Loss of interest or support from a foreign funding agency can seriously dampen foreign researcher enthusiasm for entering into a collaborative project with U.S. colleagues.

Ideally, a collaborative program with common goals would be conducted jointly, sharing timelines, deadlines, reviews, and budgets. For a number of reasons, such joint programs are not the norm. Funding agencies and research institutions face differing sets of missions, obligations, legal and regulatory requirements, and finding an operating model that accommodates all circumstances can be difficult even within the same country. One of the most mundane of obstacles is coordinating timelines, as countries follow different fiscal years.

The best approach is separate, coordinated, parallel funding, with each research partner supported by their respective country funding agencies. This model of "collaborative research with contiguous funding" would do most to encourage scientific cooperation that could spur science diplomacy. In this scenario, the partnering agencies would announce their intention to cooperate on a research program while undertaking different approaches. For example, cooperation might entail joint review, separate review, or accepting a counterpart's review and providing funding support for their researchers. This type of flexibility allows for the partnering agencies to accommodate their own requirements but allows collaborative projects to move forward with less risk of uneven support.[21] In the most recent round of the PIRE competition, 11 countries joined the program, in which PIRE collaborating scientists could gain funding through a co-funding mechanism.[22]

A similar model was successfully employed by the Collaborative Research in Computational Neuroscience (CRCNS) program involving NSF, NIH, and the German Federal Ministry of Education and Research. CRCNS has since broadened to include the French National Research Agency and the U.S.–Israel Binational Science Foundation.[23]

Future of Diplomacy through Science

Federal agencies can promote public diplomacy by exploring innovative approaches to building partnerships like the PIRE and PEER programs. PIRE has established a number of partnerships with foreign funding agencies. Fourteen organizations from eleven of the most research-intensive countries in the world have joined the PIRE program.[24] These countries have highly sought-after expertise and facilities and unparalleled access to desired research locales. Scientific agencies, ministries, and leading research institutions are among the 14 partner organizations, as some countries have committed more than one organization in the PIRE program.

---

21. This approach is being deployed in the 2015 PIRE competition with 14 foreign partners.

22. See http://www.nsf.gov/pubs/2014/nsf14587/nsf14587.htm.

23. See http://www.nsf.gov/publications/pub_summ.jsp?ods_key=nsf15595.

24. The countries are China, Finland, France, Germany, India, Japan, Republic of Korea, Mexico, Russia, Spain, and Taiwan.

The PEER model of linking research projects funded by different programs is increasingly found in other countries. For example, the Research Councils of the United Kingdom, the partnership organization of the funding councils, and the Department for International Development recently issued a Concordat declaring their intent to work together on cooperative projects of mutual interest.[25]

The European Union has a strong interest in promoting collaborative science. In December 2013, the European Commission (EC) launched Horizon 2020, perhaps the world's largest coordinated research initiative.[26] From 2014 to 2020, the EC will invest approximately €80 billion in research and innovation development, with significant emphasis on spurring economic development throughout the EU. Although the funds will be awarded to EU institutions and affiliates, the grant competitions are open to any scientist in the world, provided the work takes place in the EU.

Horizon 2020 also has significantly increased investment in programs that promote researcher mobility. The Marie Sklodowska Curie Fellowships will allow European graduate students and junior scientists to move throughout the EU and to other countries, including to the United States. Importantly, these fellowships are also open to scientists from other countries that wish to work in EU institutions. More than any other program, the mobility fellowships will likely spark new partnerships and swell the diaspora of European-trained researchers around the world.

Science can be a potent tool in public diplomacy. Judicious investment in science programs can leverage global research collaboration into an effective tool for diplomatic cooperation. The mutual benefits of science collaboration should spur more

---

25. See http://www.rcuk.ac.uk/international/funding/collaboration/rcuk-dfid-concordat/.
26. See http://ec.europa.eu/programmes/horizon2020/.

governments to look to effective deployment of science as a means for diplomacy.

12

Turning Point

Brian E. Carlson

Credit: farm4.staticflickr.com

World War I, the "Great War," represented a turning point in the nature of warfare among nations. With the benefit of hindsight, historians now perceive that 1914 saw new techniques and technologies employed on the battlefield—innovations in mechanization, industrialization, and mass movements of people—that had developed during the decades preceding August 1914. War would never be the same again.

In a not dissimilar way, the "war on terror" that followed the September 11, 2001, attacks represented a turning point in the nature of public diplomacy, especially in the ways diplomats, the military, and governments sought the loyalty (or at least the support) of publics. The changes—and not all were for the best—were most visible in spheres of military information operations and civilian-led public diplomacy.

Turning points signify and even define what are later perceived as substantive, lasting changes in the environment, in our perceptions, and in our reactions to subsequent events.

The Great War

World War I altered the landscape of the modern world in every conceivable way. When combat operations began, it was the first major, continent-wide conflict to engage most of the European (and eventually North American) nations since the previous great pan-European conflict, the Napoleonic Wars. Not surprisingly, the generals and diplomats of 1914 were largely unprepared for the differences that late nineteenth century advances in mechanization, industrialization, and invention had brought to the art of war.

Soldiers in August 1914 marched off to the battlefield dressed in uniforms not much changed from those their 1815 counterparts had worn: natty cloth campaign caps, scarlet red or bright blue coats, and white belts crossing their chests. Such parade ground uniforms were, of course, entirely unsuited to the new kind of warfare made possible by massed armies of mobilized troops, machine guns, barbed wire, trenches, poison gas, heavy artillery, and highly accurate, rapidly repeating rifles. Although Napoleon took pride in cannon that fired a ball weighing 9 to 12 pounds, a hundred years later the Germans brought out artillery that lobbed shells weighing 2,000 pounds each a distance of several miles. And they brought a lot of them.

During the nineteenth century, armies of a few tens of thousands on each side marched to suitable battlefields, collided violently, and then separated to march around some more until they found another suitable field to contest. The objective generally was to turn your enemy's flank and attack him from the side or behind. Civilian populations were not much involved. In 1914 and 1915, armies of millions of men each locked each other in ceaseless death grips at places like Verdun and the Marne. They dug into trenches and stayed in them for months, mainly because it was deadly to step out into the hailstorm of lead and steel flying almost continually above the battlements. The term "home front" was first used in World War I because for the first time the civilians and the civilian economy were very much a key part of the war.

Credit: Al Qaeda's Inspire Magazine

A Turning Point for Public Diplomacy

Humans are smart. They adapt.

In 2001, terrorists employed a new tactic, using a passenger airplane as a missile. Not only was this tactic a surprise in itself, it also represented a turning point in the nature of international public diplomacy and information operations.

The terrorists carried out an operation that would kill many people and destroy property. But, in the minds of the attackers, their action was principally meant to strike fear in American hearts. Yes, it would kill Americans, but the lives lost were incidental to the real purpose. As so many of the actions in following years in Iraq and elsewhere would prove to be, this violent, kinetic act was carried out for information purposes.

Moreover, the attacks in New York and at the Pentagon were carried out not by a state, a nation, or a government, but by members of a movement. You could not tell if the perpetrators were privates, corporals, or colonels. Unlike warfare in 1914, or in 1944, or even as late as Vietnam, attackers no longer wore uniforms. Walking through an airport, they were indistinguishable from businessmen with air tickets. Nor did they plan to occupy territory, take prisoners or hostages, obtain a ransom, or seek a surrender document.

By 2001, the media environment had changed a lot, too. In the final years of the last century, not only did most countries' embassies not have a website, but many barely used email. State-owned or state-controlled broadcasting was the norm in many countries. (Americans have a relatively unique tradition of private television and radio.) From the BBC to Radio Moscow, from Syria's SATRBC to Japan's NHK, state broadcasters have only in recent decades been challenged and supplanted by independent and numerous information sources. Some of these are domestic, private broadcasters enabled by deregulation, while others are satellite-based networks predicated on language and ethnic groups, not political boundaries.

Beginning in the late 1990s, the Internet, websites, email, and social media spread across the globe, often beyond the view of national governments long used to controlling news and information reaching their citizens. For the first time in their careers many public diplomacy and military officers faced a nimble adversary with an adept, omnipresent, creative, and constant information presence. Extremists seemed to be everywhere.

We may need more time to understand how much the world changed between the demise of America's last major nation-state adversary—the Soviet Union—and the attack by al-Qaeda extremists ten years later. Nevertheless, it seems clear that however successful old-fashioned public diplomacy was against Cold War opponents, the world after the 9/11 attacks required a different response.

In a dramatic shift from the Cold War years, after 2001 the U.S. military significantly increased its engagement with foreign audiences. In many countries, not just Iraq and Afghanistan, the U.S. Armed Forces became the face of America. Soldiers were the only Americans many people had ever seen or dealt with. This Department of Defense increase was not entirely by choice. The military sensed a gap in the civilian effort to communicate with foreign audiences and moved to fill it.

During this same post-9/11 period, the U.S. Department of State public diplomacy presence in foreign countries remained about the same, or in many cases even decreased from the high points reached in the best days of the U.S. Information Agency (USIA).

The numbers alone tell the story: at the end of 2012, the DOD had more than 352,000 active-duty troops deployed in foreign countries, of which at least 177,000 were deployed to support overseas contingencies operations in countries including Afghanistan or Iraq. [1] But that number just scratches the surface—the number multiplies considerably when factoring the total number of troops rotating in and out of various theaters of operation, many of them assigned temporarily.

By contrast, the entire U.S. Foreign Service Officer corps employed by the Departments of State, Agriculture, and Commerce, as well as the Agency for International Development (USAID) numbered no more than 15,000. With about half of those stationed in Washington headquarters or in training assignments, and many being concerned with security, computer systems, or administration, one begins to appreciate why some people in other countries believe Americans all wear Oakley sunglasses and combat boots.

America's Attention Deficit Disorder

The United States has a long history of building capacity to communicate with foreign publics in time of crisis or war, and then dismantling the infrastructure when peace breaks out. To briefly recap:

- In World War I, the Committee on Public Information (CPI) was established with nine foreign bureaus to conduct information and exchange programs aimed at foreign journalists and other opinion leaders. At war's end, in 1919, the CPI was abolished.
- Six months after Pearl Harbor, President Roosevelt set up the Office of War Information (OWI) to begin addressing both domestic and foreign opinion. Among other activities, the OWI founded the Voice of America by beginning

---

1. Defense Manpower Data Center, Statistical Information Analysis Division (SIAD), *Active Duty Military Personnel by Service by Region/Country, Report P1212 Total Military Personnel and Dependent End Strength by Service, Regional Area, and Country as of December 31, 2012*, accessed June 12, 2016, https://www.dmdc.osd.mil/appj/dwp/dwp_reports.jsp.

international radio broadcasts in 1942. But, like its predecessor, OWI was shuttered within weeks of war's end.

- In 1953, *Communist* inroads in Latin America, Eastern Europe and Asia—along with the Korean conflict—prompted President Eisenhower to ask for a U.S. Information Agency to "understand, inform and influence foreign publics in promotion of the U.S. national interest, and to broaden the dialogue between Americans and U.S. institutions, and their counterparts abroad."[2] Yet again, after the East-West contest resolved in America's favor with the 1989 Berlin Wall opening, the 1991 Soviet Union collapse, and other antagonists' apparent disappearances during the 1990s, America disengaged again. It was, in the words of historian Francis Fukuyama, the end of history.

From 1991 to 2001, the broad spectrum, single-purpose government agency that supported U.S. foreign policy with public diplomacy was gradually dismantled, like a car abandoned on an inner-city street (first the radio goes, then the wheels, then engine parts...). Radio and television divisions, once considered essential to public diplomacy and globe-circling communication, were split off from USIA, firewalled from foreign policy, and saddled with dysfunctional management (the Broadcasting Board of Governors) in 1994. The USIA budget was steadily squeezed to the point that the Agency was unable to replace retiring employees. One year USIA even offered up an entire class of newly hired officers for adoption by State. When USIA merged into the Department of State in 1999, America's public diplomacy capability was already a shadow of what it had been. Less than two years later, the "war on terror" would commence.

---

2. "USIA: An Overview" (October 1998), accessed February 16, 2015, http://dosfan.lib.uic.edu/usia/usiahome/overview.pdf.

So, Whose Job Is It?

One common characteristic of the CPI, OWI, and USIA (in its early days) was their employment of fairly aggressive information operations. These information operations—already the word *propaganda* had negative connotations—were meant to deliver convincing information to foreign audiences (and domestic ones, as well, in the case of CPI and OWI). These organizations used newsprint, posters, leaflets, radio, telegraph, and movies, as well as lecturers and speakers (such as the "Four-Minute Men," musicians, and famous people of the day) to deliver consistent messages. There was a determined effort to address both foreign military forces and foreign civilian audiences. Even such unconventional media as seed packets and soap wrappers were employed. There is little evidence to prove these tactics were effective in changing behaviors, but they represented a robust, activist approach and reflected a willingness to focus on messaging to foreign audiences.

This was a degree of activism and message focus that many U.S. military leaders and government officials found missing in the State Department's public diplomacy after 2001. Indeed, even as late as May 22, 2009, Secretary of State Clinton was still telling Congressional subcommittees that the United States is "being out-communicated by the Taliban and al Qaeda." She said that America needed a "new strategic communication strategy" to "do a better job of getting the story of the values, ideals, the results of democracy out to people who are now being fed a steady diet of the worst kind of disinformation."[3]

From the beginning, Al Qaeda's propagandists were producing high-quality videos and elaborate websites, which led U.S. Defense Secretary Robert Gates to say, "We're being out-communicated by a

---

3. U.S. Department of State, *Testimony: Hillary Rodham Clinton, Secretary of State, Before the Senate Appropriations Subcommittee on State, Foreign Operations, and Related Programs. Washington, DC, May 20, 2009*, accessed May 13, 2016, http://www.state.gov/secretary/20092013clinton/rm/2009a/05/123679.htm.

guy in a cave."[4] The terrorist propaganda and recruitment machine seemed to be in high gear.

I became a State Department liaison to the Pentagon on strategic communication and public diplomacy in 2006. At that time the fighting was worsening, with suicide bombers and foreign fighters from many countries showing up in Iraq and Afghanistan. Military commanders began to ask, "Where are these foreign fighters coming from?" And, they asked, "Why isn't someone doing something about it?"

At one point the U.S. military in Iraq discovered that a couple dozen suicide bombers had all come from one tiny village.[5] What's going on, they asked?

Gradually the U.S. military realized that the United States and its allies faced a regional if not global communication problem. The generals asked, "Who is doing the counter-propaganda against al Qaeda? Which part of the U.S. government is addressing Muslim and other youth? Where is the alternative, pro-tolerance vision? Who is countering violent extremism?"

---

4. Karen DeYoung and Walter Pincus, "U.S. to Fund Pro-American Publicity in Iraqi Media," *The Washington Post,* October 3, 2008, accessed May 13, 2016, http://www.washingtonpost.com/wp-dyn/content/article/2008/10/02/AR200810020 4223.html.

5. Joseph Felter and Brian Fishman, "Al Qa'ida's Foreign Fighters in Iraq: A First Look at the Sinjar Records," *The Harmony Project of the Combatting Terrorism Center at West Point, U.S. Military Academy,* 2007, accessed May 13, 2016, http://tarpley.net/docs/CTCForeignFighter.19.Dec07.pdf. See alsoRichard A. Oppel, Jr., "Foreign Fighters in Iraq Are Tied to Allies of U.S.," *The New York Times*, November 22, 2007, accessed May 13, 2016, http://www.nytimes.com/2007/11/22/world/middleeast/22fighters.html?pagewanted =2&_r=0&ref=todayspaper.

The State Department did not have a satisfying answer. The U.S. military began to fill the void.

Roles and Responsibilities—Public Diplomacy

This is perhaps a good point at which to discuss the roles and responsibilities of public diplomacy and military information operations. We need to understand where they are distinct and where they intentionally or unintentionally overlap.

Whether it was managed by USIA or the Department of State, all government civilian public diplomacy is premised on three fundamental missions:
- to present American values,
- to advocate U.S. policy, and
- to shape the host nation environment in our favor.

First, perhaps the most fundamental goal of public diplomacy—certainly since the time of J. William Fulbright, if not from time of the Declaration of Independence (which stipulates that "a decent respect to the opinions of mankind" compels us to explain ourselves)—has been the presentation and explanation of American ideas and values. What makes us an exceptional nation, different from other countries?

This is the public diplomacy responsibility that drives us to conduct the exchanges programs bringing foreigners here for academic study and professional training. We believe that the arts and other exhibits we send abroad, the performances by American musicians and sports figures, and the American centers and libraries in major cities are fulfilling this mandate. Why do we support English language training and foster American Studies as a discipline in foreign universities? Because they all help us explain and present America to foreign audiences.

Second, like any diplomat, the public diplomacy officer shares with political and economic officers a fundamental responsibility to be an advocate for U.S. policy. The public diplomacy officer is a counterpart to political and economic officers. In a well-run embassy, all are working from the same agenda. While the political counselor is presenting a demarche to the foreign ministry in support of some U.S. position (be it a draft trade treaty, a sanctions resolution in the United Nations, or a human rights complaint), you can bet that the public diplomacy officer is making the same case—perhaps in different words—to journalists, academics, union leaders, religious figures, or whomever may help shape host nation public opinion.

The third public diplomacy role is shaping the host nation environment to benefit American interests and objectives. The purpose is to shape host country attitudes, perceptions, and principles to make the achievement of U.S. objectives more feasible. Some might characterize this as nation-building; more often we call it programming on subjects including rule of law, anti-trafficking, anti-corruption, human rights, anti-money laundering, and drug smuggling. The purpose, common to all these activities, is to shape the host country's public attitudes, institutions, and policies in ways that will enable U.S. policy goals to be achieved. Often this is a long-term objective. In this role, public diplomacy may draw on resources from other agencies or accounts.

Public affairs officers (PAOs) often work closely with USAID, law enforcement, the military, or others. For example, in Eastern Europe and the former Soviet Union nations, anti-corruption programs have been a U.S. priority for years. Endemic corruption, a holdover from Soviet days, often reveals itself when politically connected people influence government decisions in ways that benefit them or their friends, such as through favorable contracts, zoning rules, and tax exemptions. If local officials and politicians are easily corrupted, so goes the logic, how can the U.S. government trust them to guard NATO secrets and to join in combating terrorism finance, enforcing border controls, or preventing drug and other trafficking?

Not surprisingly, effective country teams have for more than two decades addressed these issues by harnessing the people, resources, and programs of traditional diplomacy, law enforcement, and USAID, as well as those of public diplomacy. They may conduct judicial training seminars, translate and distribute publications, send key officials on exchange visits to U.S. programs, give grants to NGOs like Transparency International, or train journalists in investigative reporting.

Of course, regardless from which appropriation funds emanate, many embassy "shaping" programs serve several objectives at once. An international visitor program may expose participants to American life, culture, and values while, at the same time, teaching visitors good government principles or anti-money laundering models. A PAO may translate and distribute *The Federalist Papers* both to present and explain the principles and underpinnings of American democracy with hope that the host country would adapt some of those democratic principles in their own government. The key to identifying programs that fall under public diplomacy's third role is the "enabling factor": Are we attempting to shape outcomes? Is it our purpose to turn the host country's people and institutions into better partners for the United States?

Roles and Responsibilities: Military Information Support Operations

Let us turn now to the other major U.S. government presence abroad: the military. In broad strokes, the military resolves its communication efforts into two baskets: public affairs (PA) and information operations (IO). In a longstanding tradition, the U.S. military has separated the *inform* (PA) and the *influence* (IO) functions, believing that, as the Chairman of the Joint Chiefs put it in a 2004 directive, "PA's principal focus is to inform the American public and international audiences... IO, on the other hand, serves, in part, to influence foreign adversary audiences using psychological operations capabilities."[6]

Public affairs—for the military—is a well-developed and well-resourced activity that includes not only traditional press briefings for reporters, but sophisticated engagement techniques including photography and video (a.k.a. "combat camera") production, cooperation, and product placement with Hollywood and commercial television, hometown news about deployed personnel, business and civic leader tours, media embeds with deployed units, and background briefings for selected audiences such as bloggers, TV experts, and other message multipliers, to name just a few. Military public affairs officers will provide information and access to foreign media and will work closely with embassy public affairs staff, but the emphasis clearly is on meeting the needs of the American domestic media.

By contrast, the first mission of IO is to support the U.S. combat forces in the field by delivering information to the local population and countering enemy propaganda. Traditionally, such information activities were aimed at the adversary's troops. That once meant leaflet drops or postcards telling the enemy personnel that they are outnumbered and doomed to defeat, how and where to surrender, or

---

6. Richard Meyers, *Policy on Public Affairs Relationship to Information Operations*, CM-2077-04, September 27, 2004, in Matthew Wallin, "Military Public Diplomacy: How the Military Influences Foreign Audiences," *American Security Project* (February 2015): 5, accessed June 30, 2016,
https://www.americansecurityproject.org/wp-content/uploads/2015/02/Ref-0185-Military-Public-Diplomacy.pdf.

how to provide tips and information to us. IO might use radio broadcasts, television, billboards, and Internet or social media intended to weaken enemy resolve, mislead the enemy about our intentions, or simply to sow confusion.

As the nature of war has changed, so has the employment of military information operations. Today, we live in an era of asymmetrical warfare. Enemy forces do not line up in neat ranks across a battlefield, but rather live among the civilian population. That population may suffer the unwanted presence of warfighters among them, or may resent and resist them. The military recognizes that, especially in counterinsurgency warfare, information operations must also be designed to affect the knowledge, perceptions, and actions of the population resident where the adversary lives and fights. As Secretary of Defense Robert Gates said in 2008, "we cannot kill or capture our way to victory."[7] Winning the understanding and support of the civilian population in these environments is equally important. This in turn leads to a *military need* to address civilian audiences in foreign countries, something once the unique responsibility of the diplomat.

Out of this has grown the second mission of military strategic communication: shaping the civilian environment in ways that will make it easier to accomplish American goals. The American military leadership appreciates that they must align their actions and words, and that they must ensure that what they *do* is synchronized with what they *say* they are doing. If we say we're bringing peace and security, then we can't keep throwing cruise missiles at wedding parties.

The targets of this shaping effort are the leaders of partner nations and the general public as well as foreign military personnel

---

7. U.S. Department of Defense, Office of the Assistant Secretary of Defense (Public Affairs), "U.S. Global Leadership Campaign" (speech delivered by Secretary of Defense Robert M. Gates, Washington, DC, July 15, 2008), accessed June 11, 2016, http://archive.defense.gov/Speeches/Speech.aspx?SpeechID=1262.

and the local media. Whether it is a civil and humanitarian affairs teams digging wells, a medical or veterinary unit carrying out vaccination exercises that benefit host nation civilians, or a Military Information Support Operations team funding a women's political rights forum in Yemen, shaping activities are intended to leave a context more favorable than they found it.

Echoing Secretary Gates, Admiral Mike Mullen said about the fight against violent extremism, "We cannot kill our way to victory." Instead, he argued, in Afghanistan, we need better governance, more foreign investment, a viable alternative to poppy farming, greater cooperation with Pakistan, and more nonmilitary assistance. What Mullen was proposing was nothing less than the need to reshape the environment in Afghanistan.

While shaping the information and perception battlefield may be a military construct, it is not unique to the uniformed services. In the 1990s at the State Department, I heard then Assistant Secretary Marc Grossman tell audiences that the Foreign Service had changed a lot during the course of his career. When he joined the State Department, he said, diplomats were sent abroad to observe and to report. Today, when we send American diplomats abroad, we expect them not simply to report what they see, but to *change outcomes* in America's favor.

If you ask older public diplomacy officers, they will tell you they were changing outcomes long ago. Whether we were writing commentaries for publication under pseudonyms in Latin America, or screening "Star Wars" to audiences behind the Iron Curtain (no one missed the "Empire" analogy), or presenting indisputable graphic evidence of the American standard of living in display windows across Eastern Europe, it was public diplomacy with a policy purpose.

Whole-of-Government Public Diplomacy

Beginning around 2005 and 2006, the military determined to do, in strategic communication terms, what they perceived needed doing. The Trans-Regional Web Initiative set up websites to provide information and news in local languages to audiences in the Middle East, Africa, and Central Asia. Radio programs and television dramas using local actors and writers were created. Civil and humanitarian affairs officers were deployed, along with Human Terrain Teams intended to engage and understand local populations. Female engagement teams (female U.S. soldiers) were specifically trained and equipped to gather information and meet with female members of Islamic societies. Military commanders were encouraged to spend their discretionary funds (CERP) [8] on urgent, small-scale humanitarian relief and reconstruction projects and services. (While each grant was limited to less than $500,000, it was a substantial sum with a flexibility diplomats could only dream of.)

When questioned or criticized, the military tended to argue that these efforts were in support of public diplomacy. Reporting on Strategic Communication in 2009, the Defense Department said:

> DOD does not engage directly in public diplomacy, which is the purview of the State Department, but numerous DOD activities are designed specifically to support the State Department's public diplomacy efforts and objectives,

---

8. United States Army Combined Arms Center, Center for Army Lessons Learned, "Commander's Emergency Response Program," *Handbook 09-27* (April 2009), chap.4, accessed June 12, 2016, http://usacac.army.mil/sites/default/files/publications/09-27.pdf.

which in turn support national objectives. DOD refers to these activities as "Defense Support to Public Diplomacy."[9]

In my experience abroad and in Washington, I observed an unceasing request for more State Department involvement and guidance in these activities. Whether State officers were needed to lead provincial reconstruction teams in the field or participate in Washington planning and strategy sessions, there were never enough qualified Foreign Service Officers to meet the military's requirements.

At the November 12, 2013, Public Diplomacy Council (PDC) fall forum, a former ambassador just returned from Africa praised the way the development of Africa Command has helped State to communicate that a safe and secure Africa is in the interest of Africans, Americans, and the broader international community. As he said, State public affairs officers in Africa coordinate with their DOD counterparts to promote some very concrete U.S. security assistance priorities.

Besides messaging to achieve these goals, he continued, public affairs officers educate African publics about visits, huge multilateral exercises (African Endeavor involves more 40 African countries each year), and conferences organized by the African Center for Strategic Studies at the National Defense University. PAOs collaborate with their military counterparts on journalism exchange programs about security affairs and military cooperation. We take African journalists out on U.S. Navy ships, a relatively new phenomenon. Public affairs

---

9. Public Law 110–417, *The Duncan Hunter National Defense Authorization Act for Fiscal Year 2009, Section 1055: Reports on Strategic Communication and Public Diplomacy Activities of the Federal Government*, October 14, 2008, accessed June 11, 2016, https://www.gpo.gov/fdsys/pkg/PLAW-110publ417/html/PLAW-110publ417.htm.

officers also promote multi- regional solutions such as the African Union mission in Somalia and military training programs like the African Contingency Operations Training and Assistance program.

Lest one think PAOs are simply doing the military's message work, it goes the other way too. Military Information Support Teams (MIST), employed in Northwest Africa as part of the Trans-Saharan Counterterrorism Partnership and more and more in East Africa, work in partnership with embassy teams to achieve in-country objectives. The MIST team in Burkina Faso that worked on anti-corruption issues was particularly successful, and MIST teams in Mauritania and other countries have also worked very well. A creative MIST team in conservative Yemen was commended by State's Inspector General for working hand-in-glove with the culturally aware PAO on a women's political empowerment program, something that could never have happened without conjoined resources. Radio continues to be a powerful medium in Africa. In some cases recording a radio program and then distributing CDs is still the most effective way to get messages out. MIST teams are masters at such activities.

In some ways, the post-2001 prototype for America's relationship with foreign populations is the provincial reconstruction team (PRT) as seen in Afghanistan and Iraq. Ideally a PRT is a robust mix of diplomats, public diplomacy officers, aid workers, analysts, technical specialists, and military personnel. The most successful ones are led by a savvy diplomat and lodged in the field among the people. A PRT can bring a sophisticated, flexible, and capable USG presence to certain parts of the world. There will long remain places in the world where the United States needs a traditional embassy and its diplomats isolated behind high walls and metal detectors, venturing out only in armored Suburbans. But, a good ambassador or PAO would do well to think like a PRT leader.

Now, 15 years after 9/11 and the onset of the War on Terror, the Department of State's own public diplomacy game has sharpened. The Center for Strategic Counterterrorism Communications (CSCC) tries to provide the kind of counter-messaging operation that generals and admirals, not to mention ambassadors and special envoys including Richard Holbrooke, were demanding years ago.[10] The CSCC, established by executive order and staffed by experts from across the government, benefits from a full flow of information and analysis from the intelligence community as well as open sources. Focusing an unblinking eye on the actions, messaging, and plans of the extremists, CSCC staff devises ways to counter terrorist narratives. A Digital Outreach Team follows through, employing colloquial Arabic, Urdu, Punjabi, and Somali to counter terrorist propaganda and misinformation.

Beyond that, State has established offices and units to reach out to and engage with specific audiences, such as Muslims, youth, women, and ethnic and religious minorities. Another ambassador at the 2013 fall forum told the story of a program designed to connect and empower women through innovative business training. Using funds from different agencies, special attention was paid to multi-country empowerment programs for entrepreneurs. Nothing, he said, so grabs your attention in North Waziristan as a woman who is also a successful entrepreneur.

It seems clear from the post-2001 experience, some of which was admittedly painful, that the whole-of-government approach to public diplomacy and strategic communication with foreign audiences *can*

---

10. In Spring 2016 yet another entity, the Global Engagement Center, was established at the U.S. Department of State to fight terrorism online and counter violent extremist messaging.

produce results. But, success requires aggressive, hands-on management by the public diplomacy officer and the ambassador.

Lessons Learned

Several principles emerged from the fall forum discussion as well as from our collective experience since 2001.

First, neither the Secretary of State nor an ambassador can give orders to other federal agencies and the military. They cannot be directed to take actions or spend resources, especially if they do not believe it fits their mission. Despite the much discussed "chief of mission authority" and State's preeminence in foreign policy in Washington, each federal agency has its own Congressional committees, authorizations, appropriations, and self-determined mission.

A whole-of-government strategy or action plan coalesces only when two things occur: the State Department (and the ambassador) appear to be in sync with White House thinking, and they are providing clear strategic leadership. Strategic direction does not mean orders or instructions. It means picking up the flag and marching out in front, saying clearly, "Here is where we are going. This is what we need to accomplish." At that point, the other agencies will fall in line and support the effort with the programs and resources they have available. It's about leadership, not authority.

This was a point made clearly at the PDC fall forum by one DOD participant who said, "We've really had a shortfall in senior leadership and guidance and orientation." It is, he said, very difficult to orient the entire government on communication issues without leadership.

A second principle is to be wary of public diplomacy that is unfocused and becomes purely programmatic, rather than policy-purposed. As one PDC fall forum participant pointed out, there is a danger of falling into the trap of doing programs because we *can*, or because they *feel good*, not because they *accomplish* policy goals. Another ambassador described this kind of public diplomacy as "a Peace Corps volunteer with a budget." Instead, we need to keep the budgets and train our people to be more professional. "We need influence programs *with* a budget," he said.

Third, "Just say no." Any whole-of-government strategy suffers an unceasing vulnerability to unfunded mandates. Such mandates consist, usually, of "doing things" because some official or some organization promotes the idea, but fails to resource it. In government, and especially at embassies, the most valuable resource an ambassador or PAO has is staff. Time spent by the embassy officers and locally employed staff in assessing, strategizing, implementing, and cleaning up after "pet projects" and "good ideas" from Washington is time not spent on something locally productive.

A fourth rule of managing any interagency effort is to insist on some form of monitoring and evaluation. The starting point of any evaluation effort is to clearly state and agree upon the goals. What will success look like? How will we know if this is working? Asking these questions at the outset will often distinguish between realistic and impractical objectives. If these questions cannot be answered clearly and to the principal stakeholders' satisfaction, you can be sure you will not know when to stop the effort or try something else. If a program or project is worth doing, it is worth devoting up to five percent of the cost to some on-course monitoring and impact evaluation.

Fifth, and most important, enforcing all these rules is the task of the State Department. The authority devolves to the ambassador and the public diplomacy officer in the field. No other department or agency representative has the scope, experience, knowledge, and governmental authority to lead the required interagency effort.

Public Diplomacy Has No Scoreboard

To return to our starting point, in the years since 2001 public diplomacy officers have gained a much deeper understanding of the world around them and the tools they have at hand to deal with that world. Just as World War I marked a turning point in technology and tactics of warfare, so did America's post-2001 "war on terror" mark a turning point in America's public diplomacy. And just as the generals of 1914 had to learn to deal with industrialized weaponry, barbed wire, airplanes, and tanks, so too did twenty-first century diplomats have to learn to deal with terrorist Internet websites, IEDs on Instagram and Twitter, and beheadings committed solely for the YouTube effect.

In the early- and mid-twentieth century, life was simpler. It was possible to divide the world in two: (a) conflict zones, where the U.S. military was fighting and in charge, and (b) the rest of the world, which was the domain of the State Department and USAID. Since 2001, it has become clear that not only has the nature of warfare changed, but so has the nature of public diplomacy. No longer does the public diplomacy officer have a monopoly on America's engagement with international audiences (if she or he ever did). Today the American government engages with the world through a multifaceted, multi-purposed complex of relationships, actions, programs, and messages.[11]

---

11. The provincial reconstruction team (PRT) is an example of nontraditional diplomacy and broad-based government engagement in a foreign country. Success for a PRT depends on a clear sense of purpose combined with flexibility and an entrepreneurial spirit. PRT leadership also depends on a "train and trust" philosophy that seems incompatible with the "no mistakes, no surprises" attitude that has long prevailed in Foggy Bottom.

As much as procedures, programs, and techniques change, however, it would be wrong to think that the fundamentals of human communication have changed. Public diplomacy is about people and their ideas, perceptions, and beliefs. One can affect those ideas, perceptions, and beliefs only by listening, understanding, and making oneself relevant to the people of another country. It takes time and concentration; the struggle of ideas is not won in a single deployment or one officer's tour in a foreign land.

In a lecture several years ago the University of Southern California's Dr. Nicholas Cull said something like "Public diplomacy is not about winning hearts and minds. It is about building relationships. And, you don't *win* a relationship."[12]

We cannot expect public diplomacy to "move the needle" or "win" a campaign. Public diplomacy can, in concert with wise policy choices, build dependable, fruitful relationships. A nation's foreign affairs success is measured in relationships, not a won/lost percentage.

---

12. Dr. Nicholas Cull, USC Center on Public Diplomacy (speaking to the Public Diplomacy Council in Washington, DC, May 26, 2013).

Index

Acronyms

AFI: American Film Institute

BAPCO: Bahrain Petroleum Company

BBC: British Broadcasting Corporation

BBG: Broadcasting Board of Governors

BUBW: Better Understanding for a Better World

CERN: European Organization for Nuclear Research

CERP: Continuing Education Recognition Program

CIA: Central Intelligence Agency

CPI: Committee on Public Information

CRCNS: Collaborative Research in Computational Neuroscience

CSCC: Center for Strategic Counterterrorism Communications

CSO: Bureau of Conflict and Stabilization Operations

COCOM: Unified Combatant Command

DAS: Deputy Assistant Secretary

DOD: Department of Defense

DRL: Bureau of Democracy, Human Rights and Labor

EC: European Commission

ECA: Bureau of Educational and Cultural Affairs

EU: European Union

FSI: Foreign Service Institute

G7: Group of 7

GATS: General Agreement on Trade in Services

ICHI: Iraq Cultural Heritage Initiative

ICT: Information and Communications Technology

IO: Information Operations

ISIS: Islamic State in Iraq and Syria

JFK: John F. Kennedy

KUL: Catholic University in Lublin

MFA: Ministry(ies) of Foreign Affairs

MOOC: Massive Open Online Course

MIST: Military Information Support Teams

MPAA: Motion Picture Association of America

NATO: North Atlantic Treaty Organization

NEA: National Endowment for the Arts

NDU: National Defense University

NGO: Nongovernmental organization

NHK: Nippon Hoso Kyokai (Japan Broadcasting Corporation)

NIH: National Institute of Health

NSB: National Science Board

NSF: National Science Foundation

NSC: National Security Council

OWI: Office on War Information

PA: Public Affairs

PAO: Public Affairs Officer

PD: Public Diplomacy

PDC: Public Diplomacy Council

PEER: Partnerships for Enhanced Engagement in Research

PIRE: Partnerships for

International Research and Education

PRT: Provincial Reconstruction Team

PPP: Public-private partnership

P2P: Peer-to-Peer

Q.E.D.: Quod Erat Demonstrandum

RCUK: Research Councils of the United Kingdom

R&D: Research and Development

S/RGA: Office of Religion and Global Affairs

SATRBC: Syrian Arab Television and Radio Broadcasting Commission

SC: Strategic Communications

SEES: Science, Engineering and Education for Sustainability

STEM: Science, Technology, Engineering and Math

STS: Science and Technology Studies

TNR: The New Republic

UNESCO: United Nation Educational, Scientific and Cultural Organization

U.S.: United States

USAID: United States Agency for International Development

USC: University of Southern California

USG: U.S. Government

USIA: United States Information Agency

USIS: United States Information Service

USTR: United States Trade Representative

VOA: Voice of America

WTO: World Trade Organization

Contributor Biographies

Robert Albro is a Research Associate Professor in American University's Center for Latin American & Latino Studies and also currently Vice-President of the Public Diplomacy Council. His research and writing are concerned with the relationship of culture to questions of policy, diplomacy, security, and technology. He has been a Fulbright scholar and over the years his work has been supported by the Rockefeller, Mellon, and Henry Luce foundations. He has a Ph.D. in Sociocultural Anthropology from the University of Chicago.

Carol Balassa served in the Office of the United States Trade Representative over the course of 27 years. She headed the U.S. delegation to the World Trade Organization in negotiations on motion picture trade issues, telecommunications services, and energy services. She also served on the U.S. delegation to UNESCO in negotiation of the Cultural Diversity Convention. On retirement from USTR, she became a Senior Fellow at the Curb Center for Art, Enterprise and Public Policy at Vanderbilt. She has an M.A. in International Relations from Yale University and a Ph.D. in International Relations from the Johns Hopkins University.

John Brown, a Princeton Ph.D. in Russian history, was a U.S. diplomat for over 20 years, mostly in Eastern Europe. He was promoted to the Senior Foreign Service in 1997. A frequent lecturer for the Open World Leadership Center on the topic "E Pluribus Unum? What Keeps the United States United, " he is also affiliated with Georgetown University, where over the years he has given a graduate course, "American Foreign Policy and Propaganda: A Historical Overview." Brown's articles have appeared in numerous publications, including *The Washington Post, The Guardian, The San Francisco Chronicle, The Nation, The Moscow Times, and American Diplomacy.*

Brian E. Carlson, U.S. Ambassador, retired as a Career Minister (three-star flag officer equivalent) after 37 years in the United States Foreign Service.

From 2006 to 2010 he was the State Department's liaison with the Department of Defense on strategic communication and public diplomacy. The Chairman of the Joint Chiefs of Staff awarded Ambassador Carlson the Joint Meritorious Civilian Service Award in 2010. He currently advises nonprofit international audience research firm *InterMedia* on strategic communication.

Helle C. Dale is the Heritage Foundation's Senior Fellow in Public Diplomacy studies. Her current work focuses on the U.S. government's institutions and programs for strategic outreach to publics abroad, as well as more traditional diplomacy, critical elements in American global leadership and in the war of ideas against violent extremism. Dale has also published in *The Wall Street Journal, Policy Review, The Weekly Standard, National Review,* and *European Affairs.* Her B.A. (1979) and M.A. (1981) were earned at the University of Copenhagen, and she advanced to ABD at Tufts University (1985).

Jong-on Hahm is Special Advisor for International Research at George Washington University, and Distinguished Senior Fellow in the School of Policy, Government, and International Affairs at George Mason University, with science diplomacy expertise in Europe and Asia. She served on President Clinton's Interagency Council on Women Working Group on S&T. She received a Ph.D. in Neuroscience from MIT, an M.A. from American University, and a B.Sc. from McGill University.

Craig Hayden is Senior Professorial Lecturer at the American University School of International Service. Craig's research focuses on public diplomacy and strategic communication, soft power, and media technology in foreign policy. Craig was a Research Fellow at the University of Southern California Center on Public Diplomacy (2012-2014). He is the author of *The Rhetoric of Soft Power: Public Diplomacy in Global Contexts* (Lexington Books, 2011).

Peter Kovach retired as a Public Diplomacy specialist from the Foreign Service with the rank of Minister-Counselor. He served overseas in Pakistan, Japan, Jordan, Morocco, Bahrain, and Yemen. Kovach holds a Master of Arts in Law and Diplomacy (ABD) from the Fletcher School; a Master of Arts in Asian Studies from UC Berkeley and a B.A. in Asian History and Religion from Wesleyan University.